Bible
Speaks
today

the message of

THE SONG
OF SONGS

Series editors:
Alec Motyer (OT)
John Stott (NT)
Derek Tidball (Bible Themes)

the message of

THE SONG
OF SONGS

The lyrics of love
Revised edition

Tom Gledhill

INTER-VARSITY PRESS
Studio 101, The Record Hall, 16–16A Baldwin's Gardens, London EC1N 7RJ, UK
Email: ivp@ivpbooks.com
Website: www.ivpbooks.com

First published 1994
Reprinted 1996, 2000 (twice), 2002, 2004, 2007, 2010
This edition published 2023

British Library Cataloguing-in-Publication Data
A catalogue record for this book is available from the British Library.

ISBN: 978–1–78974–443–9
eBook ISBN: 978–1–78359–648–5

Set in 9.5/13pt Karmina
Typeset in Great Britain by CRB Associates, Potterhanworth, Lincolnshire
Printed and bound in Great Britain by Ashford Colour Press Ltd, Gosport, Hampshire

Produced on paper from sustainable sources.

Inter-Varsity Press publishes Christian books that are true to the Bible and that communicate the gospel, develop discipleship and strengthen the church for its mission in the world.

IVP originated within the Inter-Varsity Fellowship, now the Universities and Colleges Christian Fellowship, a student movement connecting Christian Unions in universities and colleges throughout Great Britain, and a member movement of the International Fellowship of Evangelical Students. Website: www.uccf.org.uk. That historic association is maintained, and all senior IVP staff and committee members subscribe to the UCCF Basis of Faith.

For Serena, with love

Contents

Bible Speaks Today

GENERAL PREFACE

The Bible Speaks Today describes three series of expositions, based on the books of the Old and New Testaments, and on Bible themes that run through the whole of Scripture. Each series is characterized by a threefold ideal:

- to expound the biblical text with accuracy
- to relate it to contemporary life, and
- to be readable.

These books are, therefore, not 'commentaries', for the commentary seeks rather to elucidate the text than to apply it, and tends to be a work rather of reference than of literature. Nor, on the other hand, do they contain the kinds of 'sermons' that attempt to be contemporary and readable without taking Scripture seriously enough. The contributors to The Bible Speaks Today series are all united in their convictions that God still speaks through what he has spoken, and that nothing is more necessary for the life, health and growth of Christians than that they should hear what the Spirit is saying to them through his ancient – yet ever modern – Word.

ALEC MOTYER
JOHN STOTT
DEREK TIDBALL
Series editors

Author's preface

The capacity to delight in physical beauty, to be attracted by members of the opposite sex, the desire to form secure and intimate relationships, and to express love and affection in demonstrably physical ways – these are all a very fundamental part of our common humanity. The Song of Songs is an unabashed celebration of these deeply rooted urges. In beautiful poetic language, the Song explores the whole range of emotions experienced by the two lovers as they work out their commitment to each other. From the aching yearnings for intimacy, to the ecstasy of consummation, from the tensions of separation and the fears of loss, to the relaxed contentment of togetherness, from coquetry and flirtation, to the triumphalism of passion: all these are traced out in the ebb and flow of a growing relationship of mutual love. So we have a strong biblical affirmation of love, loyalty, beauty and sexuality in all their variety. The language of the Song is often very florid. Its intimacies are couched in language sometimes very tender, other times seemingly coarse, crude and extravagant. Nevertheless, throughout its verses, in spite of its many metaphors which may at first sight appear quaint and comical, we have a delightful exposition of courtship and romantic love.

The Song is a unique literary genre in the Old Testament; it is the only example of an extended love poem in the Bible. It is both beautiful and enigmatic, and has been described as a lock for which the key has been lost. How then are we to find the key to its interpretation? Down the centuries, the Song has spawned an enormous variety of comments and expositions; many of these are bizarre, some fanciful, others simply downright unconvincing. This has arisen mainly because of the embarrassment of commentators in facing the explicit sexuality of the Song. In this exposition I have chosen to plough my own furrow, with only an occasional sidelong glance at other possibilities; to interact constantly with the opinions of others would be intolerably wearisome. The tack I have pursued is to view the Song primarily as a literary poetic exploration of human love. This naturalistic approach may prove too abrupt and limiting for those readers who hold to a different schema. But I would ask them to exercise grace and perseverance in the hope that something may be learned through this approach. Taking the obvious physical line of interpretation means that we have to discuss the intimacies of loving sexual behaviour. This is as delicate as walking on eggshells. However, I have bent over backwards in the attempt to avoid giving offence in the language used and I hope that I will be able to carry the reader comfortably along with me.

The Song, though unique, does not represent the totality of biblical reflection on human love relationships and sexuality. Our interpretation needs to be informed by the wider biblical context. I have not hesitated to bring into the exposition reflections on other biblical material concerning the issues raised by the Song; namely our creatureliness, our finitude, our mortality, our downright sinfulness, our ultimate destiny, our social and cultural conditioning. But beauty, intimacy and consummation can never be ends in themselves. They can never ultimately satisfy. This is not to denigrate them, but rather to recognize them for what they are. They are pointers to another world, another dimension, only occasionally and very dimly perceived, always seemingly just out of reach around the corner. These transcendental longings, intimations of immortality, are part and parcel of our complex physical, psychological and spiritual natures. Where the text of the Song prompts these ideas, I have felt it worthwhile to comment in this vein. It is almost inevitable that a consideration of human love and sexuality provokes contemplation at levels other than the plainly physical. I hope, however, that the kites I have attempted to fly are anchored to the text by threads which are sufficiently strong to enable me to avoid being cast into the same sort of mould as the exponents of the extreme allegorical method.

We live in an age when modern methods of mass communication have allowed an unprecedented expansion of the possibilities for the exploitation of human sexuality. Not that our own generation is necessarily more promiscuous than any other age. Basic human nature never changes, though cultural and social mores do. But today we live in an era when we are bombarded from every side with commercialized eroticism. From advertisement hoardings, films, TV and novels, promiscuous sexual gratification is publicly placarded as an acceptable part of our society. Love has degenerated into lust, liberty into licentiousness. The desire for instant and immediate satisfaction of every urge is paramount. Permanency in relationships is out – with the result that we have domestic disintegration, unmarried fathers, unmarried mothers and, most recently, the tragedy of Aids. The modern Christian is immersed in this society, and is under obligation to offer the hope of a better way, the way of Christian marriage, the way of unabashed delight in a sexuality within the framework of a secure and stable relationship. It is a gross distortion of the Christian worldview to denigrate human sexuality as something sinful. The agnostic poet Swinburne, in a particularly monstrous caricature, wrote the following lines:

Thou hast conquered, O pale Galilean;
the world has grown grey from thy breath.[1]

One wonders whether he had ever read the Song of Songs, with all its rompings and delightful kisses, its happy abandonment in sexual love. Our colourful Song is anything but grey. And so I hope this exposition of the Song will fulfil the aim of this series and enable the text of the Bible to speak to us today, clearly, with both relevance and power. Those who would like to get immersed straight away into the text of the Song could well skip the orientation, which sets out my approach to the Song and takes a brief look at other interpretations, as well as providing some background information.

I would like to acknowledge with gratitude the formative influence which the scholarly writing of M. V. Fox, F. Landy and P. Trible have had on my exposition. Many of their ideas are reflected in my own more popular work.

I also wish to express my thanks to the series editor, Alec Motyer, whose eagle eye has saved me from many infelicitous expressions, and whose comments resulted in a more secure and coherent interpretation of the Song. It is a sign of great magnanimity on his part that he has allowed an exposition to be presented whose main thrust falls short of the more fully orbed exposition to which his own hermeneutical instincts would lead him.

TOM GLEDHILL

---

[1] Swinburne, 'Hymn to Proserpine'.

Chief abbreviations

AV   The Authorized (King James) Version of the Bible (1611).

Davidson   *Ecclesiastes and the Song of Solomon* by Robert Davidson (Daily Study Bible, St Andrew Press, 1986).

Fox   *The Song of Songs and the Ancient Egyptian Love Songs* by Michael V. Fox (University of Wisconsin Press, 1985).

GNB   The Good News Bible (The Bible Societies and Collins; NT 1966, 4th edition 1976; OT 1976).

Goulder   *The Song of Fourteen Songs* by Michael D. Goulder (JSOT Press, 1986).

JB   The Jerusalem Bible (Darton, Longman and Todd, 1966).

Landy   *Paradoxes of Paradise: Identity and Difference in the Song of Songs* by Francis Landy (Almond Press, 1983).

Murphy   *The Song of Songs* by Roland E. Murphy (Fortress Press, 1990).

NEB   The New English Bible (NT 1961, 2nd edition 1970; OT 1970).

NIV   The New International Version of the Bible (2011).

NJPSV   Tanakh: The Holy Scriptures (The New Jewish Publication Society Version, 1988).

Pope   *The Song of Songs* by Marvin H. Pope (Anchor Bible, Doubleday, 1977).

RSV   The Revised Standard Version of the Bible (NT 1946, 2nd edition 1971; OT 1952).

Select bibliography

Avis, P., *Eros and the Sacred* (SPCK, 1989).

Bernard of Clairvaux, *The Song of Songs, Selections from the Sermons of St Bernard of Clairvaux*, H. Backhouse (ed.) (Hodder & Stoughton, 1990).

Brenner, A., *The Israelite Woman: Social Role and Literary Type in Biblical Narrative* (JSOT Press, 1985).

——, *The Song of Songs* (Old Testament Guides, JSOT Press, 1989).

Burrowes, G., *A Commentary on the Song of Solomon* (Banner of Truth, 1958).

Carr, G. Lloyd, *The Song of Solomon* (Tyndale Old Testament Commentary, IVP, 1984).

Davidson, R., *Ecclesiastes and the Song of Solomon* (Daily Study Bible, St Andrew Press, 1986).

Delitzsch, F., *The Song of Solomon* (Commentary on the OT in 10 volumes, T&T Clark, 1885).

Dillow, J. C., *Solomon on Sex* (Nelson, 1977).

Falk, M., *Love Lyrics from the Bible: A Translation and Literary Study of the Song of Songs* (Almond Press, 1982).

Fox, M. V., *The Song of Songs and the Ancient Egyptian Love Songs* (University of Wisconsin Press, 1985).

Fuerst, W. J., *The Song of Songs* (Cambridge Bible Commentary, CUP, 1975).

Gill, J., *An Exposition of the Song of Solomon* (1854; Sovereign Grace Publishers, 1971).

Ginsburg, H. L., *The Five Megilloth and Jonah: A New Translation* (Jewish Publication Society of America, 1969).

Glickman, S. C., *A Song for Lovers* (IVP/USA, 1976).

Gordis, R., *The Song of Songs and Lamentations* (KTAV, 1977).

Goulder, M. D., *The Song of Fourteen Songs* (JSOT Press, 1986).

Hocking, C. E., *Rise Up My Love: The Drama of Salvation History and the Song of Songs* (Precious Seed Publications, 1988).

Hurley, J. B., *Man and Woman in Biblical Perspective* (IVP, 1981).

Jewett, P. K., *Man as Male and Female: A Study in Sexual Relationships from a Theological Point of View* (Eerdmans, 1975).

Kidner, D., *Love to the Loveless* (IVP, 1981).

Knight, G. A. F., *The Song of Songs and Jonah* (International Theological Commentary, Handsel Press, 1988).

Landy, F., *Paradoxes of Paradise: Identity and Difference in the Song of Songs* (Almond Press, 1983).

Lewis, C. S., *Mere Christianity* (Geoffrey Bles, 1952).

——*The Four Loves* (Geoffrey Bles, 1960).

Marks, J. H., and R. M. Good (eds.), *Love and Death in the Ancient Near East* (Four Quarters Publishing House, 1987).

Mollenkott, V. G., *Women and Men and the Bible* (Abingdon Press, 1986).

Murphy, R. E., *The Song of Songs* (Hermeneia Commentaries, Fortress Press, 1990).

Pope, M. H., *The Song of Songs* (Anchor Bible, Doubleday, 1977).

Renan, E., *The Song of Songs* (Thomson, 1860).

Simpson, W. K., *The Literature of Ancient Egypt* (Yale University Press, 1972).

Snaith, J. G., *Song of Songs* (New Century Bible, Marshall Pickering/ Eerdmans, 1993).

Stadelmann, L., *Love and Politics: A New Commentary on the Song of Songs* (Paulist Press, 1990).

Taylor, J. H., *Union and Communion with Christ* (Bethany House Publishers, 1971).

Terrien, S., *Till the Heart Sings: A Biblical Theology of Manhood and Womanhood* (Fortress Press, 1985).

Trible, P., *God and the Rhetoric of Sexuality* (Overtures to Biblical Theology, Fortress Press, 1978).

Watchman Nee, *The Song of Solomon* (Christian Literature Crusade, 1965).

White, J. B., *A Study of the Language of Love in the Song of Songs and Ancient Egyptian Poetry* (Scholars Press, 1978).

Wurmbrand, R., *The Sweetest Song* (Marshall Pickering, 1988).

An orientation to the Song

1. The Song as poetic entertainment

We begin by making the almost trite observation that the Song of Songs is a literary creation. It is a love song of haunting beauty; it was meant to be sung as a celebration of love, beauty and intimacy. The Song found its early popularity within the social and religious life of ancient Israel. It was most probably sung as entertainment at local celebrations of the various harvest festivals, accompanied by dancing at a village wedding, as court entertainment at the royal palace in Jerusalem, or at happy family reunions or gatherings. Even the rabbis of the first century AD recognized its popular nature as a song, even if not with unqualified approval. Rabbi Aqiba wrote, 'He who trills his voice in the chanting of the Song of Songs in the banquet halls and treats it as a secular song has no share in the world to come.' So we must recognize at the outset the nature of the Song as poetry meant for musical recital.

With that in mind, we should not be surprised at some of the characteristics of the Song. It is cyclic and repetitious. There are recapitulations of various themes: for example, we have two similar dream sequences in 3:1–5 and 5:2–8. There are repeated refrains addressed to the daughters of Jerusalem (2:7; 3:5; 5:8; 8:4). Numerous other phrases and sentences recur in identical or near identical form in different parts of the Song: for example, the sprouting of the blossoms (2:12; 6:11; 7:13), the neck as a tower (4:4; 7:4), breasts as fawns (4:5; 7:3), eyes as doves (1:15; 4:1), browsing among the lilies (2:16; 4:5; 6:3), the day breaks and the shadows flee (2:17; 4:6), keeping a vineyard (1:6; 8:11), mountains of spices (4:6; 8:14), and many others. There are various scenes of intimacy (2:6; 3:4; 4:6; 5:1; 7:13; 8:3). I mention all this to suggest that we are meant to listen to the Song's themes. A song creates an atmosphere in which we are invited to participate. In listening to the Song, we find that it is speaking not only *to* us, but *about* us. We are captivated and drawn into its movement and ambience. Our imaginations are stimulated and we begin to identify with the lovers on their journey of love, of self-discovery and of fulfilment.

However, as we listen to the Song, we may encounter metaphors which fall harshly upon our ears, and which puncture the dreamlike fantasy world into which we have been seductively lulled. Examples are 'Your hair is like a flock of goats descending from the hills of Gilead' (4:1) or 'Your teeth are like a flock of sheep just shorn' (4:2). They jar our immediate sensibilities; but we have to distance ourselves from our initial shock, and enquire more precisely as to what is the intended impact of the metaphor. In the exposition of the text I have sought to do just that, but an initial impression of how to deal with metaphor may be gained by rapidly reading the paraphrase in Part 1. This is a very loose interpretation of the Song, intended to convey something of the atmosphere of the poem. Where the meaning of the original text is fairly clear, I have been content to stay close to a literal translation. Where the meaning requires some unpacking, I have felt free to undertake extensive paraphrasing. Where there are ambiguities and possible double entendres, I have at times resolved the ambiguity with an explicit decision one way or the other; otherwise I have preserved the ambiguity.

The Song contains a large number of words which occur nowhere else in the Old Testament, or else occur with different meanings. A handy technical exegesis of the Song which deals with these matters is the commentary by G. Lloyd Carr.[1] Precision in translation is often impossible. In matters of clothing, jewellery, anatomy and botany, there are many uncertainties. Is the girl described as a rose or a crocus (2:1)? Is her beloved like an apple tree, a lime tree or an apricot tree (2:3)? In 5:14, are they his *arms* which are being described as rods of gold, or is she referring to his *fingers*? And exactly what part of his body (in the same verse) is like polished ivory? In 7:2, is the boy admiring the girl's 'navel', or some other place? We must exercise caution here, for in striving for exact botanical or anatomical precision, the word we use might very well interrupt the flow of the poetry and ruin the atmosphere of the Song. Exact scientific translation equivalents do not always convey the required impression.

---

[1] Carr, *The Song of Solomon.*

Much of the force of the original Hebrew is lost in translation, particularly in the areas of various types of wordplay. It is virtually impossible to reproduce these in any kind of translation, so I have commented on them in the exposition as they occur. The literal translation helps to demonstrate the starkness of the original text; in particular it helps us to recognize various literary conventions such as chiasmus (the inverted sequence in parallel lines), and also helps us to see the specific emphasis which the Hebrew makes at times. Although the exposition is made on the basis of the NIV text, comparison with the literal translation will show where the NIV itself paraphrases or smooths over difficulties in the Hebrew.

Our view of the Song as a literary creation should lead us to frame questions appropriate to its literary genre. For example, we need to explore how the Song uses metaphor. We need to ask, what is the role of the daughters of Jerusalem? Do the categories of king and shepherd represent actual realities, or are they literary fictions? How does the poet use language to create the poem's own world? Are words used rationally with linguistic exactitude, or for their emotional impact? Examples we shall consider later are the wordplays on the names Solomon and the Shulammite, and the various resonances associated with the proper noun 'Lebanon'. I believe exploration of the poem along these lines is likely to be more profitable than along any other route.

There are two major consequences of this approach. First, we must realize that the two lovers are creations of a literary imagination, in the sense that the lovers are not modelled on real people. We do not know, indeed we do not need to know, much about them, other than how they feel about each other and about themselves. They are not real people acting out a real-life drama in a particular concrete situation. We do not know whether they are socially, intellectually or temperamentally compatible. We know nothing about their personalities. Were they shy introverts or noisy extroverts? Were they highly sophisticated city dwellers or simple country folk? What we do know, however, is how they respond to each other, and in as much as their responses and feelings are those typical of all men and women in love, then we can identify with them. To that extent, they are real flesh-and-blood characters, with passion and ardour flowing in their veins.

Second, this whole approach minimizes the importance of a coherent plot, a continuous narrative sequence running through the Song from beginning to end. I do not believe that the Song is meant to convey a story, a dramatic unfolding of events and encounters, with a resolution of difficulties and a grand finale. Some smaller units do in fact seem to have a unity of sequence through dialogue and locale, but overall, it is difficult to find one. Most commentators spend an inordinate amount of time and ingenuity in trying to construct an overall plot. But these always seem to be an artificial alien grid imposed externally on the rather loose association of different poems which make up the whole Song. It is all too easy to try to force the material to fit (rather reluctantly) a preconceived mould. And once that mould has been determined, all the exegesis of the constituent parts is done to support that overall structure.

This decidedly literary thrust to the exposition of the Song thus governs our agenda. However, this does not mean that other questions, such as the role of the historical Solomon or the number of main characters in the Song, the dating of the Song or its unity of composition, may simply be brushed aside. We have to tackle them, but many of our conclusions will necessarily be rather tentative since they are largely dependent on a whole set of interlocking presuppositions.

2. The role of Solomon in the Song

Questions concerning the role of Solomon in the Song, and questions of date, authorship and structural cohesion, are all inextricably intertwined. Answers we give to any one will inevitably influence our approach to finding answers for the others. Solomon is mentioned in the Song seven times: the title (1:1) ascribes the poem to Solomon; 1:5 refers to the tapestries or curtains of Solomon; 3:7, 9, 11 are all references to Solomon's sedan throne; and 8:11–12 mention Solomon as the owner of a vineyard. 'The king' is mentioned at 1:4, 12 and 7:5.

The title (1:1), literally translated, is 'The Song of Songs which pertains to Solomon'. For a full discussion of this see the exposition and also the section 'The Song in the Canon of Scripture'. While it is possible for this to be an indication of Solomonic authorship, I think that the most likely meaning is, 'The Song of Songs, attributed to Solomon'. That is, a literary editor ascribed the Song to Solomon as author, which then gave the poem the status of being classified as wisdom literature (see p. 18). On this view, no-one knows who wrote the Song. One possibility is that it emerged from an early folk tradition, and thus was the possession of the Israelite community of faith. And who better than Solomon could be chosen as its representative author, at a time of the flowering of Israel's art and culture, in a time of peace and international trade?

The reference to Solomon in 1:5 is purely incidental. The temple of Solomon was well known for its opulence. The Queen of Sheba came from afar to gawp at its magnificence. So we are not in this reference compelled to assume that the girl had actually been to the palace or temple; Solomonic hangings might have been referred to in the same manner as we refer to Queen Anne furniture – that is, the name indicates the style.

References to 'the king' in 1:4, 12 and 7:5 may well be simply a literary convention and have nothing to do with Solomon. The lover is no more a king than he is a shepherd. He is cast in these roles to illustrate different aspects of his personality and behaviour. To his beloved, he has the high status and dignity of royalty. He also grazes and pastures metaphorically in her garden. Of course, the two pictures are almost incompatible if we take them literally; but if we take them as literary stylizations, we should have no problems.

The references concerning Solomon's carriage and wedding (3:7–11) have been the subject of much debate (see the exposition). Some take the view that here a wedding is taking place between the two main participants in the Song, King Solomon and an Egyptian princess, the daughter of Pharaoh (1 Kgs 3:1). Others hold that no actual wedding is being celebrated at all. Those who espouse this version of the shepherd hypothesis (see pp. 6–9) interpret the scene as Solomon's abduction of the unwilling Shulammite maiden into his harem at Jerusalem.

The position taken in this exposition is that the two young lovers are rejoicing, on their very own wedding day, in the splendour and magnificence of their own 'royal' occasion. These verses, perhaps originally part of a song composed in honour of one of King Solomon's weddings, may have become assimilated into the popular national culture, to become part of the standard musical repertoire of every wedding celebration, just like Widor's *Toccata* in many British weddings today.

Solomon appears in 8:11–12 in a very bad light. Portrayed as 'the owner of a crowd', with his vast wealth he can obtain anything he desires. But he can never buy love. Here I take it that Solomon is playing the archetypal role of any lecherous male who thinks that women can be hired for money.

In this exposition I am taking a minimalist position concerning the role of Solomon. The two lovers are Everyman and Everywoman and have nothing to do with Solomon.

Questions concerning dating interact with this position. We no longer have to assume a tenth-century BC dating for the Song. Linguistic considerations regarding the dating of the Song are very complex and ambiguous. Are the so-called Aramaisms evidence of a late date, when Aramaic was becoming the common parlance of Israel, or are they merely Northern Israelite dialectical variations, or do they reflect a proto-Hebrew as evidenced by the languages of Ancient Ugarit (*c.*1200 BC)? Another question is whether an editor fused together a collection of originally independent poetic fragments from different chronological periods. So then a distinction has to be made between the date of the final editing process and the dates of the various constituent components. However, the debate is not settled, and we cannot pursue it here. Suffice it to say that the majority of scholars place the Song's composition somewhere between the fifth and third centuries BC. But the matter is of very marginal significance for our interpretation of the Song.

3. The shepherd hypothesis

The shepherd hypothesis presupposes three main characters: King Solomon, a country shepherd lad and a young maiden identified as the Shulammite. The girl and the shepherd boy are very much in love, but Solomon by various means tries to woo her affections, but ultimately fails. Thus we have a love triangle, rather than a simple romance between the two young lovers. Since the girl constantly repels the advances of Solomon, so that he finally gives up any claim over her, the message of the Song is seen as the triumph of faithful loyalty of true love, over against the seduction of wealth and flattery. Power and privilege cannot erode the true romance of the simple country lovers.

There are many slightly different versions of this hypothesis. In all of them, the majority of the girl's words have to be postulated as musings, dreams, soliloquies, reminiscences or flashbacks. For one very detailed outworking of the plot of the drama, see the annotations of the Amplified Bible (3-volume edition), where the speakers, the addressees and the locales are all precisely identified. *The New Bible Commentary*[2] also suggests, albeit rather undogmatically, that the shepherd hypothesis is

---

[2] *The New Bible Commentary* (IVP, 3rd edn 1970).

the best framework for the interpretation of the Song, but the details are not always worked out with great precision in the exposition itself.

In general, the plot follows some such sequence as that outlined below. The initial scene (1:1 – 2:7) occurs in the apartments of the royal palace, where there are scores of Solomon's beautiful concubines waiting around for the king to enter and choose one of them for the night. The Shulammite girl is among them, having been forcibly abducted by the king or his servants when he was on one of his inspection tours of the countryside. In 1:2, either one of the harem is voicing her desire to be selected by the king or else the Shulammite is soliloquizing about her absent shepherd lover in the countryside. 1:4 is sometimes represented as a chorus from the harem, or as a continuation of the Shulammite's yearning for her lover. The girl is self-conscious about her dark, suntanned complexion, in contrast to the painted ladies of the harem, and defends herself against their hostile stares. She cries out (1:7), asking to know the whereabouts of her lover, and the harem beauties tell her rather brusquely to go out and find him herself. She feels trapped like a bird in a golden cage. The king enters, spies the newcomer, and praises her beauty in 1:9–11. The girl meanwhile is dreaming of a rendezvous with her lover in a forest glade, while the king has gone for his meal (1:12), and in 2:7 she tells the ladies of the harem not to try to arouse the king's attentions by artificial means. In 2:8 the girl tells of how her lover came to her with an invitation to go away with him, and how she asked him (in 2:16–17) to return again at the end of the day (that is, she did not immediately accede to his request). When he did not return she became anxious and restless and went out into the night to seek him (3:1–4).

At some stage the girl manages to get away from the city completely and returns home. Perhaps Solomon has sent her back. But he never gives up. In 3:6 – 4:7 he appears in pomp and splendour, arriving at the girl's home in the country in his royal carriage, in an attempt to capture the girl's affections. He describes and praises the girl in conventional flattering tones; but no actual marriage takes place. In 4:8 – 5:1 the girl hears the appeal of her shepherd lover urging her to escape from the seductive words of the king. The situation is urgent and he doesn't waste time greeting her or praising her. She then dreams of his praises (4:9–15), and anticipates the consummation of their love on their own future wedding day. In 5:2–8 the Shulammite relates to the harem another troubling dream she had, and in reply to their mocking question she gives an impassioned description of him in 5:10–16. The king enters in 6:4 and praises her extravagantly, and tells her that even queens and concubines have praised her, using the words of 6:10. The girl interrupts this flow of praise and explains how she was abducted in the royal chariot to be taken away to the harem in the palace (6:11–12). All the harem have missed her at the palace, and they beg her to return so that they might admire her beauty. (This involves a change of attitude to her on their part.) The king again praises her in 7:1–9, but the girl makes a further refusal.

In 7:10 she reaffirms her love for the young shepherd. Solomon realizes that his pursuit has been futile and lets her go. She calls for her shepherd lover in 7:11 and waits for him, dreaming of her relationship with him. 8:5 then records her return to the village on the arm of her beloved. The girl (in 8:8) recalls her former state as a young girl and her brothers' discussion about her future. 8:11–12 represent the girl's final repudiation of Solomon in the presence of her lover, family and friends. In 8:13, the shepherd lad says, 'You who dwell in the gardens with friends in attendance, let me hear your voice!' The girl responds (8:14) with an urgent call to her lover to take her to their home on the mountain slopes.

A number of points need to be made in regard to this hypothesis. First, since this interpretation casts Solomon in the role of villain, it can hardly take the title of 1:1 as a statement of Solomonic authorship. Second, it takes the role of Solomon, in the supposed narrative plot, seriously. It makes sense of Solomon's rejection in 8:12. It takes the rural–city contrast literally. However, a number of severe criticisms may be levelled against the hypothesis. There are no examples elsewhere in the literature of the Ancient Near East of any kinds of love triangles. Also the schema of the narrative plot requires an ingenious series of dream sequences, musings and reveries, which effectively amount to a reordering of the text. Some of the scenarios seem so contrived as to be unbelievable: for example, the shepherd boy coming into the palace and whispering to the Shulammite through the lattice window of the quarters of the harem. A more serious objection is that the hypothesis requires the text to be interpreted against the natural flow of the dialogue. For example, the verses 1:9–11 are interpreted as being the gross coarse compliments of a carnal flatterer, while 1:13–14 are the beautiful sincere words of the girl's compliments directed towards her absent lover, even though Solomon is supposedly present. It is much more natural to suppose that in these verses two lovers are praising each other in a direct verbal exchange, rather than a dialogue at cross purposes. It takes a very great leap of mental ingenuity to describe as flattery and sincere praise two sets of verses written in identical styles.

However, it has to be admitted that once the hypothesis has become firmly embedded in the mind, it is very difficult to eradicate its influence when trying to read the text from any other perspective. In my opinion, the hypothesis, while taking seriously the carnality of King Solomon, is nothing more than an artificial edifice ingeniously superimposed on an enigmatic text, and ultimately is unconvincing. The Song of Songs is a cycle of songs, of Hebrew love poetry, which bears the characteristics of all poetry, namely repetitions, doublets, catchwords and metaphors, and which cannot ultimately bear the strain of a narrative plot which it is supposed to carry.

4. The morality of the Song

The main themes of the Song are romantic love, courtship, beauty, passion and mutual commitment. However, the lovers' exchanges are not merely verbal. Not only do they sing each other's praises, but they also demonstrate their love in intimate, physical ways. They kiss, fondle, embrace; they spend the night together, they consummate their love in full physical union. The girl and boy both express their yearnings for close bodily intimacy. It is this very explicit sexuality in the Song that has proved a stumbling block and a source of embarrassment to many readers and commentators.

So how do we handle it? Perhaps the happiest of contexts in which to view the Song is to consider it as love lyrics to adorn a wedding celebration. For Jeremiah, 'the sounds of joy and gladness, the voices of bride and bridegroom' (Jer. 33:11) were part of the normal festive round of life in ancient Israel. The atmosphere of joy and happiness was conducive to the uninhibited singing of songs which celebrated the intimate behaviour of bride and groom. The cheerful merriment of a wedding feast, with the wine flowing freely, provided a relaxed occasion in which it was not improper to celebrate the love and kisses and union of the happy couple. But this is not to suppose that the Song is bawdy or vulgar in any way. Its unembarrassed use of metaphor and allusion demonstrates the warmth and vitality of the God-given joys of love. It was not a thing to be hidden away in a corner, as though there were something furtive or indecent

9

about it all, but a matter that could be brought out openly in the light and a cause for public celebration. Their physical and tactile relationship was taken for granted as a wholesome part of the entire spectrum of human interaction and was not regarded in any way as a concession merely to be tolerated.

As we read the text of the Song today, however, as part of our canonical Scripture, we cannot help asking questions at various points in the Song. What are the lovers up to now? At what stage are they in their relationship? Are they transgressing the boundaries of the conventions of morality? In order to anchor the Song securely in the social context of ancient Israel, it makes sense to assume that the lovers are a betrothed couple. Now betrothal in the ancient world was very different from our modern concept of engagement. Betrothal was the point of no return, and the future of the couple was irrevocably sealed. Their marriage had been arranged; they were not isolated individuals who had casually crossed paths and happened to have fallen in love. Members of their larger family units had brought them together, and when all the negotiations between the families had been finalized and the bride price agreed and paid, then the couple were considered to be officially betrothed. All that remained was for the wedding to take place and the union to be consummated. In fact, according to the legislation of the book of Deuteronomy, a betrothed man was given exemption from military service in order that the possibility of death in battle might not prevent the consummation of their union (Deut. 20:7; cf. Deut. 24:5). It was sometimes the case that the man and the woman had never met before their betrothal,[3] and thus the relationship started from cold, as it were. But romantic love could also blossom even in the more restricted social intercourse of Israelite society (see later, on 8:5). So it is not inappropriate to view the Song as the joyous, tentative explorations of love of the betrothed couple, culminating in their marriage and full sexual union in 5:1. In our very different Western cultures, society places far fewer limits on the opportunities which young lovers may have for growing in their relationships. They have much more freedom for social interaction; and this requires the exercise of greater responsibility in the face of greater temptations.

The very untidy structure of the Song allows the lovers to come on the scene in the full flood of passionate longing. This makes it difficult for

---

[3] Cf. the arranged marriage between Isaac and Rebekah, Gen. 24.

the expositor to chart the natural progress of a growing relationship in a linear way, for the sequence of the text does not allow us to do that. If we are to regard the Song as a manual for courtship leading to marriage then we would effectively have to reorder the text to produce a more natural sequence. But in the Song, all the complex emotions of courtship are jumbled up together in a somewhat bewildering cycle of movements, and we have to untangle the various strands as we progress through the Song.

Any developing relationship will start with the first stirrings of the recognition of kindred spirits, fired by the attraction of physical beauty. Romantic affection may then begin to blossom as the couple make shy, tentative initiatives in getting to know one another. Over a period of time, or sometimes very suddenly, the two begin to recognize that something is happening between them and they long to spend more time in each other's company. As the possibility of their future together becomes clearer, their thoughts and desires progress towards more physical expressions of their mutual love. From the first holding of hands, and the cautious peck on the cheek, the relationship progresses in more tactile ways, to closer embracing and caressing, and more intimate kissing. The question is how to make sure that the degree of tactile intimacy at any stage matches the progress towards marriage. For the sanctity of marriage must be preserved at all costs, and full sexual union is reserved for that state alone.

In our Song, the lovers are portrayed in various scenes of intimacy and longing. Some of them are hot and passionate, others more tranquil and calm. The consummation of their love is celebrated in the marriage cycle. But we all know that 'the course of true love never did run smooth', and the lovers in our Song experience the agonies as well as the ecstasies of a growing relationship: the pain of separation, the fears of loss, the little misunderstandings which get magnified out of all proportion, the tensions of an insecure self-image, the lovers' quarrels, all of which are part of the warp and woof of the fabric of relationships. But the showers and the tears are compensated for by the sunshine and the laughter, the hurts and withdrawals by the joyous relief of reconciliation.

So we should look upon the Song as the joys and tensions of a young couple on their progress towards marriage. But we cannot derive a complete doctrine of sexual morality or marriage from the Song alone, for it is a unique literary genre in the Old Testament. As such, it must be informed by the wider social, moral and theological context of the Bible as a whole (see later, 'The Song in the Canon of Scripture'). It cannot be taken in isolation, as providing some definitive teaching on human sexual relationships. It is like asking the book of Ecclesiastes to provide the normative Old Testament teaching on the nature of God. If we look at the wider biblical context, we see with the utmost clarity that the ancient Hebrews possessed a very rigid moral code; premarital sexual relationships were prohibited; if, through human frailty, fornication occurred, the two partners were obliged to get married and the man was obliged to pay the bride price to the girl's father (Exod. 22:16). Adultery was considered a more serious sin, as it involved the breaking of a covenant relationship already established, and adulterers were under the threat of the death penalty (Lev. 20:10). Similarly, Christian morality is of an equally high standard; for not only are extra-marital acts condemned, but the inner thought life is subject to the moral scrutiny of God (Matt. 5:28). So the Song gives us no licence to flout the moral codes of God's covenant people. But having said that, we must remember that the Song is not a moral social tract. It is a celebration of love in all its dimensions. It is not primarily didactic, although it does (as I hope to show) teach us a great deal about human relationships. As such it is profitable for teaching, rebuking, correcting and training in righteousness (2 Tim. 3:16).

The Song contains many metaphors describing various actions relating to sexual arousal (kissing, caressing, and so on), and various euphemisms and double entendres. Commentators have two options in dealing with these. Either they leave the ambiguities unresolved, so that it is left to the unaided reader to exercise his or her imagination in unwrapping the metaphors; or else they comment explicitly, and elaborate the force of the metaphor, resolving ambiguities, planting hitherto unimagined thoughts and exposing new pathways along which to tread. The former is safer; the latter involves the risk of giving offence. To unpack metaphors and unwrap euphemisms may mean that our thoughts spiral out of control, and we end up by committing adultery in our imaginations. So if the interpretation of Scripture proves to be a stumbling block, and a cause of offence to some who believe, what then? Should a commentator be cast into the depths of the sea with a millstone around his or her neck, for having caused one of the little ones to stumble (Luke 17:1–2)? But is the offence caused by the exposition itself, or by the carnal nature of the believer, who cannot cope with his or her own reactions? There is a similarity here with the apostle Paul's struggle with the law; the law itself is holy and just and good, but it brings condemnation and itself arouses all sorts of unholy and unrighteous desires. The culprit is sin working through our members (Rom. 7:7–25). But commentators must keep a tight rein on themselves. As M. V. Fox says, 'Readers, like young lovers, have a problem of knowing how far to go.'[4] Once a particular line of interpretation has been suggested, it is difficult to avoid seeing explicit sexual allusions everywhere, until the whole work becomes (as Goulder's commentary)[5] saturated in references to genitalia, intercourse and explicit sex. That the Song is about sexual love is not disputed. But that must be seen in its widest context, for love between the sexes is more than physical expression; the lovers in the Song interact in many other ways, praising each other, going out in the country together, just quietly being in each other's presence. Their mutual commitment is not just for the purposes of physical pleasure.

What then if we cannot control our responses as we read the Song as it draws us into its net? The New Testament answer is very clear and straightforward. Jesus said, 'If your right eye causes you to stumble, gouge it out . . . It is better for you to lose one part of your body than for your whole body to be thrown into hell' (Matt. 5:29). In other words, we are not to walk into temptation open-eyed when we know our particular areas of weakness. Jesus said in effect, 'If what you read or look at causes a sinful chain of thought which you cannot handle, then don't look, don't read.' It is simply a ruthless self-discipline based on a realistic self-knowledge. Of course, this is a very general principle for maintaining moral purity; some people may be able to read the Song without being tempted to give expression to their sexual desires; others may have difficulties. It was in recognition of this that Origen wrote, 'I advise everyone who is not yet rid of the vexations of the flesh and blood and has not ceased to feel the passions of this bodily nature, to refrain from reading the book and the things that will be said about it.' He also referred to a tradition among the Jews 'to allow no one even to hold this book in his hands, who has not reached a full and ripe age'.

If we are, in a few places in the Song, required to speak about euphemisms, how are we to go about it without offence? The language we use to describe various parts of the human anatomy (what the apostle Paul describes as our 'unpresentable' parts; 1 Cor. 12:23) is a matter for delicate

---

4 Fox, p. 298.
5 Goulder.

sensitivity. We are all familiar with four-letter words, the stock-in-trade of the graffiti artist or the boorish person. These words have such power to shock that they no longer have as their primary function a communication of information. When these words are used in verbal discourse, a profound disorientation takes place in the hearer, which has a tendency to block off to a large degree any further capacity for rational discussion. They act, so to speak, as verbal hand grenades. Their use is a terrorist activity, causing wanton destruction. However, the use of clinical words for the sensitive areas also produces a distancing effect. Medical terms create a cold alienation, the detachment of impersonal scientific description. Areas of our bodies associated with deep subjective warmth, self-consciousness and self-identity need to be handled with more than clinical detachment. So we are left with the use of metaphor. We shall explore this in greater depth later. But we may say here that this device is more satisfactory as there is usually no element of shock involved; but there is a slight distancing as we mentally take time to adjust to the association of ideas between the common word being used in a different way. Take, for example, the use of the word 'vineyard': it may be taken literally, the place where grapes are cultivated; it may refer to the girl as a whole, in all her femininity; or it may have more explicit sexual references. This easy fluidity of levels of meaning is part of the charm of the Song, which teases our imaginations.

5. God, sexuality and allegory

In Genesis 1:27 we read, 'So God created mankind in his own image, in the image of God he created them; male and female he created them.' This verse thus states that the sexual differentiation of the species of humanity into male and female categories is part of the God-ordained programme of creation. The mutual complementarity of the two sexes is seen in the description of the position of the woman as literally 'one standing opposite him' (Gen. 2:18). The Hebrew implies not subordination, but equality of status and complementarity in purpose. Each makes up for what the other lacks. Each one stimulates in the other what they have in common. It is a relationship of mutual companionship, mutual help and interdependence.

Part of the image of God in humanity is expressed by the mutual complementarity of this sexual differentiation. This naturally leads us to question what characteristics of the Godhead are mirrored by this. The fully developed Christian doctrine of the Trinity establishes the oneness and complementarity of Father, Son and Holy Spirit. The early North African Church Father Augustine used the illustration of a lover, a beloved and the mutual love which binds them, in order to picture the relations of the persons of the Trinity. But we must stress that this is only a picture at the analogical level. To press the illustration and the original distinction to imply that there is within the Godhead both a male and a female principle would be an illegitimate use of the metaphor. For this polarity within the Divine is but a step away from the debased sexual fertility religions of the Ancient Near East, in which the various gods had their female consorts. The coupling of these sexual partners was supposed to induce fertility in the natural order. This concept was wholly anathema to the orthodox of Israel's religion. But this does not mean that we cannot use sexual language to describe the activity of the Godhead. God loves (Hos. 11:1), and courts and woos his people (Hos. 2:14). He is like a father to them (Jer. 3:19; Isa. 63:16). He gives them birth (Deut. 32:18). They are his offspring. Other times he is like a husband to them (Hos. 2:16). God also suffers the travail of birth pangs over his people (Isa. 42:14). But all this is at a linguistic level only. For, ontologically, God is asexual. For we can only truly speak of sexuality in the context of bodies. If God is spirit, then we cannot speak of sexuality in the Godhead.

But the Bible does in fact use the metaphor of marriage to illustrate the relationship between God and his people. The marriage is the covenant bond, the husband represents God and the wife stands for his people Israel. It is perhaps worthwhile at this stage to refer to some of these specific biblical passages. Yahweh (Israel's covenant God), speaking to his people Israel through his prophetic spokesman Hosea after a prolonged period of national apostasy (regarded as spiritual adultery), looks forward to a time of renewal with the words 'In that day . . . you will call me "my husband"' (Hos. 2:16). He later promises, 'I will betroth you to me for ever' (Hos. 2:19). Similarly, the Lord rejoices over a restored Zion, 'But you will be called Hephzibah, and your land Beulah; for the LORD will take delight in you, and your land will be married' (Isa. 62:4). In the allegory of the foundling child, Ezekiel portrays Yahweh as entering into a covenant with Israel under the picture of a marriage. 'I spread the corner of my garment over you and covered your naked body. I gave you my solemn oath and entered into a covenant with you . . . and you became mine' (Ezek. 16:8; cf. Ruth 3:9). In the well-known passage in Jeremiah proclaiming the new covenant, God laments that Israel 'broke my covenant, though I was a husband to them' (Jer. 31:32). The New Testament also makes use of this imagery. The apostle Paul spells out the parallels between the husband–wife relationship and the relationship of Christ to his church (Eph. 5:22–33). John in the Apocalypse speaks of the wedding supper of the Lamb (Rev. 19:9). There is thus considerable biblical evidence to show that the human marriage relationship can be used as a vehicle to illustrate spiritual realities.

Although no New Testament writer quotes or uses the Song of Songs in this way, many commentators have felt that they have sufficient biblical precedent to pursue a spiritual interpretation. It is argued with some justification that reflection on human love and intimacy leads inevitably to reflection on the ways of God with humankind. Thus various commentators have seen in the relationship of the two lovers in the Song an illustration of the relationship between God and Israel, or between Christ and the church, or between God and the individual believer. The many differing behaviour patterns of the lovers have been used as illustrations of the spiritual walk of the believer: the desire for and the consolations of intimacy, the articulation of praise, the pain of absence, the clouding of fellowship, the restoration of communion, and so on. But we must be rather careful in our use of such analogies. For the believer's relationship with Christ is never at an erotic level. The language used may be that of love, but it must be remembered that while God is eternal spirit, we are earthly bodily creatures. To speak of rapture and consummation and so on uses the vocabulary of love, but the metaphysical relationship between the believer and Christ is at an entirely different level from that between two lovers. To confuse the two types of relationship can lead to heretical notions and spiritual disaster.

In this exposition, the main emphasis is on the natural interpretation of the Song as a warm, positive celebration of human love and sexuality in the context of marriage. I do not pretend that this exhausts the meaning of the Song, but I do maintain that this is its primary emphasis. To those who shrink from such an approach, and would prefer a spiritualizing exposition, I would gently offer the following comments.

First, we need to be sure that an allegorical approach is not a backlash against the very explicit sexuality of the Song. For there is a real danger of driving a wedge between a 'spiritual' interpretation of the Song and one which is 'natural', with the hidden assumption that the spiritual interpretation is somehow more worthy than the other. For the Christian church has inherited a characteristic Greek way of thinking which has not always had happy consequences. For the Greeks presupposed that what was of supreme importance were the enduring invisible qualities of mind and spirit. These so-called 'higher' faculties were contrasted with the 'lower' ones associated with the tangible created order, namely the earth, the human body and its emotions and desires. This consequent negative view of the body has infiltrated the thinking of the church down the ages. It resulted in the early christological heresies of Docetism (Christ only seemed to have a body), of Arianism (Christ was only semi-human and semi-divine) and Monophysitism (Christ had only one nature, and that a spiritual one). For the church, the most enduring legacy of this way of thinking is the idea that true holiness of character can be achieved only by withdrawal from the world (monasticism) or by total sexual abstinence (the celibate life). But the ancient Hebrews had a hearty appetite for life in all its many experiences. Lacking any solid hope of an enduring afterlife, they embraced every experience of life in all its fullness. They had no philosophical inhibitions which cramped their style within the basic moral and theological framework of their unique revelation. So the allegorist must be sure that the instincts which motivate a particular reading of the Song do not flow from sources which have no secure basis in the Scriptures.

Second, those who interpret the Song following the typological analogies used by the Old Testament prophets and the New Testament apostles need to take care that their exposition does not blossom into the uncontrolled extravaganza of extreme allegorism (i.e. the sort of thing that makes the voice of the turtle dove [2:12] the preaching of the apostles; the little foxes [2:15] the sins that spoil the church; the mountain of myrrh [4:6] the hill of Calvary, and so on). It would be too easy to ridicule a true hermeneutical instinct by cataloguing the excesses of some well-meaning interpreters. But none of us is perfect, and perhaps even this exposition pursuing a naturalistic approach may have succumbed to the temptation to explore pathways only very tangentially related to the text.

6. The Song in the canon of Scripture

The Song has always been counted in the Hebrew and Christian Scriptures as one of the canonical books. Whenever its position has been questioned,

17

it has always been from the standpoint of its already accepted inclusion. In other words, the question was always, 'Should it remain in the canon?' and not 'Should it be included in the canon?' Now the process by which individual books come to be recognized as canonical is both long and complex, and it is very difficult to chart such a process with any degree of precision. At the Council of Jamnia in AD 90, Rabbi Aqiba defended the Song in the words, 'For in the entire world, there is nothing to equal the day on which the Song of Solomon was given to Israel. All the writings are holy, but the Song of Songs is most Holy.' He thought that the whole teaching of Scripture was summarized by the Song. The extravagance of his defence seems to suggest some quite serious opposition to its continued inclusion in the canon.

The Song is included in the third part of the Hebrew Bible, the Writings, which contains all the books not included in the Law (the Pentateuch) and the Prophets (the former prophets and the writing prophets). From the period of later Judaism, the Song was traditionally read at the Passover festival. It is not altogether clear why this should have been so; perhaps it was simply because of the Song's predominant theme of spring which coincided with Passover time.

But why should the Song be in the canon in the first place? Many have suggested that the process of canonization took place at the same time as the process of sacralization, that is, when it began to be reinterpreted spiritually. That these two processes occurred simultaneously cannot be doubted, but it is very difficult to establish which process influenced the other. Did the Song gradually assume canonicity on the grounds of an allegorical mode of interpretation, or was its already accepted canonicity the motivation for such an approach? It is possible that the association of the Song with Solomon played a role in its acceptance, but mere association with his name was no guarantee of inclusion in the canon; for two books from the intertestamental era, written in Greek, namely the Odes of Solomon and the Wisdom of Solomon, were never included in the canon.

The Song is sometimes classified as wisdom literature, along with Proverbs, Job, Ecclesiastes and a few of the Psalms. There is much debate about the nature and origins of wisdom literature. Some of it seems to have originated from the uncharted traditions of village folklore (like many of the proverbs). Other parts, such as Job and Ecclesiastes, seem to be an erudite questioning of orthodox theology, which could only have arisen from a highly intellectual and sophisticated elite. It has been suggested that just as Job explores the riddle of suffering, and Ecclesiastes the riddle of existence, so the Song explores the riddle of love.[6]

Many have felt perplexed by the Song's inclusion in the canon simply because of its 'secular' feel. Apart from the book of Esther, the Song is the only book of the Hebrew Scriptures where God is not mentioned explicitly. There are a few places where there may possibly be an oblique allusion to the Deity (at 8:6 and in the oath formula), but these are somewhat doubtful. The absence of any mention of God in the Song, however, does not make it a secular song, nor imply that it has thus crept surreptitiously into the canon of sacred Scripture. We need to be clear at the outset that the division between sacred and secular in the world of the ancient Hebrews was not a distinction that was recognized when applied to life in general. Of course, in the realm of the priestly cult, distinctions between the clean and the unclean, the holy and the common, were made. But in everyday life, the distinction was not recognized. Secularism, atheism and agnosticism were not acceptable intellectual options in the culture of the ancient world. The whole of life was sacred. God was both transcendent and immanent. He was over all and in all. Not that this ever led to the ideas of pantheism (i.e. that nature itself is divine). No, this idea of God permeating every area of life was fundamental to Israelite society. It was essentially a holistic view of the world. The social world, the natural order and the realm of spirituality were all mutually interlocking and interdependent parts of the whole. The social world of men and women consisted of their nuclear family, the extended family, slaves and servants, the clan, the tribe, extending to the whole of the covenant community, including the ancestors who had died and the future generations yet to come. But humankind's role in the natural order of God's creation was to cultivate the land and take care of it (Gen. 2:15). It was a world of crops and cattle and sheep, of rain and sunshine, of floods and famine, of fertility and barrenness, of life and death. But it was all God's world, thoroughly integrated with the spiritual dimension. For God was active in his own creation, to create and to destroy, to heal, to give spiritual revelation, to save his people and conquer their enemies. So we have an interlocking triangle of relationships between God as Creator, man and woman as creature, and the created world. This can be focused more precisely as Yahweh

---

[6] M. Sadgrove, *The Song of Songs as Wisdom Literature* (Studia Biblica, 1978), I, pp. 245–248.

as Israel's covenant God, Israel his covenant people, and the promised land of Canaan as their abode.[7]

So in the wisdom literature, God sovereignly superintends the whole of the moral and physical order in which men and women take human decisions and initiatives. Often God is behind the scenes, as it were, seemingly leaving them to their own devices. So in the Song, we have an expression of God's goodness in creating humankind in its complementary sexes. The mutual delight in physical beauty and sexual expression is all part of the creation upon which the Creator himself passed the verdict that it was very good (Gen. 1:31).

So the Song is a celebration of this aspect of creation. It is an invitation to contemplate our own humanity, to delight in its beauty, to sit light to its capriciousness, and to explore the possibilities involved in a relationship of love between a man and a woman. There is little moralizing in the Song (except perhaps for the idea that love cannot be bought). We have to look elsewhere in the broader biblical context for that. So if we ask the question, 'Where is God in the Song?', the answer is 'Nowhere and everywhere.' He is nowhere explicitly mentioned, everywhere assumed.

7. The unity and structure of the Song

One of the most hotly debated questions concerning the Song is that of its unity and structure. Some think that the Song is a collection of fragmentary independent poetic units of diverse origin, which have been collected and assembled by a later editor. But there is no general agreement, among those who hold this view, as to how many original units there are which have been woven together. Estimates vary from half a dozen to over thirty. It goes without saying that commentators who take this approach see no narrative plot sequence in the Song, as it is highly improbable that a later editor would try to compose a storyline from originally independent fragments. Others see the Song as a basic unity; there is an underlying unity of theme throughout the Song, even if we cannot trace an observable progression of plot. This exposition takes the view that the Song is repetitious and cyclic, but does not carry a consistent storyline. Various themes can be traced throughout the Song: the urgent desire for intimacy, the fear of loss, the celebration of consummation, the

---

7 See C. J. H. Wright, *Living as the People of God* (IVP, 1983), pp. 19, 89.

happiness of their mutual love, the praise of and delight in their physical beauty, the tensions arising from separation, the desire for public approval of their love, and the longing for its secret consummation. The Song itself is held together by the literary devices of repetition: the daughters of Jerusalem (1:5; 2:7; 3:5; 5:8, 16; 8:4), the praise poems (4:1–7; 5:10–16; 6:4–10; 7:1–10), the lost-seek-found sequences (3:1–5; 5:2 – 6:3), and various phrases which occur throughout the Song: 'browses among the lilies' (2:16; 6:2–3), 'my beloved is mine and I am his' (2:16; 6:3; 7:10), and so on. The Song meanders back and forth over its dominant themes, and is seemingly open-ended.

Those who encounter the Song for the first time are struck by what one author has described as 'the charming confusion of the Song'. There are difficulties in the demarcation of the individual units, and of the larger sections. A basic starting point is to attempt to identify the speakers. This is not so easily done as may be imagined at first sight. Although Hebrew possessive pronoun endings and verbal forms may be identified as masculine or feminine, singular and plural, there are many instances where this type of analysis does not resolve the difficulty, and so overall contextual considerations have to be invoked. As interpretations along these lines depend on the overall structural view taken by the commentator, we are left with a bewildering variety of options. Some of the units may be identified by their simple locale; others by the sustained nature of the responses of the participants to each other. Similarly a sudden change of mood may mark a division between two units; a climax of intimacy also seems to produce a natural break.

The overall structure I have postulated for the Song is a series of six cycles of movement. These coincide with those of the Good News Bible. This is only one of several possible arrangements for handling the seemingly amorphous nature of the Song, and is thus put forward somewhat tentatively. I hope it does not seem a too artificial or alien grid to impose externally on the rather loose association of different poems. It is all too easy to try to force the material rather reluctantly to fit the mould of a Procrustean bed. Within each cycle there are yearnings for love, usually some form of tension or frustration, affirmations of praise and beauty, and invitations or movements to intimacy or consummation. These appear in each cycle, but not necessarily in the same order. Each cycle ends on a note of intimacy, real, imagined or merely hinted at. However, these are not the only climaxes in the Song, and the boundaries could easily have been drawn elsewhere. A number of commentators have embarked on a complex analysis of interrelationships between their own postulated cycles, but these are often so intricate and not immediately obvious that they are hardly convincing. Since the Song is so repetitious it is not surprising that all manner of cross-relationships can be identified; but it is not clear that these can help in identifying an overall structure. Thus it is probably wisest not to be dogmatic in insisting on the correctness of one particular analysis.

The various cycles do not represent any progression in a time sequence, although the sixth cycle may be a literary culmination of the series, in that it recapitulates various themes occurring in previous cycles, and weaves them into a somewhat disjointed pattern (see on 8:5). The wedding cycle, around which the other cycles are balanced, is the literary focal centre of the Song, and its chronological climax. So we cannot automatically assume that the cycles which follow it necessarily envisage a married couple. The two troubled dream sequences occur in the second and fourth cycles enclosing the wedding cycle. In the early stages of the Song the girl is still under the authority of her brothers (1:6) and is clearly unmarried. And later, in 5:2–8, surely no newly-wedded bride would keep her husband waiting at the door at night, as she does. Similarly, it is only the inhibiting conventions of her unmarried state that give rise to her cry of frustration in 8:1. The problem of obtaining a tidy chronological sequence is linked to the whole problem of perceiving a coherent narrative plot in the Song. However, our literary approach has caused us to distance ourselves somewhat from this concern. Perhaps an illustration might help. The various cycles might be likened to a series of paintings at an art gallery where an exhibition by one artist is being mounted. All the pictures have a similar style and mood, stemming from this single artist. Each one is a particular permutation of a set of sub-themes. As we move from one picture to the next, we recognize the same underlying patterns, while noting the subtle changes in details.

Part 1
The Song as a whole

1. An overview of the text of the Song of Songs

Title and attribution (1:1)

The Song of Songs is attributed to Solomon.

The first cycle: passionate longings (1:1 – 2:7)

The deep yearnings of love (1:2–4)

The girl longs to receive her lover's kisses. His love-making is better than wine, his perfumes are fragrant. His name (his repute) is like scent wafted abroad. No wonder the maidens are attracted to him. She appeals to her lover to take her into the intimate secluded chamber where they can be alone together. The end of verse 4 is possibly an interjection by the daughters of Jerusalem, rejoicing in and extolling the lover.

Black and beautiful (1:5–6)

The girl, dark and suntanned after working in her brothers' vineyard, defends her natural beauty and complexion before the critical stares of the daughters of Jerusalem. She has not kept up her own appearance, in contrast to the city ladies.

A hesitant enquiry, an ambiguous response (1:7–8)

The girl makes a tentative, guarded enquiry as to where she might find her lover in the daytime. She is concerned lest her meandering search should be misinterpreted as being the solicitations of a harlot. The response is somewhat ambiguous; if it is her lover replying, then it could be a gentle reassurance; if it is the response of the city girls, there could possibly be an element of harshness or brusqueness here.

A filly in fine fettle (1:9–11)

Her lover likens the girl to a splendidly decorated horse, decked out with ribbons and bangles. He wants to beautify her even more.

The fragrance of love (1:12–14)

The girl describes the attractiveness of her lover in terms of the fragrances of nard, myrrh and henna blossoms. There are indications here of warm physical contact.

A duet of mutual admiration (1:15 – 2:3)

He acclaims her beauty (1:15).
She acclaims his beauty (1:16).
In unison, they describe their rustic rendezvous (1:17).
Her modest self-deprecation (2:1).
His affirmation of praise (2:2).
He is a shady apple tree to her (2:3).

Moving towards a climax (2:4–7)

The banqueting house. 'His banner over me [is] love' (2:4).
Sick with love (2:5).
Close encounters (2:6).
The adjuration of the daughters of Jerusalem (2:7).

The second cycle: springtime and showers (2:8 – 3:5)

Love in the springtime (2:8–13)

In his eager haste, the lover is compared to a young gazelle, springing over the mountains. He gives his urgent invitation to the girl, shut in behind her lattice window. There follows a most beautiful description of the exuberant blossoming of nature in the springtime.

A tantalizing tease (2:14–15)

She is inaccessible, like a dove in the crags of the cliffs (2:14).
The song of the little foxes ('Catch me if you can!') (2:15).

An affirmation and an invitation (2:16–17)

She expresses her contentment in the security of their relationship. Her lover is one who 'browses' among 'the lilies' (2:16).
She longs that she might spend the night with him and that he would be like a stag on the mountains of Bether (2:17).

A very troubled dream (3:1–5)

The girl is in bed alone at night, desperately longing for her absent lover, and fearing that she has been abandoned. She launches out into the city streets to seek him, but cannot find him. She collides with the watchmen, and asks them if they have seen her lover. She turns away from them in disappointment, and suddenly bumps into him. She seizes him in desperation and brings him to her 'mother's house'. The cycle closes with the adjuration to the daughters of Jerusalem.

The third cycle: the lovers' royal wedding (3:6 – 5:1)

Her rustic fragrant beauty (3:6)

This is probably an independent verse, praising the girl in her rustic beauty. It is uttered by the onlookers.

Solomon's sumptuous carriage (3:7–11)

A detailed description of Solomon's elaborate wedding throne. There is an invitation to gaze upon King Solomon on his wedding day. How this section fits in with the Song as a whole is a matter of much debate.

In praise of his beloved (4:1–7)

The lover praises his beloved's eyes, hair, teeth, lips, mouth, forehead, neck and breasts. He declares his intention of spending the night with her. The whole praise song is framed by two summary descriptions of her beauty in verses 1 and 7.

The lover's urgent plea (4:8)

The lover invites the girl to come with him away from the threatening and dangerous mountain ranges of Lebanon.

A lover smitten (4:9–11)

The lover is captivated and entranced by his beloved's eyes, her jewellery, her intoxicating caresses, the fragrance of her perfumes, and the sweetness of her kisses.

Moving towards a climax again (4:12 – 5:1)

Anticipation

He proclaims the purity of his beloved (4:12).
A garden locked, a fountain sealed (4:12).
A luscious garden full of fragrant spices (4:13).
A flowing stream, cascading down from Lebanon (4:15).

Invitation

The girl invites her lover to come into his garden (4:16)

Consummation

Her lover enters his garden, gathers his spices, eats his honey, and drinks his wine and his milk (5:1).

Affirmation

The lovers are encouraged to drink their fill of love (5:1).

The fourth cycle: lost and found (5:2 – 6:3)

Another dream of frustration (5:2–8)

The girl is again sleeping anxiously. She hears her lover knocking on the door at night. He is drenched with dew, and wants to come in. She is slow in responding and makes excuses for not getting up. Her lover puts his hand to the latch, and she rises in excitement to open the door. But he has disappeared, and her heart fails her. She goes out into the city to seek him, but all to no avail. The watchmen find her, treat her roughly and strip her cloak from her. The section closes with an adjuration to the daughters of Jerusalem, bidding them not to tell her lover that she is crazy with love.

The daughters of Jerusalem reply (5:9)

They ask why she thinks her lover is so special.

In praise of her lover (5:10–16)

He is radiant and ruddy. She describes his head, hair, eyes, cheeks, lips, hands, stomach, legs, stature and mouth.

An offer of help (6:1)

The daughters of Jerusalem offer to help the girl to find her lover.

Not really lost (6:2–3)

The girl replies that he's not really lost, but is in his usual haunts. She reaffirms their mutual commitment to each other.

The fifth cycle: beauty kindles desire (6:4 – 8:4)

Her awesome and terrifying beauty (6:4–7)

The lover compares the girl to Tirzah and Jerusalem. Her beauty is so awesome that he is profoundly unsettled. He praises her by describing her hair, her teeth and her forehead.

She is utterly unique (6:8–9)

She is beyond compare. All the other beautiful girls praise her in the following song.

Her cosmic beauty (6:10)

Her beauty is likened to the dawn, the moon, the sun and (literally) 'the bannered ones'.

Dreaming in the walnut garden (6:11–12)

She wanders down to look at the new growth, the blossoming vines. Verse 12 is very obscure; possibly a fantasy.

A sight for tired eyes (6:13)

The onlookers, or the lover, want the Shulammite to return, so that she might be the object of their gaze. But she does not want to be stared at as if she were a dancing girl.

Her graceful form (7:1–5)

Many commentators take this to be a description of the girl dancing in very flimsy veils. Some take it to be the words of the onlookers, others the words of the lover. The various parts of her body are praised: her feet, thighs, navel, belly, breasts, neck, eyes, nose, head and hair.

A duet of desire (7:6–10)

The lover's desire is aroused, and he longs to 'climb the palm tree' and (lit.) 'seize its fronds'. Her breasts are like clusters of dates. Verse 9 reverts to the speech of the girl, who responds by praising the smoothness of their kissing. She ends in an affirmation of her lover's desire for her.

Love in the countryside (7:11–13)

The girl invites her lover to spend the night among the henna bushes. She promises that she will make love to him there. She has old things and new things treasured up for him.

A longing for intimacy (8:1–4)

She wishes that she could kiss her lover, freely and publicly, without the embarrassment of social disapproval. She longs for physical intimacy. 'His left arm is under my head . . .' The cycle again ends with the adjuration to the daughters of Jerusalem, though in a slightly different form.

The sixth cycle: the security of love (8:5–14)

The happy couple (8:5a)

Probably the daughters of Jerusalem are here extolling the happiness of the two lovers. An independent line.

Love's arousal (8:5b)

The girl remembers how she took the initiative in arousing her lover.

Love, strong as death (8:6–7)

The girl longs for their mutual love to be on public display. Verses 6–7 are the only lines in the Song which extol the nature of love in the abstract. They represent a high point in the Song. Love is unquenchable, passionate and all-consuming. Love cannot be bought or sold.

The little sister (8:8–10)

Verses 8–9 could be spoken by the girl or by the brothers. They ponder the future fate of their younger sister, who is not yet ripe for marriage. When she is, should they decorate her or protect her? One problem here is whether 'door' and 'wall' are in synonymous or antithetic parallelism. Whatever the young sister is, the girl in verse 10 is fully mature, poised and a source of contentment to her loved one.

A vineyard not for hire (8:11–12)

Here, two vineyards are contrasted. On the one hand, Solomon's vineyard was hired out for money. The girl's vineyard, on the other hand, is not up for sale. Her love cannot be bought or sold.

The continuing cycle of desire (8:13–14)

A somewhat ambiguous ending. All the themes here have appeared previously. Probably it is a deliberately fluid ending, representing the constant ebb and flow of a love relationship.

2. A literal translation of the Song

The phrases or words marked with an asterisk (*) are in need of some linguistic explanation, and the exposition should be consulted for further information.

Title and attribution (1:1)

1:1The Song of Songs which pertains to Solomon*.

The first cycle: passionate longings (1:2 – 2:7)

The deep yearnings of love (1:2–4)

2Let him kiss me with some of the kisses of his mouth.
Indeed*, better are your caresses* than wine;
3fragrance-wise, your oils are good.
Oil of Turaq* is your name.
Therefore maidens love you.

4Draw me after you, let us run.
The king has brought me to his chambers.

We will rejoice, and we will exult in you.
We will commemorate* your caresses* more than wine.
Rightly do they love you.

Black and beautiful (1:5–6)

5Black am I, but* beautiful,
daughters of Jerusalem,
like the tents of Qedar,
like the tapestries of Solomon*.

[6]Do not look at me because I am black-black*,
because the sun has scorched me.
The sons of my mother were angry with me.
They set me keeping the vineyards.
My vineyard which is mine, I have not kept.

A hesitant enquiry, an ambiguous response (1:7–8)

[7]Tell me, him whom my soul loves,
where do you pasture,
where do you cause to lie down, at noon,
lest I should be like a veiled one*
alongside the flocks of your companions?

[8]If you do not know,
the most beautiful among the women,
go forth by the tracks of the flock,
and graze your kids
by the shelters of the shepherds.

A filly in fine fettle (1:9–11)

[9]To a mare among the chariots of Pharaoh
I compare you, my darling.
[10]Beautiful are your cheeks with rings,
your neck with bead-strings.
[11]Chains of gold we will make for you,
with the spikes of silver.

The fragrance of love (1:12–14)

[12]While *the king was on his couch*,
my nard gave its scent.
[13]A pouch of myrrh is my beloved to me;
between my breasts he spends the night*.
[14]A cluster of henna is my beloved to me,
in the vineyards of En Gedi*.

A duet of mutual admiration (1:15 – 2:3)

[15]Behold, you are beautiful, my darling;
behold, you are beautiful;
your eyes are doves.

[16]Behold, you are beautiful, my love;
indeed delightful.
Indeed our couch is verdant*.
[17]The rafters of our houses are cedars,
our roof-beams, cypresses.

[2:1]I am a crocus of the Sharon,
a lily of the valleys.

[2]Like a lily among thorns,
so my darling among women.

[3]Like an apple tree* among the trees of the wood,
so my beloved among men.
In his shade I delight to stay,
and his fruit is sweet to my taste.

Moving towards a climax (2:4–7)

[4]He has brought me to the house of wine
and his banner* over me is love*.
[5]Spread me* among the raisin cakes,
lay me out* among the apples*,
for faint with love am I.

[6]His left hand under my head,
and his right hand fondles me.

[7]I adjure you, daughters of Jerusalem,
by the gazelles or hinds of the field,
do not arouse* and do not excite*
love until it pleases*.

The second cycle: springtime and showers (2:8 – 3:5)

Love in the springtime (2:8–13)

[8]The sound* of my beloved.
Behold, he comes,
leaping over the mountains,

springing over the hills,
[9]resembling, my beloved, a gazelle
or a young stag, the hart.
Behold, standing by our wall,
peeping in at the window,
peering in through the lattice.
[10]He responded, my lover, and said to me,
'Arise, my darling,
my beautiful one, and come.

[11]'For behold, the winter has passed,
the rain has passed, has gone.
[12]The blossoms have appeared in the land;
the time of singing* has drawn near,
and the voice of the turtle dove is heard in our land.
[13]The fig tree has sprouted her early fruits
and the vines in blossom have yielded their scent.
Arise, come, my love,
my beautiful one, and come.'

A tantalizing tease (2:14–15)

[14]My dove, in the clefts of the rock,
in the hidden place of the steep ravines,
show me your appearance*,
cause me to hear your voice.
For your voice is sweet
and your appearance fair.

[15]Catch for us foxes,
young foxes, destroying vineyards,
and our vineyards in blossom.

An affirmation and an invitation (2:16–17)

[16]My beloved is mine,
and I am his,
he who pastures among the lilies.
[17]Until the day breathes,
and the shadows flee,

turn, and be like
a gazelle or a young stag, the hart,
upon the mountains of Bether*.

A very troubled dream (3:1–5)

^{3:1}Upon my bed during the nights
I sought him whom my soul loves;
I sought him, but did not find him.
²I will arise, and I will go around in the city,
in the streets, and in the open places.
I will seek him whom my soul loves.
I sought him, but did not find him.
³They found me, the watchmen patrolling around the city.
'He whom my soul loves, have you seen?'
⁴It was as a little while from when I passed away from them*
until I found him whom my soul loves.

I seized him and I would not let him go,
until I brought him to the house of my mother,
and to the chamber of her who conceived me.

⁵I adjure you, daughters of Jerusalem,
by the gazelles or hinds of the field,
do not arouse* and do not excite*
love until it pleases*.

The third cycle: the lovers' royal wedding (3:6 – 5:1)

Her rustic fragrant beauty (3:6)

⁶Who is this coming up from the open countryside*,
like columns of smoke,
perfumed with myrrh and frankincense,
from all the powders of the merchant?

Solomon's sumptuous carriage (3:7–11)

⁷Behold his sedan*, which is Solomon's,
sixty mighty men surrounding it,
some of the mighty men of Israel.

[8]All of them armed with sword,
trained in warfare;
each one his sword at his side
against the terror in the nights.
[9]A carriage he made for himself,
the King Solomon,
from the timber of the Lebanon.
[10]Its poles he made of silver.
Its canopy* gold.
Its cushions, purple cloth.
Its interior fitted out with love*,
[11]from the daughters of Jerusalem*.
Go forth, and look upon, daughters of Zion,
the King Solomon;
at the crown with which his mother crowned him
on the day of his wedding,
and on the day of the gladness of his heart.

In praise of his beloved (4:1–7)

[4:1]Behold, you are beautiful, my darling, behold, you are beautiful.
Your eyes are doves
behind your veil.
Your hair is like the flock of goats
which stream down from the mountain of Gilead.

[2]Your teeth like the flock of the shorn ones,
which have come up from the washing,
each one of them bearing twins,
and none among them bereaved.

[3]Like a scarlet ribbon, your lips,
and your mouth*, lovely!
Like a slice of pomegranate, your forehead*
behind your veil.

[4]Like the tower of David, your neck,
built in terraces*.
A thousand shields hung upon it,
all the equipment* of mighty men.

[5]Your pair of breasts like a pair of fawns,
twins of a gazelle,
browsing among the lilies.

[6]Until the day breathes,
and the shadows flee,
I will go to the mountain of myrrh,
and to the hill of frankincense.

[7]You are altogether beautiful, my darling,
and blemish there is none in you.

The lover's urgent plea (4:8)

[8]With me from* Lebanon, a bride –
with me from Lebanon, you shall come.
You shall travel* from the top of Amanah,
from the top of Senir and Hermon,
from dens of lions,
from lairs of leopards.

A lover smitten (4:9–11)

[9]You have ravished my heart*, my sister bride.
You have ravished my heart with one of
your eyes,
with one gem from your necklace.
[10]How beautiful are your caresses,
my sister bride.
How much better are your caresses than wine,
and the scent of your oils than all spices.
[11]Honey from the comb, your lips drip, bride.
Honey and milk under your tongue
and the scent of your robes
like the scent of Lebanon.

Moving towards a climax again (4:12 – 5:1)

Anticipation (4:12–15)

[12]A garden locked, my sister bride.
A spring* sealed, a fountain locked.

[13]Your tendrils*, an orchard of pomegranates,
with fruit of excellence,
henna bushes with nard plants,
[14]nard and saffron,
cane and cinnamon,
with all woods of fragrance,
myrrh and aloes,
with all finest spices of Balsam.

[15]A fountain of gardens.
A well of living water,
and cascadings from Lebanon.

Invitation (4:16)

[16]Awake, north wind.
And come, south wind.
Blow upon my garden.
Let its spices flow.
Let my beloved come into his garden,
and let him eat its exquisite fruit.

Consummation (5:1)

[5:1]I have entered my garden, my sister bride.
I have gathered my myrrh, together with my spice.
I have eaten my honeycomb, together with my honey.
I have drunk my wine, along with my milk.

Affirmation (5:1)

Eat, friends,
drink and become drunk, caresses*.

The fourth cycle: lost and found (5:2 – 6:3)

Another dream of frustration (5:2–8)

[2]I was asleep, but my heart was awake.
The sound of my beloved knocking.
'Open to me, my sister, my darling,

my dove, my perfect one.
For my head is drenched with dew,
my locks with the droplets of the night.'
³'I have taken off* my clothes*.
How then should I put it on?
I have washed my feet.
How then should I soil them?'
⁴My lover thrust forth his hand through* the hole*,
and my innards seethed on his account.
⁵I arose, I did, to open for my lover.
And my hands dripped myrrh,
and my fingers, flowing myrrh
upon the handles of the bolt.
⁶I opened, I did,
but my beloved had turned, had gone.
My soul went out at his departure*.
I sought him, but did not find him.
I called to him, but he did not answer me.

⁷They found me, the watchmen,
those patrolling in the city.
They struck me, they bruised me.
They took away my wrapper from off me,
the keepers of the walls.
⁸I adjure you, daughters of Jerusalem,
do not find my lover*.
Do not tell him*
that sick of love I am.

The daughters of Jerusalem reply (5:9)

⁹What is your beloved more than a beloved,
the most beautiful among women?
What is your beloved more than a beloved,
that in this manner you adjure us?

In praise of her lover (5:10–16)

¹⁰My beloved is radiant and ruddy,
conspicuous among ten thousand.

[11]His head, gold, fine gold.
His locks, palm fronds*,
black as the raven.
[12]His eyes like doves, by the channels of water*,
bathing in milk,
sitting upon a fullness*.
[13]His cheeks like spice beds,
towers of perfumes.
His lips, lilies,
dripping flowing myrrh.
[14]His hands, cylinders of gold,
being filled with Tarshish gems.
His stomach*, a plaque* of ivory,
covered with sapphires.

[15]His legs, pillars of alabaster,
set on sockets of gold.
His stature* like the Lebanon,
choice as the cedar trees.
[16]His inside mouth, sweet things; and all of
him is delightful.
This is my beloved, this is my friend,
daughters of Jerusalem.

An offer of help (6:1)

[6:1]Whither has your beloved gone,
the most beautiful among women?
Whither has your beloved turned,
so that we might seek him with you?

Not really lost (6:2–3)

[2]My beloved has gone down to his garden,
to the beds of balsam,
to pasture in the gardens,
to pluck lilies.
[3]I am my beloved's and my beloved is mine,
he who pastures among the lilies.

The fifth cycle: beauty kindles desire (6:4 – 8:4)

Her awesome and terrifying beauty (6:4–7)

⁴Beautiful you are, my darling, like Tirzah,
lovely as Jerusalem,
awesome as the bannered ones*.

⁵Turn your eyes away from me,
for they agitate me.
Your hair like a flock of goats,
which are streaming down from the Gilead.
⁶Your teeth, like the flock of ewes,
which come up from the washing,
all of them bearing twins,
not one among them bereaved.
⁷Like a slice of pomegranate, your forehead*
behind your veil.

She is utterly unique (6:8–9)

⁸Sixty they are, queens,
and eighty concubines,
and maidens without number.
⁹One is she, my dove, my perfect one.
One is she to her mother,
pure* is she to her who bore her.
Girls have seen her and pronounced her fortunate;
queens and concubines, and they praised her.

Her cosmic beauty (6:10)

¹⁰'Who is this who looks forth as the dawn*,
beautiful as the moon,
pure as the sun,
awesome as the bannered ones*?'

Dreaming in the walnut garden (6:11–12)

¹¹To the garden of walnuts I went down,
to see the new growth of the valley,

to see whether the vines had blossomed,
the pomegranates had bloomed.
[12]I did not know my soul set me
chariots of my people a prince*.

A sight for tired eyes (6:13)

[13]Return, return, Shulammite*,
Return, return, so that we might gaze on you.
How* would you gaze on the Shulammite
as the dance of the two camps*?

Her graceful form (7:1–5)

[7:1]How beautiful are your feet* in sandals,
daughter of a prince.
The curves of your thighs, like ornaments,
the workmanship of the hands of a craftsman.
[2]Your navel*, the basin of roundness;
may it not lack mixed wine.
Your belly*, a mound of wheat grain,
fenced in by lilies.
[3]The pair of your breasts, like a pair of fawns,
twins of a gazelle.
[4]Your neck like a tower of ivory.
Your eyes, pools in Heshbon,
by the gate of* Bath Rabbim*.
Your nose* like the tower of Lebanon,
looking out over the face of Damascus.
[5]Your head upon you like the Carmel,
and the locks of your head like purple.
A king held captive by tresses!

A duet of desire (7:6–10)

[6]How beautiful, and how pleasant,
O love, with exquisite things*.
[7]This your stature, it resembles a palm tree,
and your twin breasts, clusters of grapes.
[8]I said, I will climb up a palm tree,
I will seize its fronds*.

And may your twin breasts be as the clusters of the vine,
and the scent of your nose* like the apples,
⁹and the inside of your mouth like wine, the best,
going down to my beloved, smoothly*,
gliding over the lips of sleepers*.

¹⁰I am my beloved's,
and towards me is his desire.

Love in the countryside (7:11–13)

¹¹Come, my beloved,
let us go out into the field,
let us spend the night among the henna bushes*,
¹²let us rise early to the vineyards,
let us see if the vine has blossomed,
the grape blossoms have sprouted,
the pomegranates have burst forth.
There I will give to you my caresses*.
¹³The mandrakes have given off scent.
And over our doors all sorts of delicacies*.
New things as well as old things,
my beloved, I have stored up for you.

A longing for intimacy (8:1–4)

⁸⁺¹Who will place you like a brother to me*,
sucking the breasts of my mother?
I would find you in the streets, I would kiss you,
even they would not despise me.
²I would lead you, I would bring you to the house of my mother.
You would teach me*.
I would give you to drink some wine that is spiced,
some sweet wine of my pomegranate.
³His left hand under my head,
and his right hand fondles me.
⁴I adjure you, daughters of Jerusalem,
how* will you excite, and how will you arouse
love until it pleases?

The sixth cycle: the security of love (8:5–14)

The happy couple (8:5)

⁵Who is this ascending from the countryside*
leaning upon her lover?

Love's arousal (8:5)

Underneath the fruit tree* I awakened you;
there your mother conceived you*,
there she conceived, she gave birth to you.

Love, strong as death (8:6–7)

⁶Place me as a seal upon your heart,
as a signet upon your arm.
For strong as death is love.
Jealousy as Sheol, relentless*.
Her darts*, darts of fire, a flame of Yah*.
⁷Many waters are not able to quench love
and torrents shall not sweep it away.
If a man should give
all the wealth of his home for love,
they would utterly scorn him*.

The little sister (8:8–10)

⁸A sister we have, a little one,
and breasts she does not have.
What shall we do for our sister
on the day when it shall be spoken about her*?
⁹If she is a wall,
we will build upon her battlements* of silver;
and* if she is a door,
we will enclose her with a panel of cedar.
¹⁰I am a wall, and my breasts like towers.
Then have I become in his eyes as one bringing* peace*.

A vineyard not for hire (8:11–12)

¹¹A vineyard Solomon used to have in Baal Hamon*.
He gave out the vineyard to keepers;

each would bring for its fruit
a thousand silver pieces.
^{12}My vineyard which is mine is before me*.
The thousand are yours, Solomon,
and two hundred for the keepers of its fruit.

The continuing cycle of desire (8:13–14)

^{13}You who dwell in the gardens,
companions are listening to your voice.
Make me listen.
^{14}'Flee, my beloved,
and be like a gazelle,
or a young stag, the hart,
upon the mountains of spices.'

3. A free paraphrase of the Song

Title and attribution (1:1)

[1:1]The most beautiful of Solomon's songs.

The first cycle: passionate longings (1:2 – 2:7)

The deep yearnings of love (1:2–4)

[2]O to feel the deepness
of the kisses of your mouth!
Your gentle touch intoxicates,
your fondling strokes inflame,
a heady wine more potent
than any ancient vintage.

[3]The aroma of your presence,
the fresh fragrance of your name,
a wafted scent, a perfume sweet,
to shed abroad your fame.
With such a reputation
you are bathed in admiration,
by the virgin city maidens
who are eager for your love.

[4]My darling, take me with you.
Quick, make haste, let's run.
My royal king has drawn me
to his inner private sanctum,
the haven for our love.

The Message of the Song of Songs

How we exult in you!
The memory of your fragrant love
shall never fade away.
The mellowness of smooth mulled wine,
lingering long, and there to stay.

Black and beautiful (1:5–6)

[5]Sun-scorched am I, and stunning!
O city maidens, pale creations
of cosmetic creams.
But as for me, with darkness deep
do I with lustre shine,
the warm black depth
of distant nomad tents,
of Solomon's dusky shades.

[6]Stare not at me, so deeply dark,
avert your hostile glare.
The sun her fiery gaze has cast on me
and burnt me with her heat.
My brothers' anger also flared,
they took me, all, to task
and made me labour in the sun
to cultivate their vineyards,
their trellises to mend.

Alas! Alas!
That luscious vine, uniquely mine,
I've had no time
to tend.

A hesitant enquiry, an ambiguous response (1:7–8)

[7]O where shall I find you, my shepherd love?
Where do you graze,
where lay to rest,
amid the haze
of noonday's heat?

Tell me! Tell me! Lest I should wander
in futile search, appear to loiter,
my name besmirch,
'mongst your companions, with their flocks.

[8]Don't ask me that, most beautiful one.
Surely you know the place
of my true pasture.
Bring your own kids, and follow the tracks.
There you will find me
by the shepherds' own shelters,
and no-one will know that
you've come just for me.

A filly in fine fettle (1:9–11)

[9]A mare magnificently groomed,
a filly in fine fettle.
Sporting midst lusty stallions
of Egypt's royal chariots.
Entrancing in allure
with secret pulse of naked power
so thinly veiled, your flawless flanks
enhanced in flowing ribbons.

[10]How beautiful!
Your cheek's smooth curves
enframed by rings of brazen bangles,
which dangle down
by slender tower,
by neck bedecked by beads.

[11]We'll crown you with more royalty.
O maiden queen, with costly gems,
with rings of golden sheen
and sparkling spikes of silver.

The fragrance of love (1:12–14)

[12]My king spreadeagled sprawls,
at ease upon his sofa,

enwrapped in mists from scented shawls
enveloped by their aura.

[13]A pendant pouch of myrrh to me,
at night he lies between my breasts.

[14]A spray of henna blossom,
he, upon my fragrant vineyard,
the oasis of En Gedi.

A duet of mutual admiration (1:15 – 2:3)

[15]How beautiful you are, my precious one,
your shy coy glances their gentle invitations give,
your eyes a pair of fluttering doves.

[16-17]Indeed delightful are you, my lover,
handsome, above all others.
On nature's verdant litter,
there we lie, we rest
on greeny sward, in
Eden's secret glade,
enwrapped in nature's close embrace,
a bower of never-failing foliage,
a canopy of firs.

[2:1]What draws your eye to gaze alone
full focus just on me?
On me, a common daisy, blooming
midst myriads by the river's brim?

[2]Not so, not so, my daisy dear,
O rare exotic flower,
a stately stem in radiant bloom,
so dazzling in your bower
amid the dark of nature's thorny thicket,
of bramble and of briar.

[3]A luscious lime, a citrus tree,
a source of sweet refreshment he,
an island in the dryness of

the wild and tangled wood.
Sheltered in his shade, I rest relaxed, secure.
The sweetness of his tasty fruit,
the object of desire.

Moving towards a climax (2:4–7)

⁴He has brought me to his cellar,
I have tasted of his wine,
his glance towards me heavy
with the urgency of love.
His desire, his intent, with one purpose is bent,
our love to fulfil.
⁵O spread me out, and bed me down,
in rugs of raisin cakes, and beds of golden apples.

Come now, come soon – I faint, I swoon,
so eager to consume the fruit of our desire.

⁶I rest within his encircled arm,
his hand my contours strokes.

⁷O daughters of Jerusalem, I put you under oath,
swear to me, by wild gazelles and antelopes,
by our ancestral deity, by our covenant God,
do not disturb us, until we have drunk our fill of love.

The second cycle: springtime and showers (2:8 – 3:5)

Love in the springtime (2:8–13)

⁸Hark! His voice!
I hear him coming!
It's my beloved.
Leaping sprightly
o'er hill and dale,
effortlessly agile,
eager, alert,
⁹a dashing gazelle.

He's here! At our very wall!
Peeping in at the window,

looking through the lattice,
whispering his urgent summons:

[10]Quick! Quick!
Let's hurry, my love,
Away at nature's bidding.

[11]The winter rains, so drab and drear,
are past, and long forgotten.
[12]For nature now, with pent-up power,
bursts forth with grand effusion;
her blossoms blooming,
the doves are cooing,
[13]in concert wooing,
a seductive invitation.

A tantalizing tease (2:14–15)

[14]My shy little dove, so soft, so gentle,
so quick to fly away,
so out of reach, untouchable,
in nature's craggy cliffs, remote ravines.
Let me come near that I might hear
the softness of your soothing tones.
O please don't flee, that I might see
the smoothness of your shapely form
in nature's hidden places.

[15]Watch out! Watch out!
My eager lover boy!
There are other frisky foxes on the prowl,
wanton in their playful frolics,
raiding vineyards, causing havoc.
Eager in their haste to taste
the ripening grape of my own vine.

An affirmation and an invitation (2:16–17)

[16]In strong embrace of mutual love
so tightly held, so safe, secure.

O he is mine and I am his,
who gently feeds and pastures
in meadows of my fragrant flowers.

[17]Until the gleam of nature's morn,
until the early hours of dawn,
when sun's first ray does chase away
the shadows of the night,
turn, my love.
And there cavort and spring and sport,
a young gazelle o'er hill and fell,
upon the valleys and the peaks
of nature's rolling contours.

A very troubled dream (3:1–5)

[3:1]Throughout the long and lonesome nights,
for restless hours I lay awake with empty ache,
tossing, turning, consumed with yearning
for my absent lover.
Seeking, seeking, his presence pining,
seeking, seeking, but never finding.
Enshrouded by his absence.

[2]With urgent desperation,
into the hostile night I threw myself, exposed,
to search the silent city.

Her empty streets and squares
echoed with his absence.

[3]Darting hither, darting thither,
I met the stolid watchmen on patrol,
guardians of the sleeping city –
I asked about my lover dear;
the silence of their stares with
uncomprehending eye, their mute
reply did make.

[4]Scarce had I slowly turned away
in hollow disappointment,

when, oh! what rushing torrent of relief,
I spied my lover
and did catch and clasp.
I held him fast in hard embrace
and would not let him go
until I'd brought him to my mother's home,
the chamber of conception.

⁵O daughters of Jerusalem,
I put you under solemn oath
that you would swear to me,
by wild gazelles and antelopes,
by our ancestral deity, by our covenant God,
do not disturb us, until we have drunk our fill of love.

The third cycle: the lovers' royal wedding (3:6 – 5:1)

Her rustic fragrant beauty (3:6)

⁶Behold she comes, so fresh
from rustic countryside,
enwrapped in clouds of incense,
wreathed with the fragrant fumes
from merchant's spicy store.

Solomon's sumptuous carriage (3:7–11)

⁷In depths of rural reverie we dreamed a dream
of noble royal marriage.
Behold the sight of his sedan,
of Solomon's sumptuous carriage.
Behold its proud procession,
by honour guard enflanked;
⁸the nation's hardened heroes,
elite in skill to fight
the terrors of the night.

⁹Behold the king's exact design,
its several parts the art of
many craftsmen fine.

The timber from the famous woods
of Lebanon afar.

[10]Its slender poles of costly silver made,
the canopy of golden cloth its shade.
Its cushion covers of royal purple braid,
expensively refined.
The inner panels, luxuriously lined
with leather, by the daughters of Jerusalem.

[11]Come forth, O city maidens,
extol my royal king;
behold him crowned with family glory,
on his joyful wedding day.

In praise of his beloved (4:1–7)

[4:1]How beautiful you are,
my delectable maiden,
O daughter of delight.

Behind your frail veil's wispy thread
your timid eyes retreat,
their coy and bashful glances
your nervous invitation give.
Your flitting lashes,
the trembling fluttering of a dove.
Your glistening hair, its glossy locks,
your motion whirls their glowing curls,
they twist and turn with dancing undulation,
the distant flocks of flowing goats
which ripple down the verdant slopes.

[2]Your fresh white teeth
so clean, so smooth,
like skin of sheep so closely shorn
and washed and bleached.
Each with matching set of twins
gleaming in perfect symmetry,
and none without its partner.

The Message of the Song of Songs

[3]Your fulsome shapely lips
a silky scarlet band
around your comely mouth,
which frames your mellowed speech.

Your veil's fine web of tracery,
its gossamer of lace,
their soft fine shadow cast
upon the contours of your face.
Your temple's gentle roundness,
your curving downy cheeks
entraced with mesh so delicate,
an image of a pomegranate,
of rosy hue and membranes soft.
[4]Your stately neck bedecked
by layered rows of beads,
secure and strong, impregnable,
like David's royal tower,
majestic with its trophies,
the spoils of ancient wars.
Its serried ranks of shiny shields
adorn its panelled walls.

[5]Your shy twin breasts,
two timid fawns to stroke,
which gently graze among the cusps,
the lips of fragrant lilies.

[6]Until the gleam of nature's morn,
until the early hours of dawn,
when sun's first ray does chase away
the shadows of the night,
I'll run and spring on mountain heights,
on contours of the countryside,
her fresh and fragrant slopes.

[7]Wholly delectable you are, my darling,
flawless in your unique perfection.

The lover's urgent plea (4:8)

[8]Come with me, my darling,
from mystic mountain height,
the snowy crests of Lebanon,
from there we'll take our flight.
Magnificent in beauty,
inspiring awe and dread,
enshrouded in her misty veil
the clouds about her head.
Give me your hand, let's run, let's flee
from lairs of lurking lions
and haunts of loping leopards,
away from nature's hostile land.

A lover smitten (4:9–11)

[9]With silent glance from flashing eye,
with single spark from jewelled gem,
you set my ravished heart abeat
to burn and churn with rapid palpitation.

[10]Your tender strokes, your gentle touch,
inflame me more than wine.
The urgent tokens of your love
send shivers down my spine.
The fragrance of your perfumes sweet,
the wafting scents from flowing robes,
are better than all spices.

[11]Your heavy kiss, your liquid lips,
sweet foretaste of a promised land
to be possessed, to enter soon,
with milk and honey flowing.

Moving towards a climax again (4:12 – 5:1)

Anticipation (4:12–15)

[12]My darling sister bride,
a garden locked, secure,
a private flowing fountain spring,

her waters running pure.
A stranger has no access there
to taste her flowing streams,
nor trespass in to penetrate
her secret shady quarters.
A perfect place of privilege,
a tangled hedge about her spring
to guard against intruders.

[13]A luscious scented garden,
a paradise of Eden,
of fragrant fruit
[14]and perfumed pines,
of nature's cornucopia.
A fantasy of luxury,
its fertile groves
a garden of Utopia,
[15]of splashing streams
from mountains high,
cascading down,
so clear, so cool,
inviting.

Invitation (4:16)
[16]Awake the wind!
From every quarter stir!
and blow upon my garden,
to waft my perfumed scents abroad
to send its invitation.
Awake the wind!
and let my fragrant juices flow
in eager anticipation.

Come in! Come in!
O enter in, my lover.
Make haste and taste
my luscious fruit,
the fruit from my own garden.

Consummation (5:1)

5:1I have entered in, my precious bride,
I have taken possession of my garden,
the home of ancient promise.
I have tasted her milk.
I have gathered her honey.
I have tasted the wine from her grapes.
O delightful delirium,
O intimate union,
a fusion of fragrance,
a banquet of love.

Affirmation (5:1)

Feast, O lovers,
drink your fill,
from all restraint set free.
Let passions pent, their floodgates vent,
and cast yourselves with joyful glee
upon the tide of love.

The fourth cycle: lost and found (5:2 – 6:3)

Another dream of frustration (5:2–8)

2Restless sleeping in the night,
thoughts in motion, never ceasing,
troubled dreaming,
turning, churning through the night.

Knock! Knock! In the darkness of the night.
What intruding plight is this?
Knock! Knock! Knocking.
Who is there?
Beating in the midnight air?

Slowly waking, eyelids rubbing,
surely not my lover late
at the portals of my gate.
Urgent whispers, 'Quick, it's me.

The Message of the Song of Songs

Let me in! I'm soaked with dew,
glistening drops, dripping from my curly locks.
Quick, let me in, my precious dove.
My flawless one, my only love.'

Knock! Knock! Just who is this?
Am I dreaming? Is it him?
Should I rise to let him in?
Methinks I would my lover tease.
Just who is he that I should please his every whim?
Why not delay his coming in
and play my tricks and leave him standing,
dripping, shivering on the landing.

3'My lover dear, just keep at bay,
I've taken off my negligee.
Too late to put my wrapper on
and soil again my dainty feet,
to rise and let you in again,
into my cosy chamber.'

4He put his hand through at the latch;
I sensed the thrill, my heart did catch
with pounding jolt.
I sprang to let my lover in,
my fragrant fingers at the bolt.

5I opened wide to let him in.
But, O despair, no-one there!
Nothing but the midnight air.
He'd turned and gone,
he'd taken flight,
into the darkness of the night.

6I nearly died,
my mind went blank,
my heavy heart with sickness sank
in awful black dejection.
Into the city streets I ran,
searching here, calling there.

The eerie empty square
mockingly replied, with footsteps hollow echoing.
With urgent desperation, I sought my absent lover.
I sought but did not find him.
⁷But they found me,
the stolid watchmen of the night,
the city walls patrolling,
stern guardians of morality.
They took me for a wandering girl
of doubtful reputation.
They beat me, bruised me,
they stripped me of my outer dress
and left me crying in distress.

⁸O daughters of Jerusalem,
I put you under oath.
I beg you not to tell my lover
that I'm smitten with an illness,
a sickness of the heart,
that sent me on a wild-goose chase,
this crazy escapade.

The daughters of Jerusalem reply (5:9)

⁹O you who are the fairest
of the fair ones of your race,
just what's so great about your man
that you should bind us so?

In praise of her lover (5:10–16)

¹⁰My lover is radiant and ruddy,
glowing with rustic health.
In the full flush of manly youth,
conspicuous among a thousand.

¹¹His golden face bronzed with the sun,
with warmth of amber glows.
His waving locks luxuriant
with raven's blackness gleam,

as flowing palm-tree fronds
do shimmer in the breeze.

[12]His active darting eyes,
so full of fun,
do dance and play in unison,
two doves which sport,
in fantasy,
by ducts of flowing water,
which bathe in milky haze
and rest upon the fragrant banks.

[13]His stubbled fragrant cheeks
like garden beds of herbs,
their scent like that of
towering piles of spices.

His lips are lilies in whose cusps
are smoothly flowing fragrant scents,
delights to taste and drink.

[14]His sunburnt arms are rolls of
thinly beaten gold,
with rings of gems, imported
from Tarshish far away.

His flat taut stomach,
so white and smooth,
a plaque of ivory, whose shiny hue
inlaid with sapphire's gentle blue.

[15]His splendid rippling legs,
smooth alabaster columns, so
faintly veined,
on golden sockets standing.

His whole appearance, his stature true,
magnificent in splendour,
like Lebanon's lofty mountain height
as famous as her cedars.

¹⁶His mouth a source of sweetness,
a vintage wine to drink,
and honey from the comb.

He is altogether desirable,
absolutely lovely,
a source of never-failing fruit,
of exquisite delights.

Such is my lover,
this is my friend,
O daughters of Jerusalem.

An offer of help (6:1)

⁶:¹Tell us, O most beautiful,
the fairest of the fair,
tell us the way your lover took
that we might look, with you,
and seeking, help to find him.

Not really lost (6:2–3)

²Sisters, is that what you really think?
That he has gone astray?
He's wandering in his usual haunts,
that's where he loves to play.
In spicy gardens browsing
and plucking at the lilies.

³O I am his, and he is mine,
who gently grazes
'mongst nature's fragrant flowers.

The fifth cycle: beauty kindles desire (6:4 – 8:4)

Her awesome and terrifying beauty (6:4–7)

⁴Fair you are, my dear,
my lovely garden city,
Mount Pleasant, Tirzah
in her olden days,

resting on her sunny slopes,
a radiant crown of beauty.

In regal power and stature,
in majesty so high,
as awesome is your presence
as Salem's ancient city,
a rock of peace,
secure and wholesome,
the foundation of well-being.

Awesome as the cosmic crown,
the canopy of night,
beneath whose starry wreath we stand
and gaze in solemn awe,
agape at nature's marvel.

[5]Avert your tantalizing eyes,
your gaze which threatens danger.
Your awesome beauty has the power
to churn the depths of deep desire,
to light the fire of yearning strong
that drains me of all strength.
A helpless victim I am left,
a slave at beauty's mercy,
weak captive of magnificence.
Your glistening hair, its glossy locks,
your motion whirls their glowing curls,
they twist and turn with dancing undulation,
the distant flocks of flowing goats
which ripple down the verdant slopes.

[6]Your fresh white teeth, so clean and smooth
like skin of sheep, so closely cropped
and washed and bleached,
each with matching set of twins,
gleaming in perfect symmetry,
and none without its partner.

[7]Your veil's fine web of tracery,
its gossamer of lace,
their soft fine shadow cast
upon the contours of your face.
Your temple's gentle roundness,
your curving downy cheeks
entraced with mesh so delicate,
an image of a pomegranate,
of rosy hue and membranes soft.

She is utterly unique (6:8–9)

[8]Amid a glittering galaxy
of countless shining stars,
the myriads of choice maidens,
voluptuous virgins all,
the scores of stunning models,
bevies of beauty queens,
dozens of radiant royals,
and dusky damsels many.

[9]But one alone, unique she stands
without compare amid them all,
my precious flawless dove is she,
the special pride of mother's love.
The gorgeous girls in gathered throng
with one accord extol her praise,
upon her awesome beauty gaze,
pronounce her blessed, and with joy
they sing their happy song:

Her cosmic beauty (6:10)

[10]Behold her awesome beauty,
see she rivals nature's glory.
Her breaking forth comes as the dawn,
serene and stately in the morn.
Sun's first cold rays the gilded mountains splay,
a harbinger of promise,
of rising expectation.

Her beauty pale, as moon on high,
shines against the blackness of the night,
the lunar disc whose white reflecting light
by wisps of scudding cloud is veiled,
beyond the reach of mortal man
entrancingly untouchable,
in ethereal isolation.

Her glory as the blazing sun on high,
magnificent in splendour.
Her dazzling radiance shines forth,
her presence giving life.
The light is there for all to see
in which to bask and bathe.
Her rays of warmth new health do give
to all who sit and gaze.

As awesome as the cosmic crown, the canopy of night,
beneath whose starry wreath we stand
to gaze in solemn awe at heaven's display,
agape at nature's marvel.

Dreaming in the walnut garden (6:11–12)

[11]I wandered down in trance-like daze
to see the watered valley.
In solitude I sallied forth
to browse among the budding vines.
I dallied by the leafy trees,
the almond blossom in the breeze,
and gave myself to reverie.
[12]When all at once, I know not how,
with O what transport of delight,
I found myself placed at his side,
my royal prince, my valiant knight,
in chariot's proud procession.

A sight for tired eyes (6:13)

[13]Come back! Come back!
O Shulammite, O Perfect One!

Our hungry eyes your breathless beauty prize.
A sight to stop and make us turn, and gaze, and sigh.

What right to strip me with your stares,
as if a dancing girl who twists and whirls
to entertain the troops,
by sensual swirls entranced?

Her graceful form (7:1–5)

[7:1]O noble daughter,
how beautiful your dainty steps,
your soles in slender sandals strapped.
Your thigh's smooth curves
exquisitely turned,
as if by craftsman's skill.

[2]Your secret centre
a rounded cup of spiced wine,
a source of so much pleasure.

Your smooth curved stomach
a mound of tawny wheat,
hedged in by fragrant flowers.

[3]Your shy twin breasts
two timid fawns to touch and stroke,
so tender and so gentle.

[4]Your smooth pale neck, erect,
a tower of ivory tall.

Your eyes so cool, so calm,
deep reservoirs of stillness are,
stone cisterns, cold, profound,
a haven of tranquillity,
O noble daughter.

Your nose, its bridge a ridge so straight,
so white and fragrant as
the distant mountain ranges.

[5]Your crowning head adorns you
in wondrous majesty,
like Carmel's crimson headland,
jutting out to sea.
Your flowing locks, so black,
with purple sheen and oily lustre
gleam. A royal queen!

How are the mighty fallen!
My fearsome warrior king
brought low, hemmed in,
entrapped by trailing tresses.
By maiden's hair ensnared,
made captive by her locks.

A duet of desire (7:6–10)

[6]How beautiful!
How captivating! My delectable maiden!

[7]O tall and stately lady,
so slender and so slim,
a gracious supple palm you are
so calm in nature's sweet allure,
such teasing inaccessibility,
aloof, serene.

Your breasts so soft, so gentle,
so full with promise,
clusters of the tender vine,
O to be mine, their fruit to taste.

[8]Methinks with resolution strong,
to climb the tree, its trunk to scale,
and hold her leafy fronds,
to take her slender form,
her glistening locks caress.

Your rounded swelling breasts
to me be clusters of desire.

Your fragrant nostrils' scent
be that of luscious lime.

9The taste and motion of your mouth,
the smoothness of your silken kisses,
be as the languid flow of vintage wine
o'er sweet and liquid lips.

10It's me, it's me, it's me
he longs for,
his passion is for me.

Love in the countryside (7:11–13)

11Come, my lover, quick,
let's flee away to countryside so fresh
and in her soft embrace be folded.
Let's spend the night in scented shrubs
and gaze upon the stars above.

12Away, away, at rising sun,
at day's pale morn to watch the dawn
of nature's grand eruption.
She shouts, she sprouts,
her blossoms bursting, exploding into bloom.

13With ardour's pent-up passions
by ancient roots aroused,
with eager love I'll give myself,
I'll share with you my secret store
in awe and expectation held and hallowed long,
a den of new delights;
the novelties of love, its ancient paths as well,
are at our door, and trembling entering in,
we shall explore
the intimacies of love.

A longing for intimacy (8:1–4)

8:1O for the freedom of kinship familiar,
then would I kiss you with open abandon,
with no disapproval from many cold stares.

[2]Then would I lead you in intimate tenderness
to the house of my mother, the home of conception,
my darling, my brother.

The delights of our love are so private to nurture,
teach me to love you, your secrets to give me.
Then would I give you the wine of my vine,
with juice from my fruit in ecstasy dine.

[3]I rest in his encircling arm,
his hand my contours strokes.

[4]O daughters of Jerusalem,
I put you under oath,
swear to me,
do not disturb us until we have drunk our fill.

The sixth cycle: the security of love (8:5–14)

The happy couple (8:5)

[5]Here she comes
in rustic freshness wreathed.
Upon his arm she comes
from desert grazing grounds afar,
so shyly presenting for eager approval
her young country lad.

Love's arousal (8:5)

Underneath the fruit tree's bowers,
heavy, ripe with golden showers,
'neath the shades of family tree,
branches of maternal pedigree,
there I stirred your sleeping form,
where your mother brought new birth
in agony of ecstasy writhing.

Love, strong as death (8:6–7)

[6]Emblazoned on your arm parade me,
the public seal of secret love

for all the world to see,
the sign of mutual love,
of access to your intimacy.
O love, like death remorseless in your grip of power.
Your victims, helpless borne, in passions churn,
smitten by your fiery darts
with holy conflagration burn.
Your hollowed hunger, like Sheol's shades,
is ne'er assuaged.

[7]No thundering waters
of nature's primal myth,
no cosmic chaos in her ceaseless motion,
its flame can ever quench.
No overflowing torrents, no flashing floods,
can sweep away her overwhelming potion.

Away, false wealth!
No silver, fruit of toilsome labour long,
of many years a hoard,
can e'er have power
to purchase love's freely given gift.
Away, false love!
Beneath contempt
your mercenary mind
of base intent.

The little sister (8:8–10)

[8]We have a young sister,
her bosom not yet budded,
so what shall we do
and how to present her,
when she starts getting noticed,
when she's ripening for love?

[9]If she's a wall,
so plain yet so pure,
we'll adorn her with turrets,
with towers of silver.

But if she's a door,
too anxious to please,
too free with her favours,
we'll protect her with panels,
with partitions of pine.

[10]But I am a wall,
my defence is impregnable,
resisting invaders.
My breasts are like towers,
firm and assertive,
erect and protruding.

Such is my posture,
such is my poise,
in him I can foster
contentment and ease,
a source of well-being,
of succour and strength.

A vineyard not for hire (8:11–12)

[11]Look at Solomon,
Lord Luxury's estate –
Wealthville unlimited,
acres of vineyards,
vines without number,
virgin vines and
queenly concubines.

He let out his land
for others to farm,
for silver he lusted
to trade in the vine.
But that is a fate
that cannot be mine.

[12]My very own vineyard
is not up for sale.

I cannot be hired,
I cannot be sold.
But to him whom I love
I freely dispose
of my favours and fruit;
they are his for the tasting,
my beloved's alone.

Begone, wretched lecher,
seducer of old;
your silver take with you,
o'er me it's no hold.

The continuing cycle of desire (8:13–14)

[13]My gracious one,
all glorious in flower,
radiant in public display,
in rapt attention held,
surrounding suitors
straining on your
every word;

O to hear your voice,
your private plea to me
alone:

[14]'Flee! Flee! Bolt away
to the secret grove,
there to sport, there we'll cavort.
Spring like a stag
o'er the hills and the valleys,
the clefts and the crannies,
the fragrant contours
of the smooth rolling slopes.'

Part 2
An exposition of the Song

Song of Songs 1:1

4. Title and attribution

King Solomon was famous for his skill as a composer of songs. In 1 Kings 4:32 we read, 'He spoke three thousand proverbs and his songs numbered a thousand and five.' So it is quite natural to presume that here, in the title, Solomon is being taken as the author of the Song. A literal translation of the Hebrew would read, 'The Song of Songs which pertains to Solomon.'

The Hebrew preposition *lāmed*, here translated by 'pertains to', is an extremely common relational word with a very wide range of usages.[1] It is used in the headings of many of the psalms (e.g. Pss 11, 12, 13) of which David is regarded as the author ('A psalm *of* David'). Thus we could very legitimately have here the Song of Songs *by* Solomon. However, the use of the preposition *lāmed* does not necessarily commit us to a particular view of authorship. It could indicate just as easily that there is some other connection with Solomon. We have seen already that there are a number of difficulties in regarding Solomon as the author of our Song, so it is better if we consider some of the other possible interpretations of this heading. If our Song is not *about* Solomon, or *by* him, then it is possible that the poem was dedicated *to* Solomon, or that the Song was placed in the Solomonic collection of songs. Possibly the poem was recognized as being in the then well-known Solomonic style. Yet a further possibility is that the Song was just Solomon's favourite song (a simple *lāmed* of possession). But the most likely meaning is that conveyed by the translation 'The Song of Songs attributed to Solomon.' That is, a later literary editor

---

[1] R. J. Williams mentions nineteen distinct classifications of the usage of *lāmed* in *Hebrew Syntax* (University of Toronto Press, 1967).

ascribed the Song to Solomon as author, so giving the poem the status of belonging to the category of wisdom literature. On this view, no-one knows who wrote the songs. Either they emerged from an ancient popular folk tradition (and thus were of anonymous authorship), or else they were a product of the intellectual elite of the court wisdom school. Either way, Solomon came to be considered by later generations as the patron of wisdom, and if it be true that the Song may be considered as part of wisdom literature, it was natural that his name should become attached to the Song as its putative author. (We have the same sort of consideration to invoke in the question of the authorship of Ecclesiastes.)

One indication that the title in 1:1 is a late editorial attribution, from a different hand from that of the main body of the poem, is the fact that the Hebrew word for the relative particle 'which' (*ʾăšer*) is used only here. In the poems themselves, another form of the word (*še*) is used throughout.

The title of the Song gives us our first example of the literary phenomenon of assonance, which occurs very frequently in the poem. This is a simple literary device, similar to alliteration, in which words are linked together with similar-sounding consonants, in order to make the poetry flow better and more memorably. Here in the title, the repetition of the 's' sound makes for a somewhat startling introduction. In the original Hebrew, this is even more pronounced. Of course, the assonance in the translation is entirely coincidental. In the poem itself, the original assonance can be reproduced in translation only by introducing a loose paraphrase.

The phrase *Song of Songs* is generally recognized as a superlative of quality. The meaning, thus, is something like the most beautiful of songs, the most musical of songs, the number one, the top of the charts. Examples of this type of expression indicating a superlative of quality are 'the holy of holies' (Exod. 26:33, literal translation; NIV, 'the Most Holy Place'), 'vanity of vanities' (Eccl. 1:2, AV), and possibly 'heaven of heavens' (1 Kgs 8:27, AV), 'king of kings' (Ezek. 26:7) and a 'slave of slaves' (Gen. 9:25, literal translation). If we paraphrase the title as 'the most beautiful of Solomon's songs', we not only see an indication of its excellence, but we also preserve the ambiguity of the meaning of the reference to Solomon.

We might legitimately pick up a clue here right from the title of our Song, that our lover is the model or type of the 'fulfilled man'. For Solomon's name in Hebrew (transliterated *šĕlōmōh*) would immediately invite a play on the word *šālôm*, meaning peace, wholeness, prosperity, fulfilment. The beloved is later in the Song called the Shulammite (6:13), and she herself brings *šālôm* to her *šĕlōmōh* (8:10). This hint of mutual happy fulfilment sets the tone for the rest of the Song. But more on this later (see at 6:13).

So let us now listen to the sublime Song itself.

Song of Songs 1:2 – 2:7

5. The first cycle: passionate longings

1. The deep yearnings of love (1:2–4)

The first voice that we hear in the Song is that of the girl. There is a surprising preponderance of her speech in the Song. Athalya Brenner has worked out that the female voices constitute 53% of the text, male voices 34%, the chorus 6%, and headings and dubious cases 7%.[1] Certainly the girl bares her emotions much more than the boy. She voices her yearnings, her anxieties, her fears and her delights in a much more colourfully expressive way, and more frequently than her lover does. She is the one who invites him to intimacy, she is the one who so often takes the initiative. As a result, a number of commentators speculate on the possibility of the writer of these poems being a woman. As Athalya Brenner[2] has said of the verses attributed to the girl, 'These are so essentially feminine that a male could hardly imitate their tone and texture successfully.' Be that as it may, there is no inherent implausibility of a female author. Both Deborah (Judg. 5) and Miriam (Exod. 15:21) are represented as singing victory songs which they may well have composed. Perhaps it is a feminine characteristic to express desire for security, for love, for respect and appreciation. That these are desires which are common to both sexes is hardly open to dispute. It is the *articulation* of them which is perhaps more difficult for the male. But throughout our study of the Song, we must beware of casting the two lovers in stereotypical roles. For the Song subtly undermines the common typecasting of the male–female roles as dominant–submissive,

---

[1] Brenner, *The Israelite Woman*, ch. 4, 'Women Poets and Authors', pp. 46–50.
[2] Ibid.

active–passive, leader–follower, protector–protected, and so on. In the Song we have complete mutuality of desire, boy towards girl, girl towards boy. (When I use the terms lover [male] and beloved [female] in this exposition, I do this without implying any of the aforementioned stereotypes.)

We know nothing about the age of our two lovers. It is natural to assume that they were young teenagers. If marriage took place in the late teens, then our couple (not yet married) would be only just a few years beyond puberty. But this is to assume a misplaced concreteness of background. The couple are representative types of Everyman and Everywoman. They articulate our own most private and intimate longings, and as we read, we are drawn into their passions and tensions. They are literary fictions of an author of creative genius. Similarly, the background to these verses cannot be determined with any certainty. Some assume that this scene represents the girl as a captive in the harem of King Solomon, and she is pining for her absent shepherd lover. Others say that this is the arrival of Solomon's bride-to-be, an Egyptian princess, in the royal court (1 Kgs 3:1). Others see it as the idyllic scene of the simple country girl, the Shulammite, yearning for her shepherd boyfriend. We have to be content with a lack of specificity concerning the scene. Perhaps it was meant to be ambiguous, so we can all identify with them.

What matters is that the girl is giving vent to her deepest feelings. She wants to be kissed by her lover, and not just a formal peck on the cheek from cold, passionless lips. She wants to feel his mouth's deep kiss inside her own, and to know his fond embrace. *Let him kiss me . . .* gives the depth of her longing. She is very tactile. She wants to be touched and to be held; not just as an object of his desire, but because she wants to be stirred to give herself to the one whom she loves. She is not interested in her own self-fulfilment apart from her lover. Her self-fulfilment is achieved by her self-abandonment, just as his fulfilment is found by his captivation by her beauty (see later).

In the Hebrew, the words for kiss and kissing may be onomatopoeic; that is, they portray the sound of what they describe. 'O that he'd give me some of his smacking kisses' that take her breath away. She then describes the effect of his love-making (or caresses) upon her. The word for love-making is a plural noun (*dōdîm*) found also in Proverbs 7:18, 'Come, let's drink deeply of love till morning; let's enjoy ourselves with love', and in Ezekiel 16:8, 'Later I passed by, and when I looked at you and saw that you were old enough for love, I spread the corner of my garment over you.' The context of those verses makes it clear that what is meant is some sort of erotic activity rather than love in the abstract. 'Truly' (or 'indeed', or simply *for*) 'your caresses are better than wine'. This is the first mention of the common association in the Song of wine and sexual activity. It occurs also at 1:4, 'We will praise your love more than wine'; 2:4 (lit.), 'He has taken me to the house of wine'; 4:10, 'How much more pleasing is your love than wine'; 5:1, 'I have drunk my wine and my milk'; 7:9 (lit.), 'Your palate [i.e. the taste of your mouth] like the best wine'; 8:2, 'I would give you spiced wine to drink.' At the linguistic level there is a pun here, a play on the Hebrew words to kiss (*nāšaq*) and to drink (*šāqâ*). At the metaphorical level, the wine flows smoothly over lips and teeth (7:9) as do kisses. Also wine is savoured, its memory lingers long (1:4d). Moreover, at a less precise level, drinking wine (2:4) is associated with feasting at a banquet, and in 5:1, where there is the most explicit intimation of intercourse, the act is metaphorically described as eating the honeycomb and drinking wine and milk. In a seduction scene in Proverbs, eating and drinking are metaphors of sexual activity: 'Come, eat my food and drink the wine I have mixed' (Prov. 9:2, 5). Of course, it is now well known that wine is not a stimulant, but rather a depressant. It lowers our inhibitions, so we loosen up and become less guarded. It appears to act as a stimulant, but in fact it depresses our physical alertness and potency.

We should not be disturbed by the change in person addressed in 1:2 (*Let him kiss me . . . for your love . . .*) for it is a common phenomenon in Hebrew poetry.[3] It is not necessary to invent possible scenarios, either actual or mental, to rationalize this change (i.e. a change in the person addressed), or to assume that her yearning transports her into her lover's immediate presence. But a few modern translations tidy up the Hebrew.

The girl goes on to extol the fragrance of her boyfriend's scents. The fact that the men of ancient Israel used perfume should not make us think that they were effeminate. They did not have water on tap, and standards of personal hygiene could not have been very high, when water for washing had to be carried some very considerable distances. So 'oils' or *perfumes* were something of a necessity to mask the odour of the natural man!

Verses 2b and 3a are examples of chiasmus, a poetic device which breaks up the uniformity of the description. There is an inversion in the

---

[3] See on 8:2.

second line of the order in the first (i.e. ABC/CBA), as shown in the literal translation:

> For *good* your *caresses* than *wine*.
> With respect to *fragrance*, your *oils* are *good*.

The chiastic pattern simply adds variety of interest in poetic expression. The girl's description moves on from the physical *fragrance* of his *perfume* to the metaphorical fragrance of his character. His *name* represents the totality of her lover, his stature, his public reputation; even the mention of his *name* within earshot causes her to be alert, so closely does she identify with him. His reputation, though, is not just her own private concern. He has standing among all the other *young women*. These are possibly potential rivals to the girl, but she is so secure in her relationship with him that she can afford to allow him to bask in their admiration. Love is jealous (see 8:6), even possessive, yet paradoxically it can be shared generously when its foundation is secure. *Perfume poured out*, or 'Oil of Turaq', is a bit of a problem. It could be just a kind of proper name; or it could be perfume that is wafted abroad as from an unstoppered bottle; or else it could be the perfume made from the greeny-yellow sap of some exotic pine tree. Either way, his fragrance causes heads to turn, and she is delighted that it should be so. There is again a wordplay between 'oil' and *name*, which have two consonants in common. The 'maidens' who are so attracted to him are any beauties of marriageable age who are looking for a husband ('virgins', AV).

The contemplation of his *kisses* and caresses, and the remembrance of the beauty of his whole personality, sets off a desperate urging of desire. She wants him to seize her, and run off with her so that they can be alone together in the seclusion of his private *chambers*. She calls her lover *the king*. If we want to think that he is Solomon, then obviously he is king. But it is more likely a literary device. She wants to accord her lover the dignity, nobility, the honour of royalty. He is her *king*. She is proud of him. An association with royalty may be an enhancement of self-esteem and public honour. The glory rubs off a little. Some commentators here mention the fact that in some Ancient Near Eastern marriage ceremonies, as in those of the Orthodox Church today, the bride and groom were called king and queen for the period of the wedding festivities (see later at 3:7). However, our lovers are not yet married here. That state is reflected only in the third cycle (3:6 – 5:1). The NIV here has *Let the king bring me* . . . rather than the

Hebrew 'The king has brought me . . .' But her lover has actually brought her into the private place. If they are a royal couple, then it refers to the luxuriously decorated rooms of Solomon's splendid palace. If they are a poor country girl and a young shepherd lad, then it may refer to the shelters mentioned in 1:8. But the precise location is immaterial. It is all a flight of fantasy. And she is breathless at where her imaginings have taken her. But the Song, as it were, draws down the curtain here, as elsewhere in the poem, leaving the lovers in their secluded intimacy, and leaving the reader to speculate as to what they get up to. This is part of the literary artistry of the Song; it keeps us in suspense, and sets us imagining, and usually draws a veil over the most intimate scenes.

This verse also illustrates another contrast that permeates the Song, between the public place and the place of privacy. The lovers wander in and out of these locations, either separately or together. They want to parade their love in public for all the world to see. Yet they want to enjoy it privately together in the secret place. However, the secret place alone in solitude can be a place of desperate yearning and loneliness. The public place can be a place of both joy and isolation. She cannot kiss him in public, and the social mores of the day prevent their public intimacy (see 8:1). She might see her lover in the far distance, on the wide open spaces of the hillsides, and fear his isolation. For she might think that he is totally content in his aloneness, and therefore does not need her.

Right at the very beginning of this first cycle of the Song, our love-dazed girl is articulating her deepest yearnings. It is impossible to say whether these are the result of her highly developed capacity for fantasy, or whether they are based on a previous history of intimacy (so that her first taste has whetted her appetite for a repeat performance or for even deeper experiences of familiarity). Within the Song itself, it is very difficult to chart a clear development of the lovers' progress. There appears to be only a series of cycles of intimacy in which it is impossible to say what *stage* of their relationship the lovers have reached. The only exception to this is the third cycle depicting their wedding. We have postulated that the Song pictures a betrothed couple beginning to explore the delights of an increasingly tactile relationship, culminating in the consummation of their union on their wedding night. This framework for viewing the behaviour of the lovers in the Song starts from the presumption of an irreversible commitment to each other. And as an arranged match, their future is secure. If romance is not there at the beginning, as was quite possible in such cases, then the couple are starting from cold and stoking the fires as they gradually get to know one another. So our girl in the Song knows how it is all going to end, and in her mind's eye keenly anticipates the delights of her marriage bed. That is still in the future, but she is already securely launched on the pathway of delightful thrills of new discoveries.

We in our Western cultures, however, tend to start off with an emphasis on basic human biology and sexuality, and only later begin to think of personal human friendship and what that might lead to. So the pressure is on to explore and experiment outside the context of a developing relationship, a relationship which ought to have always in view the goal of a permanent union in marriage. But this is not a question of relative cultural mores. The biblical pattern stands as a moral norm. Even though our concept of engagement is looser than that of the betrothal of the ancient Hebrews, that does not mean that we abandon the biblical priority of marriage. It does mean that we have to be more tentative and circumspect in the degree to which we can allow a tactile relationship to develop, especially when there is still uncertainty as to whether love will mature and lead to marriage. What must be safeguarded is the honour and sanctity of the married state, and nothing must be done which would bring shame and regret if for any reason the relationship were to be terminated.

When two lovers are beginning their adventure together, when they feel the first stirrings of mutual attraction, they want to touch each other. That first moment of physical contact, however slight, however brief, however tentative, represents a movement forward, which is irreversible. Having been touched, she can never revert to the state of not having been touched. She can only move forward. They touch, they embrace, they kiss, with varying degrees of passion. Here she has tasted, and with passion wants a repeat, because it is already a foretaste, as every kiss is, of even deeper levels of intimacy and penetration and intermingling. And her mind has possibly rushed far ahead of her real degree of love and knowledge of her lover, and of self-knowledge. Fantasies move far beyond what the realities are capable of bearing at any given moment.

The second half of 1:4 slows down the breathless passion of the girl in 1:2–4a. A number of commentators, on the basis of the plural *we*, assign this verse to a group of bystanders (the daughters of Jerusalem of verse 5?). But as Pope says, 'Virtually any difficulty, real or supposed, may be obviated by invoking additional characters to whom the troublesome words may be assigned.' So the shepherd hypothesis here puts these words on the lips of the harem, addressing the absent lover in the presence of King Solomon. We need not resort to such an unsatisfactory expedient. It is enough for the girl to continue speaking in praise of her lover, including in the *we* herself and all the nubile maidens who admire him. She wants her lover to absorb the greatest amount of praise possible, and she can only contribute her own portion to that. Again, if it seems too improbable that the love-intoxicated girl wants all the world to praise his love-making capacities, we must remember once again that this is a literary device, not anchored concretely in the real world, only in the mind of the author.

There are problems with the word translated by the NIV as *How right*.[4] The Hebrew *mêšārîm* is used elsewhere at 7:10 and in Proverbs in conjunction with wine, with the implication that it is 'smoothly flowing' (literally, level or upright; Prov. 23:31). So we could translate it as 'more than smooth wine do they praise you'. Or, less probably, the comparison may refer to the other 'upright men'. So then, they exult in him more than in other handsome men. Others speculate even further, on the basis of cognate languages, that it has overtones of virility.

The usage of the plural *they* in *How right they are to adore you* is an impersonal usage, and we do not have to identify the persons. It is passive in meaning, '. . . are you adored'. So his love-making, his caresses, are savoured or commemorated more than the taste of a smooth wine. The memory of it lingers long. The caresses have an intoxicating effect and make her heady, and yet happy and relaxed. No wonder she praises the one who can bring her such bliss. She also finds an intense pleasure in the anticipation of her love-making. In fact, the exquisite pleasure of fantasy may surpass the pleasures of the reality itself. Indeed, the occasional disappointment of the failure of their amorous escapades may stimulate her erotic imaginations to new levels. Her thought life then acts as a compensatory mechanism against the realities of their love-making, which fluctuate in pleasure according to time, mood and environment. Here, right at the very beginning of the Song, the lovers are thrown into a relationship which is intensely sensual and physical. The girl has a passionate yearning for her lover. But can it really be described as love? Could it just be nothing more than an obsessive infatuation, petulant, and demanding immediate satisfaction? We have to wait until later in the Song to resolve those

---

[4] RSV, 'rightly'.

questions. But we in our own generation live in an age when the physical aspects of a relationship between a man and a woman are deemed to have the highest priority. If things don't work out at this level, it is said, there is no hope of a satisfying relationship at any other level. Now of course there has to be some spark of physical attraction to allow any romantic relationship to get off the ground, but the physical aspect is only one side of a many-sided partnership. A growing physical intimacy has to be matched by a steadily increasing mutual self-knowledge; of intellect, temperament, goals, moods, maturity, emotions, and so on. Compatibility in these areas is of infinitely greater importance than the capacity to please one another to the highest degree in the physical realm.

It may seem strange to be considering first the hot passionate yearning of the girl for her lover. For the type of kisses she desires to receive are at the extreme end of a continuous spectrum of degrees of intimacy. It may have begun with a formal peck on the cheek, which signals 'Yes, I'm interested, but let's see what develops.' There may be aggressive stolen kisses, a presumptuous cheeky invasion of privacy, assuming a greater degree of intimacy than she is allowing herself to give. Or after a longish period of cautious shy circling of each other, she may receive a first awakening kiss when all at once she realizes that things are different now, on an altogether different plane. As emotions get more strongly aroused, so does the desire for the deep surrender of a lingering passionate kiss, *the kisses of his mouth*, a foretaste of a hitherto unexplored deeper union and communion. But that perhaps is still very much in the future. The anticipatory aspect of any romantic kissing has been well portrayed in the lines

Graze on my lips, and if those hills be dry,
Stray lower, where the pleasant fountains lie.[5]

Much fun has been made in the literature down the ages of the act of kissing; from Jonathan Swift's 'Lord! I wonder what fool it was that first invented kissing?', to Andy Warhol: 'Two people kissing always look like fish.'

I suppose the latter wishes to draw attention to the unfocused, glazed look of the lovers, and their rather gormless appearance in attempting to devour each other. But the reductionism of a scientific attempt to describe

---

5 Shakespeare, *Venus and Adonis* (1593).

osculation will inevitably destroy the mystique. For it is not an act to be analysed, but rather to be participated in. For I suppose most of us would not feel free to gaze indefinitely on a couple engaged in prolonged romantic kissing; it would amount to an invasion of privacy, from which we would naturally withdraw. It is only the lonely voyeur who obtains second-hand gratification by these means.

But in kissing, as in so many other things, once the appetite is roused, the demand becomes insatiable:

> 'May I print a kiss on your lips?' I said.
> And she nodded her full permission;
> So we went to press and I rather guess
> We printed a full edition.[6]

So our girl in the Song is longing to indulge in 'the wanton kissings of the tongue'.[7] And she longs to be like the girl described in William Browne's lines:

> A winning kiss she gave,
> A long one, with a free and yielding lip.[8]

Our lovers, in their physical contact, find that, as Alfred Tennyson puts it:

> Our spirits rushed together
> At the touching of the lips.[9]

The union of their love has been sealed with a kiss, they now mutually possess each other, and the knowledge of such security makes them feel like gods: 'Sweet Helen, make me immortal with a kiss!'[10]

2. Black and beautiful (1:5–6)

For the first time in the Song, the girl gives voice to her insecurities, her fears and her self-doubts. She is unsettled by the uncertain reaction of the

---

[6] Lilienthal, *A Full Edition*.

[7] Aristophanes, *The Clouds*, line 51.

[8] Browne, *Britannia's Pastorals*, Book 3, Song 2, line 193.

[9] Tennyson, *Locksley Hall*.

[10] Marlowe, *Doctor Faustus*, XIV.

daughters of Jerusalem to her deeply suntanned complexion. She is troubled by her relationship with her brothers, who were angry with her. She is conscious of her own low self-esteem, brought about by her enforced neglect of her own personal appearance. How can she accept herself, if she is not accepted by her friends and her relatives? Her first words are probably spoken in a defiant, petulant tone. Yes, she is black, yet she is also beautiful. She is conscious of her own beauty, which is of the wild, unkempt, natural variety, and yet she is uncertain of the attitude of the daughters of Jerusalem towards her. Her 'blackness' of course is not the natural pigmentation of her skin. It is not a question of her race. She is, rather, deeply suntanned and windswept, having been exposed to the elements in her work among the vines on the hillsides. It is not altogether certain what the import of the conjunction and/but is in 'Black am I, and/but beautiful.' Is she responding to the critical appraisal of the city girls, 'Yes, I may be dark, and suntanned, which is not beautiful according to your accepted criteria of beauty, but I am conscious that I am beautiful in my own eyes, and in the eyes of my lover'? Or else is she saying, 'My beauty consists in my blackness, not in spite of it'? In other words, is she beautiful because of her suntan, or in spite of it? The first would be the interpretation of 'black and beautiful'; the second, of 'black but beautiful'. It is difficult to decide between these two. Probably the second is more appropriate. She is perhaps conscious of her low standing in the eyes of the city girls who look down in lofty disdain on those who have to perform manual labour. So she is defiantly proclaiming her beauty against those who prefer a more cultivated type of beauty.

The identity of the *daughters of Jerusalem* is uncertain. Most commentators take them to be the members of Solomon's harem, or else to represent the cultured elite of the upper-class ladies of Jerusalem, the high-society ladies who move in court circles. For both of these cases, darkness would not imply beauty. They would be incompatible. Their beauty would be of the light-skinned variety, produced by weeks of cosmetic treatments. This was the case of the girls of King Xerxes' court harem, where there were 'twelve months of beauty treatments prescribed for the women, six months with oil of myrrh and six with perfumes and cosmetics' (Esth. 2:12). It seems that in those days, gentlemen preferred blondes. Of course, this is a matter of personal or cultural preference. In Africa today, the most popular forms of feminine cosmetics are skin lighteners. Western Europeans have a tendency to parade a dark skin as the symbol of health and beauty (whether the product of a holiday on the Riviera or the sun lamps of the beauty parlour round the corner). Light-skinned people prefer to be darker, dark-skinned people prefer to become lighter. I think that the most that can be said about this is that it must be some sort of cosmic joke of the Creator. Plato thought of it this way: 'The dark in complexion are said to have a manly look, and the fair are called the Children of the Gods'![11]

But whatever the identity of the *daughters of Jerusalem*, they play an important literary role. They act as a foil, as a sounding board, for the expression of the girl's deepest feelings and emotions. They draw out from the girl the articulation of her yearnings; seldom if at all do they play any active role in the drama. They may well be a literary fiction, like the wall through which the two lovers Pyramus and Thisbe speak in Shakespeare's play *A Midsummer Night's Dream*, and which comments independently on the relationship of the lovers. Perhaps another role they play is in highlighting the city–country contrast which occurs throughout the Song. The city represents civilization, human-centred achievements, culture, sophistication, architectural splendour, wealth, power, affluence and self-assertive independence. The countryside in which the lovers live represents the natural order of simplicity, of being at one with the created order, a passivity or at least a cooperation with the natural order of things, with no attempt to impose or dominate the way things are. The city–country contrast is illustrated here by the *tents of Kedar* and *the tent curtains of Solomon*. She is black and swarthy as the tough goat-hair hides of the tents of the desert nomads of Arabia; she is dark like the tapestries in Solomon's splendid palace in Jerusalem. (Some commentators emend *Solomon* to read *Salmah*, in parallelism with *Kedar*, but this is neither natural nor necessary.)

The girl is made self-conscious by the stares of the city girls. Any stare is an intrusion, an invasion of our privacy. If it is held too long, it provokes embarrassment, hostility and defiance. If we are the victims of a stare, we are threatened by a critical appraisal of our external credentials. The real 'us' is masked by our external appearance, and we feel the stare might penetrate behind that mask and threaten us at the deepest level of our being. So we turn away, or confront the one staring at us with our defiant questioning. We don't like being weighed up by others, lest we be found

---

[11] Plato, *The Republic*, V.

wanting. We feel disrobed, defenceless and naked. Perhaps the girl in our Song is conscious of the fact that those of her own sex can be far more harsh in their criticism of her than her male companion can be. Yet that criticism is brought about by the threat of her beauty. Her wild, sensual, unkempt beauty is a threat to their artificially cultivated beauty. Her blackness is both enviable and contemptible. They envy her because they do not have this natural beauty. They despise it, because they know they can never have it. They are wary of each other, they are half envious of each other, half fearful of each other. Her beauty threatens their ordinariness. Yet she in half her heart would like to be in their place. So she is not at ease with herself. She fears her own vulnerability.

She is deeply tanned (6), an intensive of the original word for 'black', because *the sun* has literally 'cast her glance on her'. (This is an unusual phrase, found elsewhere only in Job 20:9; 28:7.) *The sun* has burned her with its heat. The reason is that she has been outdoors working in the vineyard. There is a play on the word for 'become angry' here. Her brothers' (stepbrothers, the sons of my mother) anger 'grew hot' or 'burned against her'. She has been doubly burned, by *the sun* and by her brothers' anger. Why her brothers should have been angry with her we do not know. We can only speculate. Perhaps it was because they disapproved of her flirting or of her chosen lover, and they put her in quarantine as it were, out of harm's way, where they could keep an eye on her.

An alternative view is that the brothers, having allocated the girl to family duties in the vineyard, became angry because the girl's inevitable neglect of her appearance would reduce her chances in the marriage stakes.

Be that as it may, she was under their authority; this alone is sufficient to indicate that she was unmarried. She was under the protective shield of the family home. The father nowhere appears in the Song; he is presumed dead, or otherwise offstage. The mother hovers enigmatically on the edges of our consciousness (1:6 here; 3:4, 'my mother's house, to the room of the one who conceived me'; 6:9, 'the only daughter of her mother, the favourite of the one who bore her'; 8:5, 'there your mother conceived you, there she who was in labour gave you birth'). Not only is our girl's social status low, as a manual labourer, but her family status is now questionable. She has offended in some unspecified way.

She ends up rather pathetically saying that she has not kept her own *vineyard*. This is not of course to be taken literally. Her *vineyard*, which is her very own (the Hebrew is emphatic), represents the totality of her personality in all her feminine allure. She has been forced to keep her brothers' *vineyards*. Her own *vineyard* she had not kept. Her outdoor work has forced her to neglect the cultivation of her own appearance. That is why she is so wild-looking, yet attractive. It is interesting to note how fashions change. The wild look is expensively and artificially cultivated these days as something attractive. The close-to-nature cult of the primitive savage look is deemed to have an intense seductiveness and sensual allure. Ovid recognized this in his lines,

> Her head was bare
> But for her native ornament of hair;
> Which in a simple knot was tied above,
> sweet negligence, unheeded bait of love! [12]

Her *vineyard* represents everything that conveys her essential femininity. Her looks, her complexion, her dress, her status, her sexuality – all those considerations which would make her attractive to a man. That she has not been able to keep up her appearance is a cause of her low self-esteem. She is a prisoner of her circumstances, and longs to be free to be herself. And yet there is the pride that she exhibits in her own natural beauty, a power which, as we shall see, she knows how to wield to good effect.

The *vineyard* represents a halfway stage between the city, with all its sophistication and human-made culture, and the countryside, in all the wildness of its natural disorder. Viniculture is the cultivation of nature. A *vineyard* has to be cultivated. It has to be cleared of stones, ploughed and dug. It has to be sown, planted, watered and pruned. It has to be walled in and protected (see Isa. 5:1–10). So also the girl in all her femininity has to be cultivated, or otherwise she will 'go to seed'. Hers is a natural beauty, but it needs to be enhanced and guarded (see later). Some modern commentators take another view of this verse. They introduce rather implausibly an explicitly sexual dimension here. Some interpret it as, 'I have not guarded/preserved/taken care of my sexual being', the implication being that she has been promiscuous, she is not a virgin, and therefore has violated the moral norms of her religious and social

---

[12] Ovid, *Metamorphoses*, 'Meleager and Atlanta', line 68, translated by Dryden.

upbringing. Others say it means, 'I have not cultivated, sown or ploughed my vineyard', the implication being that she is a chaste, pure virgin with no previous sexual experience. Both these views make a too precise identification of her vineyard with her own sexuality, and the more general interpretation is to be preferred. It is intrinsically improbable that the girl is bemoaning, or even parading, her own history of unchastity, in the light of the whole tenor of the Song as being a celebration of mutual love, fidelity and loyalty.

In these verses we are brought face to face with the problems of our own self-image. How do we view ourselves? When we look at our reflections in the mirror, do we like what we see? Can we accept ourselves as we really are, with all our quirks, idiosyncrasies and limitations? Do we like the way we look? Or are we always wishing we were like someone else? Can we accept our own temperaments and personalities, or are we always hemmed in by a crippling self-consciousness that paralyses our emotional and social lives? Inferiority complexes can lead to a sense of worthlessness and self-rejection and self-hatred. So how do we cope and come to a more balanced sense of self-worth, and to a degree of psychological, emotional and social integration and poise?

We can approach this from a number of angles. At the basic physical level, there is only a limited amount that we can do to improve our physical or outward appearance (see later, on 1:9–11). But even that limited enhancement can work wonders for our self-esteem and sense of well-being. For we are psychosomatic beings, and the old adage *mens sana in corpore sano* (a healthy mind in a healthy body) rings very true. A little attention to our physical well-being, by enjoyable exercise, by how we dress, by a little application of eau de cologne or of aftershave, can give an almost disproportionate, positive boost to our own self-esteem and enable us to face the world with more gusto and confidence.

Similarly also, our basic temperament types and personalities are things that we have to accept as a given. We may be introverts or extroverts, happy-go-lucky phlegmatics, or intense intellectuals, or dreamy romantics; we may be driven by relentless ambition or just be content to let life bring what it will. All these may be the results of our genes or of our early social environment, or of the way we were treated by our parents or siblings. But at some stage we have to accept that this is the way we basically are, and that we can transform our temperaments only to a very limited degree. This is not to encourage a negative passivity, but rather to explore how our basic character traits can be used to their greatest advantages. For example, a withdrawn introvert can blossom into a gentle counsellor, but he or she never will be the life and soul of a party. If we are in need of encouragement, we can always encourage ourselves with the thought that the people whom we admire most and who are so different from ourselves are so often the very people who wish they could be otherwise. If we cannot accept ourselves as we are, then we either totally withdraw into ourselves, or else put on a mask, projecting a presentation to the outside world which we think is more acceptable than our real personalities. But we all know that wearing any kind of mask palls after a while; we become suffocated and tired. They are painful to wear, for the external mask jars against the inner contours, causing tension and friction. Better to be ourselves, and allow others to see our weaknesses, than constantly to bear the strain of going on stage with alien gaudy make-up.

At a spiritual level, we are all made in the image of God (Gen. 1:26–27). This is a glorious subject to ponder, and we can consider it here only very briefly. We all bear the imprint of our Creator, and however distorted and disfigured that image has become, there is always hope of renewal. For the Christian is one who is accepted by the Creator; whose broken image is being transformed from one degree of glory to another by the Spirit (2 Cor. 3:18); who is a new creation in Christ (2 Cor. 5:17). All this is not merely at a theoretical level; it is at work now in all those who believe. But the work will be completed only when we see Christ face to face, in his unveiled glory. For now, the rough edges are being smoothed down gradually and that which is twisted made straight. So in all these ways, here a little, there a little, we are being transformed, enabling us to come to a happier acceptance of who we are, and a more confident trust in our Creator God in whose image we are being renewed.

3. A hesitant enquiry, an ambiguous response (1:7–8)

The elements of uncertainty, tension and shame which we encountered in verses 5–6 are carried through here in verses 7–8. But, whereas in the previous verses the girl's uncertainties were expressed in regard to her relationship to the daughters of Jerusalem, to her brothers and to her own inner self, here her fears are concerned with her lover and his companions. In verses 5–6 the controlling metaphor is that of cultivating a vineyard, whereas in verses 7–8 it is that of shepherding or pasturing. The girl directs her anxious question to her lover in verse 7, and she receives an enigmatic, perhaps a teasing response. The NIV assumes that it is her friends who reply to her in verse 8, thus requiring that the question in the previous verse be directed at her absent lover (so she would be expecting no response from him). Alternatively, one can perhaps more naturally assume that the girl is posing her question directly to her lover, in which case the words represent his own reply. I take the latter to be the case.

The lovers are together in the early morning, and she is trying to arrange a rendezvous for a midday meeting. Her tone is urgent, perhaps complaining or fearful, even doubting; why hasn't he told her before of his whereabouts? Is he playing hard to get? Does he really want to meet her in the middle of the day, perhaps in the presence of his fellow shepherds? Would he not then resent her presence?

She directs her plea to (literally) 'the one whom my soul loves'. This latter phrase indicates the involvement of her whole person with her lover. For the girl, her love bathes and suffuses every aspect of her being and of her life. Her life is 'shepherd-shaped'. She is not in love with an idea, or a fleeting fancy. She's not just in love with love, but with him, a real handsome shepherd boy, teasingly out of reach throughout much of the day somewhere in the vast open spaces of the hillsides, and she wants to be with him. She asks him (literally), 'Where do you pasture, where do you cause to lie down at noon?' The verbs 'to pasture' and 'to cause to lie down' normally would take an object. He would pasture his flock, and cause his sheep to lie down. But here in the words of the girl, the verbs are intransitive. No objects are given. Now this indicates a subtle undercurrent to her words. For the verb 'to pasture' or 'to graze the flock' (rāʿâ) has the same consonantal root as the word meaning 'darling' or 'intimate companion' (raʿyâ). Not only so, but to *graze* is also used metaphorically as a description of some sort of erotic activity (6:3, lit., 'He grazes among the lilies'). Elsewhere in the Old Testament, the phrase 'One who pastures harlots' has clear sexual connotations (Prov. 29:3, lit.). So there is perhaps a veiled double entendre here. The girl is asking for a secret rendezvous with the possibility of some loving encounter between them. She may have *herself* in mind as the object of his causing to lie down at noon.

She is intent on going out to find him. But how can she do so with propriety? If she has no specific directions, she will be wandering around blindly in search of him, and she will be in danger of being mistaken for a prostitute, plying her trade among the other shepherds. *A veiled woman* has been the subject of much discussion. Literally it means 'like one who wraps herself up'. Others have emended it to a similar verbal root meaning 'like one who wanders' or 'goes astray'. Now not all prostitutes were veiled, as Tamar was (Gen. 38:14–15), and not every *veiled woman* is a prostitute. But it does seem likely that the implication of the girl's words is that she does not want the shame of being thought a harlot. Perhaps it is a veiled threat to her lover. 'If you don't tell me, I'll be taken as a loose woman. Now you wouldn't want that, would you?' Or perhaps it gives an indication of the depth of her urgency, a throwing of caution to the winds, as she throws herself with bravado into this reckless act in which she has to brave the wolf whistles of the shepherds.

His reply is very enigmatic. Does he in fact tell her where to meet him? Does she in fact go? Does she find him? It is all very uncertain. She is desperate for his company, almost at any price. She wants to be with him all the time. She wants to know where he works, who his companions are. Is he enjoying others' company, while she is on the outside, excluded from this camaraderie? There is a sense in which 'togetherness' can be stifling, cloying and claustrophobic, a sense in which it leads to ossification and stagnation and introversion. The girl wants his exclusive company, but that will constrict him and confine him. He can enjoy life in his own mannish professional world, which excludes the woman. Her presence would break up his circle of intimacy, his clubby companionship. So in this sense, her presence diminishes him. He must be free to develop his own interests, of which she will remain an external observer for ever. So she must allow him this freedom. His love for her is only a part of his total being; his professional life runs in parallel. So he answers teasingly, perhaps to discourage gently, perhaps to encourage her. If she comes with her own little flock of kids, then it will not be so obvious why she is out on the hillside. He directs her to the temporary huts or shelters (the word is normally translated as 'tabernacles') where they can meet together alone. The shepherds will not be there at siesta time, and they will not return before night. The couple would feel the freedom of delight in being alone together in a hut in the wild open spaces.

But perhaps he wants to be with his companions and her presence would be an intrusion into his masculine world. For not all the world loves a lover. Then again, perhaps he wants to be utterly alone, an isolated individual, alone with nature in all its awesome splendour. For aloneness in the open can be a very wonderful thing. On the sea, in the air, in the barrenness of the rolling hills, not seeing another living soul for miles around. It can be an almost mystical experience, communing with oneself and with the Creator. Possibly the boy is aware of his own finitude, his own insignificance in the grand order of things. He loves the solitude of nature, yet it is not an easy familiarity but one that is tinged with fear and respect. For nature can be very capricious. And so he contemplates his own existential loneliness, an aching void which none other can fill except his God; and the ephemerality of all his closest human relationships is come in upon him. Perhaps this is why he wants to be alone.

Some have seen in the word *miškan* (tabernacle) a cultic significance. But this is hardly an obvious connection. There is no religious or cultic vocabulary in the Song; no mention of priest, temple, sacrifice, altar, ritual, cleanliness, or any such thing. At one time, a theory originally propounded by T. J. Meek gained popular support. The theory has taken on a variety of forms. It basically states that the Song is an expurgated edition of what was originally a song celebrating the sacred marriage of a god and goddess of fertility. Various backgrounds in Mesopotamia, Syria and Canaan have been proposed. While it is certain that even in the darkest days of Israelite apostasy the temple worship was polluted by these fertility cults (see Ezek. 8:14; Zech. 12:11), this gives no ground for assuming that our human love song ever had a basis in such a depraved environment. Similarities in language, particularly the images from nature, are no basis for supposing an original for the song in an alien cult whose whole ethos was an abomination to the orthodox spokesmen of Yahwism, the prophets such as Hosea, Jeremiah and Ezekiel.

These verses prompt us to reflect on the degrees of aloneness and togetherness which it is appropriate for a developing relationship to sustain. We may sometimes be tempted to think, especially in the early days of courtship, that the ultimate joy consists of being in the other's presence every hour of the day and night. But this starry-eyed romanticism needs to be tempered by the fact that each one of us needs to have a degree of 'private space', to enable us to stand apart and evaluate and come to terms with the growing friendship. To be crowded out by the other partner can often lead to a growth of resentment and hostility. We need to be able to breathe freely, without the sense that we are under inspection all the time. We need to be given time to grow into a relationship without a constant pressure bearing down upon us. We must give each other time and space to go our own ways and pursue our own interests. And this requires much trust, a letting-go by the partner, and then a coming together again. The degree to which we can participate in the other's enthusiasms needs to be considered with some hard-headed realism. A confusion of expectations in this area can end up in bitter frustration unless a new modus vivendi is achieved. But of course new interests can blossom and flourish within the relaxed harmony of love.

4. A filly in fine fettle (1:9–11)

The hesitations, tensions and ambiguities of the last four verses are now for the moment laid aside and dissolved, as it were, in the lover's poem of praise and admiration for his beloved. Perhaps the rather tenuous link between verses 9–11 and the previous verses is through the catchword *rāʿâ*, the verb 'to pasture' and the noun translated by the NIV as *darling* in verse 9 (perhaps better as 'friend' or 'companion'). Where there is no obvious thematic link between sections, there may be a loose linguistic link by the idea of a 'catchword', though this may be apparent only in the original Hebrew and not in translation.

The girl is her lover's 'friend' or 'companion'. Obviously it is a term of affection (as we would use the term 'girlfriend'), implying a very special relationship. She is not just another conquest, to be shown off to all and sundry to enhance his own status; nor just a plaything, to satisfy his every whim or fancy; nor a subservient menial, a kind of living doll, who flatters and praises him in public, soothes his bruised ego in private, and whose life revolves so remorselessly around the centre of gravity of his career, profession, social standing and total well-being.

No, she is a girl in her own right, with her own mind; no cringing yes-girl this. She knows her man, can tease him or flirt with him, and can hold her own in the company of others. She is his friend. They are companionable together. They have interests in common. They have different interests. They are able to give each other space to develop their own interests. They are able to encourage each other in their own separate pursuits. They can be proud of each other's achievements. They are distinct personalities, each with different types of needs – emotional, social, physical, intellectual or psychological. The recognition of this enables them to be companions. They are not just squeezing the juice out of each other, but giving each other room to grow. Recognizing how different they are, they do not try to force each other into preconceived moulds, or have unrealistic expectations of each other. They support each other when necessary, but they do not serve as 'crutches' for each other. Their 'togetherness' is not mutual self-absorption, not an egotism of two, but a relaxed harmony of two distinct and very different personalities. They are not as like as two peas in a pod – for that makes for boredom and ossification. The very differences act as a stimulation for growth. Their separate worlds make for growth and experience in dimensions of which each would have been unaware had they been moving in their own isolated and separate ways.

The girl in verses 9–11 is obviously dressed in her 'Sabbath best'. She is no longer in her workaday clothes, tending the vineyards. Her lover sees her in her festive outfit, decked out with all the finery of shawls, veils, sashes, bangles, headbands, earrings, tiaras, headdresses, and so on.[13] Even if our girl is a simple country girl, she will still have her special jewellery and clothes set aside for family, festive or religious gatherings. She is 'dressed up', not just dressed to kill. She has already made her kill; the king is made captive by her tresses (7:5). She actually enjoys dressing up. It makes her feel good. It enhances her sense of self-worth as a simple human being. Not that she is trying to be someone she is not. Nor is she trying to cover up her own deep and private insecurities and inadequacies whatever they may be. She is taking advantage of her own natural beauty, and displaying it to good effect.

Her lover compares his girl to *a mare* among *Pharaoh's chariot horses*. The NIV is an interpretative paraphrase here. There is nothing in the Hebrew text about being harnessed to a chariot. The comparison of the girl to a horse has puzzled some commentators and readers. One has even suggested that she has very large haunches, suitable for much childbearing! Others, that she is very fleet of foot. She does not look like a horse. She is gloriously decked out like one of Pharaoh's chariot horses. The immediate point of comparison is the way both girl and horse are gloriously festooned with ribbons and other decorations. Wall paintings from the tombs of ancient Egypt show Pharaoh's horses with feathered headdresses and studded leather halters and bridles, and finely decorated with drapes and beads.

---

[13] See Isa. 3:18–23 for the type of finery worn by the upper-class ladies of Zion.

Her rounded *cheeks* are enhanced by large circular *earrings* which emphasize the roundness of her face. Her neck is decorated by row upon row of strings of brightly coloured beads. This enhances her height, her stateliness, as well as giving a slight hint of inaccessibility and protection (see 4:4, 'Your neck is like the tower of David'; and 7:4, 'Your neck is like an ivory tower'). Although verse 11 is spoken in the first person plural, *We will make you . . .* , it is probable that the lover is continuing his own speech. It could be 'the royal "we"', or a plural of self-deliberation, or a literary fiction in which he seems to be inciting all men everywhere who have an eye for female beauty to enhance her natural advantages, with yet more decorative power. But perhaps this is all too subtle; and it may be that it is simply the case that the couple have just begun to think of themselves as a unit (and others perhaps have come to know that they are on their way to marriage), and each one delights to use the word 'we' for an individual action.[14]

The exact nature of the *silver* and *gold* jewellery mentioned in verse 11 is uncertain. But whatever it may be, his sole intention is to make her yet more 'royal'. He wants her to be seen to her best advantage. Her beauty is enhanced by the jewellery with which he will adorn her. Not that he is going to make her like an overdressed glittering Christmas tree. There is something vulgar about the extravagant use of jewellery. But a single sparkling gem can set off the girl's radiant beauty more than a thousand golden necklaces.

There is one further aspect of the comparison to a mare that needs to be considered. *Pharaoh's chariots* were pulled by stallions, hitched in pairs, so that a female horse among them would cause quite a stir. In fact, there is an incident that has been recorded in which, during the Egyptian military campaign against Qadesh, the prince of Qadesh released a mare among the Egyptian cavalry in order to send them into chaos. But the mare was quickly killed by an Egyptian soldier, thus saving the day for the Egyptians. So if our lover is saying that the effect his beloved has on him is the same as that which a mare has amid a host of military stallions, pawing the ground and neighing lustily, then that puts a very different light on the picture. He is saying that his beloved sends him into a frenzy of desire which is the ultimate in sex appeal. The GNB takes this line of interpretation with

---

[14] I owe this thought to Alec Motyer (private communication).

You, my love, excite men
  as a mare excites the stallions
    of Pharaoh's chariots.

King Solomon made a military and trading pact with the pharaoh of Egypt, through a marriage alliance. He married Pharaoh's daughter. His import–export trading with Egyptian horses, selling them to the Hittites, is recorded in 2 Chronicles 1:14–17. This, another link with Solomon, is, however, very indirect, and may be totally coincidental.

The horse is a very sensual animal. No-one can stand close alongside a large magnificent racehorse, or a ceremonial parade horse, without sensing something of the vibrancy, the thrill, of so much potential power hidden within those large glistening flanks. There is a sense of awe at the aesthetics of such power.

Our lover senses a similar power within his girl, a kind of animal magnetism, and it unsettles him, by her sheer physical proximity. This allure, this attractiveness, is made more deadly by the exposure of skin; a thinly veiled body. A partially clothed figure is always more suggestive than a completely clothed or completely nude figure. This is common psychology. What is suggested, or hinted at, works far more powerfully on the imagination than what is fully exposed. As one film star has put it, 'Sex appeal is 50% of what you've got and 50% what other people think you've got.'[15]

The enhancement of our physical attributes with which nature has endowed us is something not altogether to be despised. As Robert Herrick has written:

Art quickens nature;
care will make a face.
Neglected beauty perisheth apace.[16]

But this has not been a universal opinion. Listen to the words of James Thomson:

Loveliness needs not the foreign aid of ornament.
But is, when unadorned, adorned the most.[17]

---

[15] Sophia Loren.

[16] Herrick, 'Neglect'.

[17] Thomson, *The Seasons*, 'Autumn'.

That very austere North African theologian Tertullian, writing in the third century AD, had decided views on the matter:

> Against Him those women sin who torment their skin with potions, stain their cheeks with rouge, and extend the line of their eyes with black colouring. Doubtless they are dissatisfied with God's plastic skill. In their own persons they convict and censure the Artificer of all things.[18]

Shakespeare's characters express similar views:

> I have heard of your paintings too, well enough;
> God has given you one face, and you make yourself another.[19]

Of course, such an interest can degenerate into a narcissistic obsession with our own self-image. But our self-esteem is in some degree linked with our external appearance. A drab unkempt appearance may be deliberately cultivated in order to signal a rejection of the normal conventions of society. On the other hand, it may be a sign of a poor sense of self-worth. Again, smart dressing may be a facade behind which we hide our feelings of inadequacy, or an attempt to project a new and more acceptable image. But whatever the inner motivations, it always is a boost to our own self-confidence to know that we are looking our best. Of course, fashions change so rapidly, and we all want to avoid being thought of as outdated; to wear last year's outfit is unthinkable; but to wear the clothes of the previous generation may be the new avant-garde fashion. The purpose of high fashion is both to hide and enhance. Bulges in all the wrong places may be concealed skilfully by the deliberate cut of a dress or suit. The scope for all this is much wider in the case of feminine beauty. A long facial profile can be counterbalanced by a rounded hairstyle. A well-endowed torso can be partially concealed by a long flowing dress with vertical patterns. Smallness of stature can be compensated for by high hairstyles and high heels. We know instinctively what suits. But those of us who are blind in these matters may need a little help from the whispered advice of our closest friends. So just like our lovers in these verses, we can enhance our mutual attractiveness by taking a little thought over our personal

---

[18] Tertullian, *The Apparel of Women* (c.220 AD).
[19] Shakespeare, *Hamlet*, Act 3, Scene 1, line 148.

appearance. This is not to be despised, and from careful sowing of such small seeds we may reap an abundant harvest of delight.

5. The fragrance of love (1:12–14)

The lover's praise of his girl in verses 9–11, and his determination to embellish her further, has the natural effect on her: she finds her lover irresistible, and she soliloquizes and dreams to herself; her perfumes give off their fragrance. *The king* (12) is her lover, again part of the royal fiction, and not part of a love triangle. The translation *while* is a Mishnaic usage of a term which in classical Hebrew usage is normally translated as 'until'. She dreams of her lover on his (lit.) 'couch', a low settee or divan used for eating from, or for sleeping on. Whatever she imagines her lover doing on his couch, whether eating or sleeping or lying with her, the 'couch' in this context has definite erotic connotations. And she speaks of her love and her lover in terms of very fragrant spices. *Perfume* (12) is nard, or spikenard, a very expensive perfume or ointment from a plant native to India. The scarcity of this exotic fragrance made it extremely expensive.[20] Origen, one of the great Fathers of the early church, observed that the actual spikenard plant emits its scent only when its hairy stem is rubbed, thus hinting at some erotic connotations. At 4:13–14 the plant itself is mentioned as part of the maiden's luscious garden. The second fragrance that is mentioned is *myrrh*. It belongs to a thorny shrub or tree which exudes from its bark and stems a fragrant resinous gum. The pleasant odour of the gum contrasts with its very bitter taste. It is mentioned six times in the Song (at 1:13; 3:6; 4:6, 14; 5:1, 13). The third fragrance is that of the *henna blossoms*. In the springtime the shrub is covered with *clusters* of tiny yellow-white flowers of very pleasant odour.

Whether our girl was able to afford all these types of perfume is irrelevant. She may not have possessed them, but she knew what they were and how attractive their smell was. And she perhaps dreams that she is on the 'king's couch' alongside him, and that her nard is yielding its fragrance and performing its seductive work upon him. The other mentions of *myrrh* and *henna blossoms* refer to her lover. The girl perhaps goes to bed with a little leather pouch of *myrrh* suspended around her neck and

---

[20] See Mark 14:3. An alabaster flask would cost a manual labourer a whole year's wages in New Testament times.

dangling between her breasts. *Resting* (13) is rather weak. The verb usually (but by no means always) means 'to spend the night'. What we are undoubtedly meant to infer is that it is not only her *sachet of myrrh* which spends the night between her *breasts*, but her lover as well. The tense of the verb could be future or present. Incidentally, it was myrrh that the wife of easy morals used to perfume her bed, to attract her lovers between the sheets while her husband was away on his trading expeditions (Prov. 7:17). However, we are not to assume that our couple are of that type of character.[21] In verse 14, the *cluster of henna blossoms* is 'in' (not *from*, as NIV) *the vineyards of En Gedi*.

En Gedi (literally, well/spring of kid) was an oasis on the western boundary of the Dead Sea, set among inaccessible cliffs, in the suffocatingly hot area of the Rift Valley. The oasis was a luscious land of freshness and fertility in an area of incredible barrenness and heat. At various times in its history it was a place for the production of exotic cosmetics and perfumes. David, at one point in his flight from King Saul, found refuge and asylum here. The parallelism between verses 13 and 14 makes it clear that since the lover is represented by the pouch of *myrrh* and the *cluster of henna blossoms*, so the girl herself is represented by *the vineyards of En Gedi* (the latter parallels her breasts). We have already come across the vineyard as a metaphor for the girl (1:6). Here the metaphor may have more explicitly sexual or erotic undertones. A spring or fountain or well (a source of flowing water) is a picture elsewhere in the Old Testament for the sexuality of the female.[22] Later in the Song itself (4:12) the girl's virginity is expressed by the phrase 'a spring enclosed, a sealed fountain'. *Gedi* (kid) may possibly have sexual overtones.[23] Be that as it may, the girl regards her own sexuality as a luxuriant oasis in a deep ravine, and her lover as a sprig or *cluster* of henna within her oasis. She represents an oasis of fertility in a very barren environment.

The word that is used in verse 13 for *my beloved* (*dôdî*) has the same consonants as the Hebrew for 'David'. The etymology of the proper name David is very much open to debate, though many have speculated that it means something like 'loved one'. So some have even suggested that

---

[21] See section on 'The morality of the Song' (pp. 9–14).

[22] See Prov. 5:15, 'Drink water from your own cistern, running water from your own well,'; Prov. 9:17, 'Stolen water is sweet; food eaten in secret is delicious.'

[23] See Gen. 38:17 where Judah, thinking that Tamar, his daughter-in-law, was an unknown prostitute, offered her a kid for her services.

David was the lover of the Song, as David was also a great musician. But this line of argument can also support Solomonic authorship, since Solomon's alternative name was Jedidiah (which has the consonants *d-w-d* hidden within it; 2 Sam. 12:25), meaning 'beloved of Yahweh'. All this is very speculative, and not much weight should be placed on its significance.

The Song is very rich in its descriptive power in that much use is made of all the five senses (tasting, touching, seeing, hearing and smelling). We have been introduced already to all these aspects, and we shall come across much more in the rest of the Song. It might be worthwhile at this stage to pause and consider this in general (we shall look at specific metaphors in more detail as we meet them). In everyday life, let alone the spiritual life, is it not true that we look and look but never perceive; we listen and listen but never hear (cf. Isa. 6:9)? Sheer familiarity with the ordinariness of life dulls our senses. We become hard of hearing, we do not perceive. This is not something merely physical, but mental. We do not take time to consider, to hear and listen. The ordinary, the humdrum, the everyday experience, may become a source of wonder and rest if only we stopped and took time to ponder, and think, and imagine. We need to slow down and savour our environment; the light and shade produced by the winter's sun breaking through a dirty window pane; the taste and smell of hot, freshly ground coffee; the feel of the coat of a beautiful dog as it is stroked; the happy sound of children's laughter down the street; the sight of a glistening cobweb heavy with dew. Did not Jesus say, 'Consider the lilies of the field' (Matt. 6:28, RSV)? We are not at the moment thinking of spiritual lessons. Rather, we are talking about a heightening of our awareness of our environment through our sense perceptions. We are not talking of 'the deeper hue that Christless eyes have never seen',[24] but something much more mundane; of looking at all life as a gift from a benevolent Creator. Let us take deeper breaths as we pass the fresh bread bakery. Let us linger over the face of a gnarled old man we meet in the street. Let us appreciate the fine features of a beautiful girl. Let us savour the fragrance of expensive perfume.

Then are we truly rich, not because we possess these things, but because we are able to enjoy what others possess. Surely that is a bonus, a gift and a capacity worth having from our Creator God.

---

[24] See Wade Robinson, 'Loved with Everlasting Love'.

6. A duet of mutual admiration (1:15 – 2:3)

Here we have a series of short exchanges between the boy and the girl, of crisp point and counterpoint. The symmetry of the speeches is somewhat obscured by the NIV; but the Hebrew itself highlights the balanced structure of the verses. Verses 15 and 16 both begin with *How beautiful*. The girl in verse 16 then introduces the idea of their verdant bower, which is taken up in the next verse by the boy. In 2:1 the girl rather deprecatingly compares herself to *a rose of Sharon* and *a lily of the valleys*, which elicits the counter response from the boy, *like a lily among thorns*. The girl's final response in 2:3 begins with a similar refrain, *Like an apple tree among the trees of the forest*. A division at the end of 2:2 is somewhat artificial, since 2:3 continues her admiration of her lover, though in soliloquy form – she addresses him in the third person. Perhaps she is dreaming or fantasizing as to how their love will be consummated. There is a progression of theme from 1:15 to 2:7; mutual compliments using imagery from the natural order (doves, verdancy, cedars, firs, rose of Sharon, lily of the valleys, an apple tree) lead to dreams about being together in some leafy bower where they can be alone, undisturbed and relaxed. This privacy leads inevitably to the blossoming of desire (2:4–5) and to the intimate embrace and fondling of 2:6, concluding with the adjuration to the daughters of Jerusalem.

The boy begins the exchange by describing his girl as *beautiful* (*yāpâ*). The Hebrew adjectives for both *beautiful* and *charming* (*nāʿîm*; 16)[25] can be used equally to describe both male and female. English is not quite so flexible in this regard; we would hardly call a grown man 'beautiful'. She is *beautiful*, more than 'pretty'. Prettiness invokes the idea of a homely domesticity, of apple pie, happy sociability, of smiles and laughter and rollicking fun, a non-threatening, playful, childish innocence. Beauty, on the other hand, bears the connotations of awesomeness; there is a hint of remoteness and inaccessibility and stateliness; she is statuesque, with an almost unreal perfection which threatens mere ordinary mortals. We shall come across this threatening aspect of the girl's beauty later in the Song at 4:9; 6:4–5, 10; and 7:5.

The boy then describes her *eyes* as *doves*. This is the first time *doves* are mentioned in the Song. They also occur at 5:12, where his eyes are described very enigmatically as literally 'doves by brooks of water, bathing

---

[25] The woman's name Naomi derives from the same root.

in milk, dwelling by a fullness'. It is possible that the expression implies that her *eyes* are like the 'eyes of doves'; that is, they have an iridescent quality, a scintillating pearly-grey speckled with flecks of brighter colours, as in Swinburne's 'Félise':

Those eyes the greenest of things blue,
the bluest of things grey.

But it is more likely that he is referring to the shape of her eyes, as oval-shaped, like the body of a dove with its neck stretched down to pick up scraps from the ground. Egyptian tomb paintings portray the eyes in an exaggerated almond shape. The shape of the eye may be made more pronounced artificially by painting and shading. In 2 Kings 9:30 we read that Jezebel 'painted her eyes' (RSV) in her attempt to be attractive to Jehu. In Jeremiah 4:30, Jerusalem, personified as a harlot, is said to 'enlarge [her] eyes with paint' (RSV). Similarly, in Ezekiel 23:40, the harlot Oholibah paints her eyes. The Old Testament seems to associate eye-painting among the Hebrews with women of doubtful character.

Other possibilities are that the girl's eyes are somewhat timid; they glance and flutter and dart around, like a pair of shy doves. Similarly, the dove was proverbially a model of innocence; see Jesus' words 'Be as shrewd as snakes and as innocent as doves' (Matt. 10:16). The human eyes, together with the mouth, are the most eloquent expressions of our inner feelings. There are bright sparkling eyes, indicating a vivacious personality; there are shifty eyes, hiding guilt and deception, never holding the gaze of an enquirer for the necessary length of time for normal contact to be made; there are mocking eyes, contemptuous eyes; there are arrogant eyes; cruel, despotic eyes; eyes full of fear and apprehension; eyes that indicate exhaustion or hopelessness; eyes that are dead with despair or vacuity; dreamy eyes that focus on another unseen world; lustful, leering eyes, full of depraved intent. Our eyes mirror exactly our inner disposition. Did not Jesus say, 'The eye is the lamp of the body' (Matt. 6:22)? Whatever this enigmatic saying may mean, surely it conveys at least the idea of our 'inner light' shining through our eyes? Of course, when the Song talks about the girl's eyes, it refers to the totality of her eyes: the pupils, the iris, the eyelids, the eyebrows, the eye pouches, and the lines beneath the eye. Our eyes are the focus of attention in any act of communication. They are the initial means of contact. The boy says, *How beautiful you are ...! Your eyes are* . . . Now we can alter artificially the impact of our eyes, with false eyelashes, resiting eyebrows, and underlining the lids to enhance the visual impact of our faces. Of course, when this is overdone, it becomes grotesque, as in a clown, or in 'the harlot's cheek, beautified with plastering art'.[26] I suppose that the correct balance to strike is just that little extra help which makes one wonder whether the beauty is natural or not.

The girl replies in 1:16 in similar terms, literally 'Behold, you are beautiful, my lover.' The masculine form of the adjective is used. We would have to say that he is *handsome*. She considers him *charming*, attractive, delightful (*nāʿîm*). Beauty and handsomeness are subjective terms; beauty is in the eye of the beholder. But beauty is not just skin deep; for a truly beautiful personality will shine through, whatever outward mask we wear with which nature equips us. We may be very ordinary, plain or even ugly by conventional standards, but a beautiful spirit will inevitably shine through. But of course our self-esteem does in some respects depend on how we view ourselves. That is why we try to 'take care of our own vineyards'. If we 'go to seed', that indicates a lack of proper self-respect and self-esteem, and a degeneracy of spirit.

So our lovers praise each other's beauty. Surely this is no mere flattery; they are not out to gain short-term advantage by mouthing falsehoods; but they give each other heartfelt praise. The psychological effects of praise and affirmation are beneficial to our well-being. They make us 'feel good'. We are made to feel important and valuable to others. Surely this is an important part of any relationship. It is the oil that makes the machinery of everyday life run smoothly. It is an added fillip on grey days. It is the un-expectedness of it, the surprise element, that gives us the boost we need. But to set out on a programme of mutual affirmation can often be artificial and sterile in its basic self-serving mechanisms. Much of our ability or willingness to articulate emotion or praise is culturally or temperamentally conditioned. Many men would rather die than praise their wives. Perhaps we all need to break down barriers of reserve and inhibitions in this respect. Of course, it can go to the other extreme, where all our relationships are at a very superficial level of mutual back-scratching, at the sort of level of 'how to win friends and influence people',[27] which is at worst self-serving manipulation.

---

[26] Shakespeare, *Hamlet*, Act 3, Scene 1, line 51.

[27] The title of Dale Carnegie's book, first published in 1936.

The duet is continued by the introduction of the secret bower motif. Their *bed* is in the countryside. The word used here for *bed* implies some sort of canopied bed, with fancy carved panels and perhaps decorative screens. Possibly we are meant to hear hints of a sumptuous royal bedroom here. But no, their *bed is verdant*. They are lying together on the green sward of the forest with a canopy of evergreen fir and cedar trees above them.

The Hebrew says 'our houses' (plural), indicating that they have a vast choice of shady groves to which they can retire in privacy. The Song is permeated with the theme of love in the countryside. We have already met the girl's attempt to meet her lover at the shepherds' huts (1:7–8). The lover also urges her to come with him out in the open to the countryside in 2:8–13. In 4:8 we have his invitation to her to come from (to?) Lebanon. In 7:11–13 we hear her invitation to him to spend the night among the henna bushes, where they will make love together. In these verses (2:16–17) there is an implied contrast between the city or town, with all its human-made civilization, and the naturalness of unspoilt creation. Perhaps it is a literary device, a convention, to show that the lovers are doing only what is natural, what is part of God's created order. Of course, we have to be careful here. This does not give carte blanche for unlicensed sexual freedom. The theme of love in the springtime (2:8–13) conveys the idea of the lover's identification with the blossoming, flowering, bursting forth of nature after its long winter sleep. Here they are not communing with nature, but with each other; the backdrop of the created order is an encouragement to them to participate in the natural order of things. But 'nature' in the Song is never personified or given a divine status. We in our Western tradition are used to such personification through the Romantic nature poets (Tennyson, Wordsworth), and we can talk quite harmlessly of nature's bidding, beckoning, imitation, and so on. But this type of language was too close to the language of the Canaanite fertility religions for it ever to be embraced by the authors of the Old Testament. The idea of copulating gods and goddesses behind the fertility cycle of the seasons was absolutely anathema to the faith of Israel. Hence the guarded quality of its language. The natural backdrop is a literary device. Our lovers are free from the trappings of convention, of society, of civilization, in order to express themselves fully to each other.

The girl continues the duet by modestly, self-deprecatingly, calling herself *a rose of Sharon, a lily of the valleys* (2:1). She is hardly *a rose*, more like a crocus; Sharon is 'the Sharon', the low-lying coastal plain south of the promontory of Mount Carmel. She is *a lily of the valleys*; not our well-known English flower; rather a tall flower, with one or two clusters of six-petalled trumpet-like flowers at the top of a single thin stem. These flowers would be commonplace in the countryside – so she is virtually saying there is nothing special about her, there are many more like her. Nevertheless, commonplace flowers can be extraordinarily beautiful. Did not Jesus himself say, 'Consider the lilies of the field, how they grow . . . even Solomon in all his glory was not arrayed like one of these' (Matt. 6:28–29, rsv)? Perhaps the girl here is fishing for compliments. If that be the case, it certainly has the desired effect. The boy replies that she is like a lily among thorns compared with the other young women. All others are as briars and brambles compared with her beauty. There may also be the additional element of the unlikelihood of such a beautiful flower growing in such hostile surroundings. This is a common theme in the folk litera-ture of love: the poor maiden, a menial drudge, dressed in rags, living in a hovel, yet possessing extraordinary beauty. The handsome prince is attracted by her, rather than by all the wealthy court maidens of the palace, whose beauty pales into insignificance in comparison with that of the heroine.

Finally the girl basks in the security of her lover (3). The phrase *Like an apple tree among the trees of the forest is my beloved among the young men* parallels *like a lily among thorns is my darling among the young women*. There is much speculation about the nature of the *apple tree*. Most agree that it cannot be our modern apple, not native to Israel at that time; it must be a sweet citrus tree such as the apricot. (Note: its fruit is sweet to her taste.) But here is a case where literary sensitivity in translation must override considerations of strict botanical accuracy. 'Apples', with their ready availability and their refreshing taste, are much more appropriate than 'apricots', which jar somewhat with their relative unfamiliarity. So our girl finds other men tasteless and unrefreshing compared with her lover. Finding a wild *apple tree* in an uncultivated woodland is an occasion of spontaneous happiness. Most of our deeper pleasures are serendipitous. By chance, they pass unexpected on our way, and we seize the moment and drink deeply of the pleasures of the moment. 'Apples' are also mentioned in the Song at 2:5; 7:8; and 8:5, seemingly with some erotic connotation. Here, that possibility is in view; *his fruit is sweet to my taste*. She enjoys his intimate and sweet kissing.

Perhaps more importantly, however, she delights *to sit in his shade.*
Here there is a strong indication of the role of the male as protector of
the female. He provides the security in which she can shelter and
blossom. It was considered an abnormal reversal of the established order
that a woman should protect a man (see Jer. 31:22, NIV mg.). This male
role is not merely one of finance, or overall head of the family, but
one of emotional and psychological strength to the woman. Of course,
in the times of ancient Israel, women worked, laboured, marketed,
bought and sold, just as much as men, or even more so. But their status
in society was almost totally governed by their attachment to their
menfolk, whether fathers, brothers or husbands. A woman without some
male protector was considered most pitiable, and without real identity.
Hence the Old Testament legislation concerning the protection of
the orphan and widow. A girl was always under her father's authority
until she got married. Of course, much in our Western society has
radically changed since then, and a woman's self-identity is no longer
dependent in any way at all on an attachment to a member of the
opposite sex. But where there is a relationship between a man and a
woman, the male is more often likely to be looked to as the provider of
protection. As Matthew Henry, commentating on Genesis 2:21–25,
quaintly observes,

> The woman was made of a rib, out of the side of Adam; not made out of
> his head to rule over him, nor out of his feet to be trampled upon by him,
> but out of his side to be equal with him, under his arm to be protected,
> and near his heart to be beloved.

These verses of mutual admiration prompt us to ask the question as to
exactly what it is that we most admire in our partners or spouses. For
in the first full flush of youthful ardour, the haze of romantic passion in
which we float may often prevent us from seeing the obvious. For we may
be completely blind in failing to perceive the solid qualities or underlying
weaknesses which are self-evident to outside observers.

> O me! What eyes hath Love put in my head,
> Which have no correspondence with true sight:
> Or, if they have, where is my judgment fled,
> That censures falsely what they see aright? . . .

O cunning Love! With tears thou keep'st me blind,
Lest eyes well-seeing thy foul faults should find.[28]

Yet the analysis of the reasons for our mutual attraction is not just a tiresome chore imposed on impatient youngsters by the dull aunties and uncles of this world. For such heart-searching can bring us to a deeper self-knowledge, and may prevent us from unhappy entanglements which we may later live to regret. Better to withdraw now, than to blunder on in a hopelessly unsuitable match. Do we admire our partners because they resemble us in so many ways, or because they are the exact opposite of us? To be so alike is very safe, yet has the seeds of dull conformity within it. To have diametrically opposed temperaments and interests can lead to a tempestuous relationship, yet with the potential for many exciting surprises. Do we respect them for their incisive intellectual abilities, or for their earthly practical natures? Are they full of robust common sense, or are they impractical daydreamers? Are they exciting to be with, or are we going to be bored with each other after a few weeks? Have we not all at some time or another looked at a couple who have degenerated into a vegetable-like existence and exclaimed, 'Help! I hope we don't end up like that!'? Let us make sure that there is much to stimulate us in our partners, seeing in them a rich vein of precious rock, to be explored and mined in an ever-deepening relationship.

7. Moving towards a climax (2:4–7)

We have already noted that these verses are a continuation of the girl's soliloquy, which transports her into a fever of desire culminating in some very close intimate behaviour. This progression to some sort of climax is very obvious. However, a number of the details are very unclear, and we cannot be certain of their exact interpretation. We need to consider these in turn, before looking at the general meaning of the passage as a whole.

Her lover this time has taken the initiative (perhaps in the girl's imagination) and he has taken her to what is literally in the Hebrew 'the house of wine'. Many take this, as NIV, to be a banqueting hall, as though there is a wedding celebration or some cultic festival in view here. But so far in the Song, there has been no hint of a formal marriage. Others take it to be a

---

[28] Shakespeare, 'Blind Love', Sonnet 148.

tavern, or a rural drinking place. However, since there is a rapid progression to intimate behaviour in this scene, it seems inappropriate to postulate these literal locales, as the lovers are still in the countryside. The greeny sward and the canopy of conifers are still their place of love-making. So it is better to link this idea with what immediately precedes it (that is, 'his fruit is sweet to my taste'), which is also an indication of intimate behaviour. Since, as we have already seen, wine is associated in the Song with the idea of kissing, it seems better to interpret the 'house of wine' metaphorically as his mouth, into which he invites her to enter, to enjoy their deep kissing.

The second half of verse 4 is also problematical. The traditional translation (*his banner over me* [is] *love*) has become the theme line of much popular hymnody and choruses. The problem is the word *degel*. The majority of the Old Testament occurrences of this word appear in the book of Numbers (Num. 1:52; 2:2–3, 10, 17, etc.). In these contexts the NIV uniformly translates the word as 'standard', that is, a pole, bearing some identifying flag, ensign or insignia, to act as a rallying point for the tribes and clans of Israel on their march through the wilderness. Some take the word to mean some sort of military unit. However, the military connotations here seem inappropriate, unless we like to think that the boy has made a 'conquest' and is staking out his claim over the girl whose heart he has captured. Goulder, in his commentary, always on the lookout for precise erotic identifications, implies that the standard, *banner*, pole or rod is a phallic symbol, so that the boy is aroused and ready for love-making. Perhaps the best way to interpret this troublesome word is to look for similar roots in cognate languages. There is an Akkadian word with the same consonants which means basically something to do with sight, or appearance, or glancing. So we then have the interpretation, 'His glance towards me was intent on love-making.' (The glance then represents his wish, his desire, his purpose.) This same root *d-g-l* appears with the troublesome 'bannered ones' at 6:4 and 6:10 (see later).

In 2:5 we have problems with the verbs and their forms and meanings. They are masculine plural imperatives. This raises the question of whom she is addressing. Fox calls this a 'rhetorical imperative, a strong way of expressing a wish for what is already the case'. However, her words seem to be addressed directly to her lover. But Pope suggests that the words are addressed to no-one in particular, but are an outcry under the pressure of extreme emotion. Whatever the request may mean, its purpose is that her lovesickness might be alleviated. The traditional translations for the two almost synonymous verbs are 'support, sustain, revive, strengthen, refresh'. Alternative possibilities are 'preparing a bed' (in Ps. 3:5) or 'spreading out of a couch' (as in Job 17:13). So the verse could be translated as in NIV and RSV, or as

> Spread me out among the raisin cakes.
> Lay me out among the apples.

Of course, the latter would represent some flight of fancy. The raisin cakes have pagan cultic connotations.[29] The cakes were made in the shape of a nude female with exaggerated genitalia. So there are strong erotic associations here.

The girl is aroused, and she is weak, sick, and *faint with love* and desire. The seeming hopelessness of love is portrayed in Dryden's line: 'Love's a malady without a cure.' She is not pretending to be sick, as Amnon did in his ruse to get Tamar to wait on him in his bedroom (2 Sam. 13:5). She is swooning with desire. She has that ache in the pit of her stomach, she has that loss of appetite which can only be cured by her being 'spread out' with her lover, and by eating and drinking of the delights of love-making. That is the only cure for her malady. She sees herself held in the strong embrace of her lover as they lie together under their leafy shade, her head locked in the strong left arm of the boy while with his right hand he gently caresses her. She allows him to explore her body, the smooth mountains and valleys of her shapely contours. She has surrendered to his advances and acceded to the request of her lover to

> License my roving hands, and let them go
> Before, behind, between, above, below.
> O my America, my new-found land.[30]

How far they go in 'making love' is not for us to know. The poem fades away in a haze of passion, and the author closes down the scene of intimacy with the words of the refrain, addressed to the *daughters of Jerusalem* by the girl, not to *arouse or awaken love until it so desires*. The theme

---

[29] They are mentioned in Isa. 16:7 and Hos. 3:1.
[30] Donne, 'Elegy 19'.

of lovesickness also appears in the Egyptian love songs. At first sight, the verses of the following extract seem to convey a ruse similar to Amnon's, but the last line shows that it is a sickness that only his beloved will understand, something beyond the diagnostic skills of the doctors:

> I will lie down inside
> And then I will feign illness.
> Then my neighbours will enter to see
> And then my sister will come with them
> She'll put the doctors to shame
> for she will understand my illness.[31]

That the girl is already aroused is clear. It is hardly likely that she needs the further stimulation of aphrodisiacs. In this state of excitement, she makes this somewhat obscure request to the *daughters of Jerusalem*. This is the second time they occur in the Song. Previously they appeared at 1:5. Again we cannot postulate too literal a scene. It is hardly likely that they are peeping through the pines, spying on the lovers' intimate caresses. No, they are much more likely to be a literary fiction, a foil or sounding board for the thoughts and desires of the girl. She begs them solemnly, puts them on oath as it were, and causes them to swear not to *arouse or awaken love until it so desires*. She binds them to swear *by the gazelles and by the does of the field*; they are both female deer, shy wild animals of the open hillsides. The gazelle and stag are symbols of alert potency elsewhere in the Song, but that symbolism does not seem to be warranted in this particular context. In any oath-taking, one always swears by some higher authority. The NEB translates 'by the spirits and goddesses of the field'. This is a very unlikely reference to primitive animism, which formed no part of ancient Israelite religion. The NEB took its lead from the Septuagint, which translated it as 'in the powers and strengths of the field'. The desire to swear by a spiritual authority is a universal instinct. Probably the best interpretation of the meaning of this adjuration is found by supposing that this is indeed the case; for the Hebrew for hinds (*ṣĕbā'ôt*) may suggest the idea of Yahweh of Sabaoth (the LORD of armies or hosts), and the Hebrew for *does of the field* (*'ayĕlôt haśśādeh*) may suggest the similarly sounding El Shaddai (the ancient patriarchal name for God). Perhaps there

---

[31] Part of an Egyptian love song, quoted by Fox, p. 13.

was a reluctance to mention explicitly the names of God in a poem that was full of human sexual love.

The two words *awaken* and *arouse* are two different forms of the same Hebrew root, meaning to awake from sleep, or to arouse, excite, to bestir something or someone. It never has the idea of 'disturb' or 'interrupt' elsewhere (cf. GNB). *Love* here is love-making, or sexual desire. The problem here is to determine the thrust of the request. There are a number of possibilities. If we can accept the translation 'interrupt', we then have 'do not disturb or interrupt our love-making until we have had our fill' (i.e. 'until we are satiated'). Alternatively, it might mean, 'Do not force love-making or a love relationship; let it blossom naturally in due season, for the process cannot be hurried artificially.' Perhaps another interpretation is, 'Don't start the process of loving exchange until the opportunity and appropriate occasion is present for its consummation.' Delitzsch suggested, 'Don't interrupt the sweet dream of love she is enjoying by recalling her back to the reality of the present situation.' This implies that it is the author or narrator who is speaking, and not the girl herself. But the author hardly ever appears in the Song. The only other possible place of the author's appearance is in 8:6–7 in the poem describing love 'strong as death'. It should be pointed out that this adjuration occurs again at 3:5, and in a slightly different form at 8:4. It seems to act as a brake on the proceedings, as if the lovers were being doused with some cold water to cool down the ardour of their passion which is being aroused perhaps at an inopportune time. However, at 5:1, where there is the most unambiguous and explicit reference to full intercourse between the lovers, they are encouraged to drink their fill and become intoxicated with love.

Perhaps we need to stand back a little from the intensity of our passage, and survey it with a cool objectivity and detachment. Our lovers are well on their way to full physical communion either in fact or in fantasy. (I prefer the latter interpretation here.) What then is there to teach us here about our own love relationships and our thought lives and fantasies? The first thing that needs to be said is that our imaginations often run far ahead of our physical reactions and they in turn run far ahead of what our actual relationship may be able to bear at that particular moment. When the physical outstrips the fully personal, emotional and psychological integration of two lovers, the danger signals should start flashing. Adulterous thoughts, thoughts of fornication, are all too easy to entertain in the abstract, divorced from a relationship that is developing healthily at its own pace. It seems that the girl in the Song recognizes that here. She wants their love to be consummated, but she is in great tension, because she knows that the time is not yet ripe. In speaking to the daughters of Jerusalem, she is speaking to herself. She is basically telling herself to cool it, to wait for the appropriate time. For the Christian, the appropriate time is always within marriage, never outside it. We are all so clever at rationalizing our own desires, at excusing our own lack of self-discipline of our bodies and of our thought lives. But we need to be ruthless in this matter, as Jesus himself taught (Matt. 5:29–30). If what we see, touch, feel, read or hear causes a wrong chain of thought to originate in our minds, then we are to be severe on ourselves, and shut our eyes, and refrain from touching or reading or watching. Not that the desire or instincts are in any way wrong in themselves. What is wrong is when those desires run away with us, and spiral totally out of control, and find their fulfilment in illegitimate ways.

One very startling biblical example of how an initial love went wrong is Amnon's affair with Tamar (2 Sam. 13). He was overwhelmingly attracted to his beautiful half-sister, who seemed to him to be totally unobtainable and out of his reach. He allowed his passions to overwhelm him, and once he had indulged them, he had no further use for her. There is no more poignant statement in the whole of the Old Testament of how love can be totally corrupted by lust. We read that 'the hatred with which he hated her was greater than the love with which he had loved her' (2 Sam. 13:15, RSV). As Shakespeare says of lust, 'Past reason hunted; and no sooner had, Past reason hated'.[32] This very perversion of what is so noble and good has its own terrible cycle of maturation and death. As James writes in his epistle, 'Each person is tempted when they are dragged away by their own evil desire and enticed. Then, after desire has conceived, it gives birth to sin; and sin, when it is full-grown, gives birth to death' (Jas 1:14–15).

As well as falling under the objective moral judgment of God, the pursuit of lust is also subject to the law of diminishing returns (i.e. the frustrations of pursuing an ever-increasing pleasure only to be met by an experience of ever-diminishing intensity). What promises so much, in fact yields so little. The physical exhaustion and the psychological self-disgust are the natural consequences of isolating the desire for immediate pleasure from the love and respect for the person.

---

[32] Shakespeare, Sonnet 129, lines 6–7.

However, our passionate love-struck girl, with all her ardent desires and yearnings, will, like all young lovers, have to learn to wait. For it is only in the security of their future marriage that she will be able to experience the fulfilment of all her deepest longings.

Song of Songs 2:8 – 3:5

6. The second cycle: springtime and showers

1. Love in the springtime (2:8–13)

After the passion of the last poem, a new cycle of songs begins here with a beautiful description of an invitation to a meeting in the countryside in springtime. The adjuration of 2:7 produces a calmer atmosphere; and yet the continuing cycle of love evolves. In 2:16–17 there are hints of intimacy. The tension of absence is introduced in 3:1, and is resolved in great relief as the lovers are brought together again in intimate contact at 3:4. The cycle closes, as did the last one, with the adjuration to the daughters of Jerusalem not to arouse love before it pleases. It is likely that within this overall cycle, verses 2:8–17 constitute a single unit. It begins with *mountains, a gazelle* and a *stag* (8–9), and closes chiasmic-fashion with gazelle, stag and mountains (17).

The verses of this poem have such simple evocative power that any comment seems almost superfluous. The text is so marvellously alive that any comment will appear to be very pedestrian. Beautiful poems can too often be reduced to dust and ashes by dry academic analysis. But, for the purposes of our exposition, we can divide the poem quite naturally into the girl's eager anticipation (8–9) and the boy's urgent invitation (10–13).

The NIV captures well the girl's thrill and excitement as she hears her lover approaching. Her sense of anticipation is almost tangible, as her boy leaps and springs over *the hills* towards her. He is as fleet of foot as a young *gazelle*, with boundless energy, an alert ear, a lightness of touch. Within no time at all, he is at her *wall, gazing through the windows*, eager to catch a first glimpse of her before she comes out to him. And then he invites her to come away with him to enjoy the explosion of nature in the springtime. The girl reports his speech as something in the past, thus indicating that it is her remembrance of a past event. She reports her anticipation in the present tense, to give immediacy and excitement to the statement of her feelings. Another way of dividing up the poem is to note the rural–domestic–rural sequence. The rural countryside motif is an expression of untrammelled freedom and exhilaration, of energetic enthusiasm and adventure. The countryside represents the thrilling liberty of the natural order of things, of excitement, or potential for new growth, new experiences and new relationships. It represents adventure, travelling new and unexplored pathways, taking the risks that a new liberty entails.

The domestic scene as a literary motif, on the other hand, represents safety, security, the acceptance of society's norms and conventions. There is the possibility of dullness and decay and of drab conformity. This motif can indicate a prison within which free spirits are confined. The girl is there in her house (*our wall*) together with her mother and brothers. And her lover regards her as being shut in by society. That is why he beckons her so urgently to join him in the wide outdoors, away from the drab darkness of suffocating domesticity, to enjoy the scents of the blossoms, to feel the wind blowing through their hair as they skip hand in hand across the hills. The barriers between these two types of existence are dramatically and forcefully represented by the *wall*, the *windows* and the *lattice*. She must penetrate these obstacles in order to join her lover, not just physically, to be with her boy, but emotionally and psychologically. This is stated tersely in Genesis: 'That is why a man leaves his father and mother and is united to his wife, and they become one flesh' (Gen. 2:24). For the girl, in her domestic environment, is known far more intimately by her brothers and her mother than by her lover. She must take the huge risk of abandoning her former undemanding securities to throw in her lot with a boy who is as yet a somewhat unknown quantity, and so face an adventure of increasing knowledge and self-knowledge, of expanding horizons, and of an uncharted future. She must leave the shelter of the patriarchal or matriarchal household, and find a new life on a different footing, a life of mutual exploration and of new delights, to be entered upon with trembling uncertainty.

The boy's invitation is a model of literary construction. The wonderful passage on the explosion of nature is framed between the words of invitation, almost identical, at 2:10 and 2:13, *Arise, my darling, my beautiful one, come with me*. There is a strong sense of temporal movement in the poem, from the past through the present to the future. The cold *rains* of the drab gloomy winter are now completely gone. They are a thing of the past. And now the tiny spring *flowers* are sparkling forth among the new shoots of the undergrowth. The turtle *doves* are cooing, the time for *singing* (or alternatively, 'pruning') has come ('pruning' probably breaks the parallelism – all the other activities are more of the natural order of creation, the singing being that of the birds). Some have suggested that the phrase *our land* is not a natural usage for indigenous inhabitants, and therefore leads to the suggestion that the girl is a foreigner, a non-Israelite. Goulder makes much of this theme;[1] according to him, the main message of the Song is to convey that marriage to foreigners is acceptable. So then the Song represents a counter thrust to the exclusive nationalism of Ezra and Nehemiah (Ezra 9 – 10; Neh. 13:23–31).

There is the hint of future blessings in the references to the *fig-tree* and the *vines* in blossom. The sterile fig of early spring is the precursor of the edible fig which is produced on new growth and matures in the late summer. (A tree that does not produce this *early fruit* will not yield a crop of real figs either; see Matt. 21:18–19.) The *vines* in blossom are also a harbinger of the luscious grape harvest to follow. So we have a movement from seeming barrenness to the full flower of fertility; from dark days of the past to the blossoming of new hope in the future.

Our lovers are part and parcel of this explosion of new life and new hope. Not that there is any explicit identification with any sexual element of fertility. For fertility and reproduction of the species are themes which barely surface in the Song. The renewal of nature is seen not in any sexual way (as was the case of the Baal fertility cult, which the prophets of Israel so forcefully opposed); rather the great Creator God, the covenant God of Israel, Yahweh of Hosts, stood over and behind the natural order, both transcendent and immanent. He is the sustainer and upholder of all that is. The way he works in the cycle of the seasons is a mirror of his workings in the lives of his people: from the secret growth in days of darkness, to the exuberance of new life. All this is expressed so brilliantly through the words of the prophet Isaiah. The exuberance of this eschatological passage reflects very clearly the exuberance of the lovers in their new-found freedom:

---

[1] Goulder, pp. 74–78.

As the rain and the snow
    come down from heaven,
and do not return to it
    without watering the earth
and making it bud and flourish,
    so that it yields seed for the sower and bread for the eater,
so is my word that goes out from my mouth:
    it will not return to me empty,
but will accomplish what I desire
    and achieve the purpose for which I sent it.
You will go out in joy
    and be led forth in peace;
the mountains and hills
    will burst into song before you,
and all the trees of the field
    will clap their hands.
Instead of the thorn-bush will grow the juniper,
    and instead of briers the myrtle will grow.
This will be for the LORD's renown,
    for an everlasting sign,
    that will endure for ever.
(Isa. 55:10–13)

Love in the springtime is of course a well-known literary motif, and the theme of blossoming romance in the countryside represents a poetic fantasy of escapism. But in actual practice, the bright flame of love can transfigure the most mundane of circumstances. The office, the college library, the work canteen and the factory production line: all can be bathed in a new transforming light in the eyes of those whose hearts are suffused with love. The fragrance of the blossoming vines may be replaced by the aromas of the coffee bar; the season of singing replaced by heavy-metal music pounding through headphones; the mountains and hills may perhaps become the inner-city area past the gasworks, which the lovers have to cross in order to be in each other's company. But whatever the circumstances, the lovers smile with happy benevolence on all and sundry who cross their paths, and in times of separation the constant yearning is for the thrill of seeing each other again, to hear that urgent invitation once again: *Arise, come, my darling; my beautiful one, come with me.*

Christopher Marlowe, in his poem 'The Passionate Shepherd to His Love', captures well the identical themes of our verses:

Come live with me and be my love,
and we will all the pleasures prove,
that valleys, groves, or hills, or fields,
or woods and steepy mountains yield.

2. A tantalizing tease (2:14–15)

How closely these two verses are connected with the scenario of 2:8–13 is a matter of some debate. The boy's eager invitation seems to be left hanging in mid-air. And so are we, the readers; we are kept in suspense. Is his invitation accepted? Does the girl join him in his flight across the hillside? It is not at all clear. Some have taken the boy's words in 2:14 to contain an element of mild disappointment because of his girl's inaccessibility. She does not show her face through the lattice, she does not let her voice be heard. Perhaps she is too shy and tentative; perhaps she is teasing him coyly, 'I won't show myself, I won't come out to you. It's up to you to come out and chase me.'

Whatever the connection with 2:8–13, the boy's words in verse 14 are tender, delicate and gentle. He calls her by a pet name, *my dove*. The dove is a shy, timid bird, easily put to flight at the slightest hint of threat. Perhaps the girl herself is retreating from the boy's advances. Perhaps she considers him too threatening, and she flies away like the dove, to the inaccessible crannies and *clefts of the rock*, the secret places of the steep ascents. Whether she is retreating in order to egg him on, while she delights in the thrill of the chase, is uncertain. What is certain is that her moods change; sometimes she is swooning with desire (2:5), other times she is troubled by her own self-image (1:5); here she may be bashful, or just coquettish. Some have seen in the references to *clefts* and crannies some sexual innuendo. We cannot be certain. The whole purpose of double entendres is that the ambiguities are unresolved. To plant the suggestion is a kind of tease. Hills, valleys, mountains of incense, mountains of 'Bether' (separation), all occur in the Song and can be interpreted at different levels of meaning. However, here, at the surface level of meaning, it is possible that the girl is playing hard to get, and she is deliberately setting a challenge to her lover. She knows she will ultimately be caught, but wants to sustain the thrill of anticipation by delaying the act of self-giving by prolonging the chase. Or perhaps she sees herself as independent and free like the dove, able to determine her own future destiny; to choose her own resting places and vantage points; free not to be captivated by love. Her independence may be too valuable to her. Her lover may even envy that freedom of hers, and prize it for himself. But as soon as he takes her independence from her, he paradoxically loses what he most prizes. At a more physical level, the same paradox occurs. He prizes her virginity, her purity, her enclosedness. But as soon as he takes her, he loses what he values.

According to the NIV, the boy here wants the girl to show him her *face*, and to cause him to hear the sound of her *voice*. But the NIV is somewhat misleading, for the word lying behind the translation *face* is the Hebrew word *mar'eh* which means 'appearance' (and translated as such at 5:15) and not the word *pānîm*, the usual word for face. In 5:15 the lover's appearance (i.e. his form, his stature) is like the Lebanon. Here, he wants to see her form. While this may mean no more than that he wants to see *her*, it could be extended to mean that he wants to feast his eyes on the totality of her person.

The imagery of the *dove* in the rocks may lead us to infer that he wants to be alone with her, far from the madding crowds, alone in the secluded crags, the overhanging hiding places of the rocky outcrops of the wilderness, there to make love to her, there not just to gaze on her *face*, but also to see and gently touch the rest of her beautiful and wondrous form, and to hear her shy and mellowed responses. Perhaps they murmur 'sweet nothings' to each other, private love talk on which it is improper to intrude, the sweet verbal nonsense and irrationalities of the communication of the lovers. There is a well-known cartoon in a *Punch* magazine from the Edwardian era in which two high-class and star-struck lovers are sitting on a park bench, holding hands and gazing into each other's eyes. A crusty old gentleman with large side whiskers sits reading his newspaper at the other end of the bench and looks at them through the corner of his eye. The lovers say to each other, 'Darling!' 'Yes, darling?' 'Nothing, darling; only *darling*, darling!' The rest of the caption says, 'Bilious old gentleman feels quite sick.'

There is a language between lovers which is appropriate for their ears only. Similarly, there are sights which only lovers are allowed to see, such as the various stages of the intimacies of undress. The boy wants to see her beautiful 'form', her breasts, her body, her thighs. He is so easily aroused by what he sees. He would like to undress her in the secrecy of the wilderness and to explore her form. For he knows, like every male, that a partially clothed female figure is more alluring than a fully displayed body. The partial concealment is partial disclosure. The hint of what remains concealed is what arouses the desire for total possession. As Michael Frayn has said, 'No woman so naked as one you can see to be naked underneath her clothes.' Of course, this whole matter of nakedness, nudity, of clothing and undress, is very complex.

Nakedness in the Old Testament is nearly always associated with shame, humiliation and degradation. Slaves and prisoners of war were paraded naked, as indicated by the prophetic symbolic acts of Isaiah and Micah (Isa. 20:2–4; Mic. 1:8) who went around 'with buttocks uncovered' (RSV) to symbolize the coming captivity of the people of Israel. David's envoys to the Ammonites were humiliated and sent back to the king half shaved and half naked (2 Sam. 10:4). The condemnation of a harlot was to have her 'nakedness' exposed by publicly lifting up her skirts over her head (Jer. 13:22, RSV). In the Garden of Eden, after the couple's disobedience, they were covered with shame and became self-conscious, aware that they were naked, a nakedness which indicated a defencelessness, a vulnerability.[2] It is almost certain that Jesus himself was crucified naked, the ultimate in public exposure and degradation. The opposite of nakedness is nudism, exposure without shame, a revelling in a natural state of undress. Who has not felt the thrill of the freedom of shedding one's clothes in private? But we can only be secure in that if we can be sure of no intruders. Nudism can very quickly flee into nakedness at the slightest hint of disturbance. But nudism, a sort of 'back-to-nature' mentality, is a pathetic fallacy that needs to be 'exposed'. For, as C. S. Lewis[3] has pointed out, we are less ourselves when fully unclothed than when we are dressed. At the public baths, what is on display is something that is common to us all, our human frame. Our real identity is masked by our nudity. Our real selves are more fully expressed by our outer clothing, which expresses our personality more than nudity ever can. The apostle Paul, speaking in the completely different context of the Christian's resurrection body, writes of this desire:

---

[2] Gen. 3:7; cf. Gen. 42:12 where the text reads literally 'the nakedness of the land', implying its vulnerability and its defencelessness.

[3] Lewis, *The Four Loves*, ch. 5.

> Meanwhile we groan, longing to be clothed instead with our heavenly
> dwelling, because when we are clothed, we will not be found naked ...
> because we do not wish to be unclothed but to be clothed instead with
> our heavenly dwelling.
>
> (2 Cor. 5:2–4)

We shall return later to this theme of nakedness and shame in the exposition of 5:1.

The refrain at 2:15 concerning *the little foxes* has teased commentators for millennia, and no certain conclusion can be reached. Who is mouthing these words? And to whom is the command addressed? The NIV puts them on the lips of the boy, but it is more likely that the girl speaks them. The masculine plural imperative *catch for us* is probably a rhetorical imperative, addressed to no-one in particular. The words have been thought by some to be a snatch of an ancient folk tale, or from a nursery rhyme. *Foxes* are guileful creatures in ancient fable and folklore. But here, their threat seems to be minimized.[4] They are *little foxes*, playful creatures that romp wantonly through *the vineyards* destroying the blossom. In the Samson story, the foxes are easily caught and are used as firebrands to destroy the harvest fields of the Philistines (Judg. 15:4–5). They are not like the leopards and lions in the mountain ranges of the Lebanon (4:8) which constitute a serious and dangerous threat; rather they are viewed with some condescension, even affection. What then is all this about?

Murphy[5] speculates that this little ditty could simply be the girl's response to her lover's request to *hear* her *voice*. So she accedes to this by singing a snatch from a catchy folk tune whose meaning has no actual relevance to their situation. So any form of words would act as a response. Alternatively, Murphy suggests that since the boy has just compared her to someone who is inaccessible in rocks and crevices, she replies rather saucily that she (the vineyard) is not as inaccessible as all that.

Conscious of the attraction that her feminine charms hold for all young men, she is reminding her lover playfully that there may be others who may be tempted to mount a raid on her *vineyards that are in bloom*, and that he had better show a bit of masculine chivalry towards her. Not that there is any hint of possible unfaithfulness or promiscuity here. The lovers

---

4 See Landy, p. 240.
5 Murphy, p. 141.

are devoted to each other, their relationship is closed, and no outsiders can trespass in. But by this playful banter she is gently warning him not to take her too much for granted.

The role of teasing in any relationship is a very delicate and sensitive one. For the playful or humorous exposure of weakness may often be carried too far. We are all very fragile creatures, and it is so very easy to go over the brink and destroy the other's self-esteem and provoke a hostile response. Constant teasing can destroy a relationship by an insensitive wearing down of the partner's self-respect. It all depends on how thick our skins are, or on our ability to laugh at ourselves. Sometimes we may be able to brush off humorous remarks like water off a duck's back. Other times, they may be too close to the bone, and we are hurt. Yet there is a positive role for teasing. It helps us to stop taking ourselves too seriously, and knocks us off the pedestal on which we so often place ourselves. It also can act as the stimulus to overcome our suddenly exposed faults, and we can come to a healthier knowledge of ourselves. We all too often live in a fool's paradise, and teasing is probably the most painless way of growing up and of becoming more mature.

Teasing can often take on the character of playful innocence. It causes pricks of pleasure which spark off a catalytic reaction of cascading fun, stimulating each other to a heightened sense of self-awareness; the adrenalin flows with the frisson of the unexpected sharpness of repartee. As Shakespeare puts it:

. . . a lover's pinch, which hurts,
and is desired.[6]

3. An affirmation and an invitation (2:16–17)

After the uncertain teasings of 2:14–15 we return to a reaffirmation of the fundamental theme of the Song – the mutual belonging of the lovers. In any relationship that is secure at its most fundamental level, there is always room for teasing, for play, for frolicking adventure; also there is always the possibility of nagging insecurities, of doubts, of longings for deeper levels of intimacy, or fear of loss. But for now, all hesitations are gone, and the girl reaffirms in verse 16 the depth of their mutual belonging.

---

[6] Shakespeare, *Antony and Cleopatra*, Act 5, Scene 2.

He belongs to her just as much as she belongs to him. They own, they possess each other. Their relationship is totally symmetrical. The whole of each belongs and is available to the whole of the other. As Paul says of the marriage relationship, 'The wife does not have authority over her own body but yields it to her husband. In the same way, the husband does not have authority over his own body but yields it to his wife' (1 Cor. 7:4). But here in the Song we are not just talking about bodies. Their bodily sharing is an expression of their mutual love and loyalty, of their determination to treat each other as whole persons, and not just as instruments for mutual self-gratification. This reciprocity, this mutuality, is something that shines out from the Song, something of a protest against the male dominance and macho masculinity which sin brought into the world (Gen. 3:16). But this sensitivity towards the female is known to the prophets of the Old Testament. Hosea especially was aware of the delicacy and fragility of this mutuality. There was a tendency for a woman to call her husband 'my Baal'. This word has connotations of ownership, authoritarianism, of domination rather than complementarity. But Hosea, mouthing the words of Yahweh to his people, says, 'You shall no longer call me "my Baal", but you shall call me "my husband"' (see Hos. 2:16). Of course, all this is in the context of Israel's apostasy away from Yahwism, when they embraced the indigenous Canaanite fertility cult. Yahweh was viewed by the prophet Hosea as the rejected husband, and Israel was viewed as the unfaithful wife. So the whole idea of the covenant between Yahweh and his people Israel was pictured as marriage, with all that that involves, namely loyalty, faithfulness, mercy, compassion, and so on. This is looked at in detail in the whole of Hosea's prophecy.[7] But for the moment, we see in Hosea the difference between a husband–wife relationship based on mutual loyalty and compassion, and a master–servant relationship based on authority, submission and fear. The whole ethos of the Song is far removed from any hint of the latter.

It is just because the betrothed couple are mutually and irrevocably committed to each other in regard to their future marriage that the physical side of their relationship can be expressed more freely. Of course, for the Bible believer, the final consummation of this is an act that is reserved for the married relationship alone. The lovers in our Song are thinking about this, and dreaming and fantasizing about the fulfilment of their

---

[7] See D. Kidner, *The Message of Hosea* (The Bible Speaks Today, IVP, 1981).

relationship. They have tentatively started out on the pathway of the physical expression of their love for each other in some intimate ways already. The girl's lover *browses among the lilies*. We have seen in 1:7 the first reference to 'pasturing'. The refrain here in 2:16 is repeated in its entirety at 6:3. Also at 6:2 the lover goes down to his garden (lit.) 'to pasture in the gardens, to pluck lilies'. As we have already seen, the verb 'to pasture, to graze, to feed' normally requires an object, such as 'the flock'. But here it is totally inappropriate to assume such in this context. He cannot be pasturing his flock among the lilies. His sheep and goats are hardly 'lily-eaters'. We have already seen that the boy describes his girl as a 'lily' among thorns (2:2). She describes his lips as lilies (5:13) which drip with flowing myrrh. So it seems probable that to 'browse among the lilies' is a metaphor to represent some very close intimate behaviour such as kissing or fondling some tender part of each other's body. It is totally speculative to attempt to be more precise in this matter. The metaphor, drawing as it does from the realms of gardening and shepherding, and combining them in such a surrealistic way, is meant to evoke an atmosphere of fantasy and make-believe.

Verse 17 is an enigma; it is totally ambiguous, and we cannot be certain of what is happening. What is certain is that the ambiguity is deliberate, a double entendre that makes us travel along opposite directions, to tease us in exploring the fantasy world that has already been suggested to us in 2:16. The clause about the day breaking and the shadows fleeing reappears at 4:6. The second half of 2:17 reappears, with slight modifications, at 8:14. The basic question about 2:17 is, is it an invitation to her lover to intimacy, or is it a command to him to depart and then return later? A further related question is regarding the time referred to by *Until the day breaks and the shadows flee*. Is it until morning, or until evening? We have no clear reference to a similar phrase in the Old Testament to help us out here. *The shadows* of the day lengthen and *flee* as the sun sets. Alternatively, *the shadows* of the night disappear as the sun rises. Reference to the day 'breathing' (see literal translation) could mean the cool breeze of the day (cf. Gen. 3:8) blowing as the sun rises, throwing off the suffocating darkness of the night. We cannot be certain whether 'shadow' means, in this context, the general darkness of the night, or the precise geometrical shadow cast by objects illuminated by the sun. I take the reference here to be the former, thus indicating the morning. But does the girl want him to turn away from her or towards her? The same ambiguity exists at 8:14, in spite of the more precise 'flee' (NIV 'come away') there. She wants him to *be like a gazelle or like a young stag on the rugged hills*. The unit began at 2:8–9 with the lover bounding over the mountains and hills like a young stag towards his girl. The unit closes here with a similar reference. So the natural reference is now to motion away from her, as is the case in 8:14. Thus literally it might mean that she is requesting him to go away and fly through the night, and come back again to her in the morning. But that does not make too much sense.

If we view the time frame differently, we could interpret it as the girl, having received him at the lattice of her home in the morning, telling him to fly away and come back in the evening, a more appropriate time for their secret meeting. It is more likely that the phrase is meant to be a subtle indirect invitation to the boy to come and make love to his girl all night (until the morning). This requires us to view the metaphor of the *stag* and *gazelle* as an indicator of young and ardent sexual potency (the Babylonian fertility-cult literature uses this metaphor in a similar way), and the rugged hills (literally: 'the mountains of Bether') as euphemisms for the girl's shapely body on which he is to skip and cavort. Bether has been taken as a proper noun, but no certain geographical reference has been found. Alternatively, it has been seen as a phrase indicating separation or division (from the root *b-t-r* meaning to divide); either as the mountains which divide the lovers, over which he has to spring and bound in order to meet her; or else as mountains which are cleft, or divided (hence RSV 'rugged mountains', indicating mountain range upon range receding into the distance). More precisely the 'cleft mountains' could represent the girl's breasts which her lover now has access to. A less likely possibility is that indicated by the Jerusalem Bible, 'Mountain of the Covenant', which picks up the reference in Genesis 15:17–18 to the making of the covenant with Abraham when the smoking fire pot was taken between the cleft halves of the sacrificial birds.

So the ambiguity of the language indicates the ambiguity of human responses. She wants him; she does not want him. This is a tension which every one of us feels. We dislike dependency, yet we cannot do without it; we long for its succour, but wish that things might be otherwise. What strange creatures we are! We want to be free, yet we want to possess and be possessed. We want to maintain independence, yet the loneliness of independence drives us to the desire for intimacy. And intimacy in turn leads us to the 'chains of love'. Any actual relationship will have to be a compromise. It is possible to suffocate our partners by an overwhelming desire for an unhealthy intimacy, by a cloying togetherness which stunts any development of different interests, and we limp along, leaning on each other as psychological and emotional crutches. Alternatively we can each go our own separate ways, with barely a meeting of minds, let alone bodies. But the adventure of courtship, both within and outside marriage, entails the ability to be flexible enough to cope with these tensions. There is some truth in the saying that only those who have learned to live with the responsible freedom and independence of singleness are qualified to cope with the togetherness and mutual dependency of marriage.

4. A very troubled dream (3:1–5)

If we try to link 3:1–5 with the literal scenario of 2:8–17, then we might suppose that the girl's prearranged rendezvous with her lover did not materialize. He did not show up, and she is in great agitation, longing for her absent lover. However, since it is impossible to be certain of any progression in the events lying behind 2:8–17, it is better to think of 3:1–5 as an independent unit. At a metaphorical level, 2:17 represents a longing for intimacy; 3:1 shows a similar longing that has not been fulfilled. Unfulfilled dreams and fantasies lead to a desperate fear of isolation and of loss.

So in 3:1 we have a sudden change in mood. It progresses from yearning for his presence, through fear of loss and abandonment, to panicky action, leading to a rushing torrent of relief when she finds him, clutches him, and will not let him go until they have consummated their relationship. The unit closes in 3:5 with the same adjuration we met in 2:7, which seems to indicate some climax to their physical relationship.

Most commentators take these verses as the girl's very troubled dream which ends, however, in a happy climax. There is a similar, though not identical sequence starting at 5:2 and continuing to 6:3. We shall compare and contrast them when we consider the fourth cycle of poems. It is unlikely that the scenes in 3:1–5 represent actual reality, for it is highly improbable that the young woman would go off in the middle of the night all by herself to search for her absent lover in the city streets and squares. Also the speed of the action seems too compressed to represent an actual event. The adjuration to the *daughters of Jerusalem* at 3:5 is probably a literary convention as before at 2:7. Thus it is best if we take the whole unit as a dream expressing the girl's insecurities.

The text itself is very vivid and stark, and needs little direct explanation. The girl is lying in bed, half asleep, half awake, restlessly yearning for her lover's presence beside her. The literal Hebrew 'in the nights' could mean 'all throughout the long hours of the night', or, more probably, 'night after night'. Obviously, the lovers are not married, for it is his continuous unexplained absence that causes her yearning. Her whole heart was knit together with that of her lover, but the physical absence was intolerable to bear, gnawing away at her inmost being. Her thoughts, her imaginings, her flights of fancy drive her to desperation. Nothing can satisfy her but her lover's actual presence. She seeks him throughout the long watches of the night, as if the very strength of her desire could achieve his presence with her. She determines (2) to get up and search the *streets and squares* thoroughly, in order to *find him*. It is irrational, impractical, impossible. She seeks and seeks but does not find. And panic is setting in. Instead, *the watchmen* find her, and they gaze at her in mute incomprehension of her question. For she assumes that everyone knows her lover's identity and that he is lost. As soon as she turns away from them with heavy heart and dull disappointment, she suddenly collides with her beloved, and seizes him and will not let him go until she has brought him to her *mother's house*, and *to the room of the one who conceived me*. This moment of relief, ending in the climax of consummation, is closed by the adjuration to the daughters of Jerusalem not to awaken love until it pleases.

'The house of my mother' could be translated more exactly as 'my mother-house', with the possessive 'my' qualifying the compound unit 'mother-house'. Then 'mother-house' could literally be the chamber where motherhood becomes a reality, that is, her womb. The phrase occurs again at 8:2 where again some intimate activity is implied (drinking spiced wine, drinking from the juice of the girl's pomegranate), leading on to the embracing of 8:3 and the adjuration at 8:4. So again, motion to *my mother's house* leads us in two opposing directions; to the literal homestead, which is an unlikely place for the secret love-making of the unmarrieds; and metaphorically to the girl's own secret place, to the entrance to her womb, the 'chamber' (1:4), the innermost sanctum of intimacy to which she longs to bring her lover. That this is the meaning is confirmed by the request the girl (or is it the author?) makes, that love should not be awakened or aroused until there is an appropriate opportunity for it to be fulfilled. Her dreamings have led her to explicit sexual fantasies, which cause her to be aroused when there is no hope of satisfaction, except in the physical presence of *the one my heart loves*. But she is still alone, and her fantasies are an exercise in frustration, so it is better that she not be aroused at all.

A number of themes are introduced here which it is profitable to explore. First of all, we see here the pain of love. There are both agonies and ecstasies in love, as well as the warm glow of contentment. The path of true love never did run smooth. There is a place for pain in every true relationship, the pain that gives one the opportunity to grow in love and bear one another's burdens; the pain that learns to live with limitations, with frustrated desires, with unfulfilled ambitions. The pain of love may mean a surrender of one's ideals, or a realization that one's ideals were misconceived.

Second, in these verses we have the pain of separation; the hollow aching provoked by the continual absence of the loved one. If the absence is too prolonged, then heaviness results. As the writer of Proverbs puts it,

> Hope deferred makes the heart sick,
> but a longing fulfilled is a tree of life.
> (Prov. 13:12)

But a prolonged absence can play havoc with our emotional stability. It is only partially true that absence makes the heart grow fonder. The coals which blazed so brightly when together may so easily smoulder and be extinguished when forced apart and left alone. The longer the absence, the greater the scope for fantasizing about the relationship. And the imaginations of the heart and mind may not correspond to the actual reality in the flesh when the lovers reunite. Similarly, the absence gives free reign to fear of loss, to jealousy, to insecurity. What is my partner doing now, who is benefiting from his or her attentions, is he or she being enticed away, or lured into more immediate relationships? Absence without reassurance can give way to speculative doubts. Are we right for each other? Are we compatible? We rationalize our fears, we counteract them because we cannot bear the possibility of being wrong, the pain of rejection, the loss of self-respect brought about by discovering that we have made mistakes, that we have fooled ourselves for too long. Separation also gives room for thought, for reflection and contemplation. But it needs to be followed by true communication, by honest dialogue, by a refusal to be bowled over by infatuation or desperation. The girl in our Song takes the initiative to resolve the impasse of her uncertainty. To live too long in uncertainty is debilitating, and needs as far as is possible a stroke of initiative to resolve it. The girl's initiative here is irrational. But love is a brand of madness. Not that it just makes us do irrational things, but love is a madness of the soul. It so disorients our senses, our rationality, it so takes possession of our hearts and minds, that all else is carried before it in its flood. Its tide is unstoppable, its fire unquenchable (8:6–7). The onset of love, of 'being in love', is entering a whole new dimension of existence. The lovers feel as though they had never lived at all before they met each other.

A third theme that arises from these verses is that of dreams and fantasies. Our subconscious fears are brought to the surface in our dreams. In this particular dream, the girl's basic insecurities surface in this nightmare, which repeats itself in a more violent form in 5:2. She is basically frightened of loss, of abandonment, and this terrible haunting dream is an indication of this. Her fears are compounded as she exposes herself to ridicule, as she flouts the conventions of society, and is confronted by *the watchmen*. The reality of the dream is more frightening to her than the barely articulated fears that hover uncertainly at the threshold of her consciousness. But her dream is also an expression of her deepest wish to be united to her lover. And so she enacts in her dream what she so dearly longs for in reality, and has possibly not yet experienced. As is often the case, the fantasies are a form of wish fulfilment. But they also represent a dissatisfaction with the current state of their own relationship.

Song of Songs 3:6 – 5:1

7. The third cycle: the lovers' royal wedding

1. Her rustic fragrant beauty (3:6)

The first cycle of poems ended at 2:7 with the adjuration to the daughters of Jerusalem not to awaken or arouse love prematurely. This same adjuration again brings down the curtain, as it were, on the second cycle, the scene of intimacy which ends at 3:5. A new cycle begins at 3:6 which continues through until the consummation of 5:1. It might be worth taking a preliminary overview of the whole cycle before looking at its various parts in more detail.

The cycle begins with 3:6, which I take to be an isolated independent verse, unconnected with what precedes and what follows; an exclamation of the breathtaking beauty of the girl, creating an atmosphere of ethereal beauty and fantasy. 3:7–11 is a description of Solomon's sedan chair used on the day of his wedding. 4:1–7 is the first of a number of descriptive praise poems detailing the charms of the lovers, culminating in the invitation (4:8) to come to (or is it from?) Lebanon. 4:9–11 depicts the lover absolutely smitten by the beauty of his girl. 4:12 – 5:1 moves progressively towards a climax: in 4:12 he praises her virginity; in 4:13–15 she is a luscious spicy garden; 4:16 is the girl's eager invitation; 5:1 is the actual consummation of their love, closing with an affirmation of the fulfilment of their passion, possibly by the author. So from 4:12 to 5:1 we move from anticipation, to invitation, then to consummation and a final affirmation. 5:1 represents a high point of the poem, and is the exact centre of the Song, with 111 lines from 1:2 to 4:15 and 111 lines from 5:2 to 8:14. It acts as a kind of fulcrum or centre of gravity about which other counterbalancing scenarios are suspended.

So back to 3:6. One of the first questions to ask is, 'Who is speaking these words?' It could be the daughters of Jerusalem, or the girl's companion, or the author of the poem obtruding on his own creation. Whoever it may be, it is certain that the question is not a request for information. It is a rhetorical question whose answer is obvious. It is the girl herself who is *coming up from the wilderness*. Following M. V. Fox,[1] I take the verse as an exclamation of surprise and admiration, thus, 'Look who's coming up out of the wilderness.' This type of rhetorical question also occurs at 6:10, 'Who is this that appears like the dawn . . . ?', and at 8:5, 'Who is this coming up from the wilderness, leaning on her beloved?' In both of the latter cases, the answer is obvious; it is the girl herself who is coming up. There is no attempt made in the following verses to answer it. But, in particular, this interpretation then implies that verses 3:7–11, which refer to Solomon's wedding carriage, have no connection with this question. In other words, there is a disjunction between verse 6 and verse 7. Verse 7 is not the answer to the question in verse 6. The whole verse represents an announcement of her dazzling appearance. Behold, she comes! It is an awesome manifestation, her royal epiphany. However, the conjunction between the two verses is technically quite possible. But then the interrogative 'Who?' must be interpreted as 'What?' if we are to take the literal answer to be Solomon's sedan (a feminine noun in Hebrew). *This* in verse 6 is feminine singular, and could refer either to the girl herself, or to Solomon's sedan. But I think the cycle begins more appropriately with this exclamation of her glorious appearance.

She is *coming up from the wilderness. The wilderness* is the open countryside where the shepherds graze, not the barren sandy wastes of the Arabian wilderness. But we should not take this phrase too literally. She is not just coming in from a cross-country safari. The phrase is an idiom meant to evoke an atmosphere of awe, majesty, almost of unreality. The meaning of the idiom is more than that of its constituent parts. She comes *like a column of smoke*, enshrouded by the fragrance of exotic and expensive perfumes. It is no use trying to locate the *column of smoke* in terms of the campfires of the shepherds, or of the dust devils, the vortices of the hot winds of the countryside. For the atmosphere evoked is surreal. It suggests that her beauty is not of this world (we shall come across this suggestion later at 6:10). Perhaps a modern equivalent would be the way

---

[1] Fox, p. 119.

in which pop groups perform through a haze of artificially produced mist, and are lit up by kaleidoscopic and stroboscopic lights. Or when we have photographs of our loved one taken against a leafy background, and the edges of the photo deliberately made hazy, to give the impression of an unworldly, ethereal apparition. The famous painting by Botticelli of the birth of Venus, being blown upon the shore on a seashell by two heavenly beings, is an example of how classical artists evoke an atmosphere of fantasy. And I think that is what the author of the Song is attempting to do here. William Wordsworth creates a similar atmosphere in his lines:

> She was a Phantom of delight
> When first she gleamed upon my sight;
> A lovely Apparition, sent
> To be a moment's ornament;
> Her eyes as stars of Twilight fair;
> Like Twilight's, too, her dusky hair;
> But all things else about her drawn
> From May-time and the cheerful Dawn;
> A dancing Shape, an Image gay,
> To haunt, to startle, and waylay . . .
> And yet a Spirit still, and bright
> With something of angelic light.[2]

This lovely apparition is captured in these lines of Tennyson:

> Half light, half shade,
> She stood, a sight to make an old man young.[3]

2. Solomon's sumptuous carriage (3:7–11)

As we have mentioned previously, there are many problems associated with this unit. The NIV translation makes 3:7 connect smoothly with 3:6, a position held by most commentators. These are the only verses where King Solomon appears as an integral part of the poem, and not just as a foil against which to contrast the simplicity, poverty and faithfulness of

---

[2] Wordsworth, 'She Was a Phantom of Delight'.
[3] Tennyson, 'The Gardener's Daughter'.

the boy. *Solomon* is mentioned at verses 7, 9 and 11. It is obvious from verse 11 that a marriage is taking place, indeed Solomon's own marriage. But which one? For Solomon had 'seven hundred wives of royal birth' (1 Kgs 11:3). Presumably he did not have a sumptuous wedding for each one of them. But it is most likely that 'seven hundred' is a round number. However, it is certain that Solomon would have had a grandiose ceremony for his marriage to the Egyptian princess (1 Kgs 3:1), the daughter of Pharaoh, for this was a political alliance. Solomon's marriages to foreign women were in defiance of Yahweh's command to the Israelites, and they led him astray and turned his heart after other gods (1 Kgs 11:1–13).

The unit divides up into three sections: the description of the *sixty warriors*, the construction of *the carriage* itself, and the command to the *daughters of Zion* to go forth and applaud the king on his *wedding* day. Obviously the poem has some original connection with one of Solomon's weddings. But now it appears in the Song rather abruptly. We have already assumed that our lovers are representatives of Everyman and Everywoman, and that the role of Solomon in the Song is minimal. Furthermore we have distanced ourselves from the idea that a strong narrative thread can be found in the Song. This enables us to avoid the difficult questions posed by the passage to those who see such a sustained element of plot; questions such as, Is the throne moving? Is it portable? Is it in a wedding procession? Where is it going to, and where is it coming from? Who sent it and for what purpose? Who is sitting in it? Solomon himself? The girl? The boy? The queen? Or is it empty with nobody in it at all? Answers to all these questions depend very much on one's set of presuppositions about the nature of the Song.

My own view is that this unit provides a focusing context for the whole of this third cycle (3:6 – 5:1). Here the lovers are getting married and celebrating their own wedding. The allusion is rather indirect, however. The lovers are perhaps singing a snatch of a wedding song originally sung at one of Solomon's own nuptials, which had gradually been assimilated into the popular musical choruses sung at village weddings. At their own banquet, the couple and their guests are celebrating their own 'royal' occasion. All this sets the legitimate context for the only explicit description of the lovers' physical union, at the end of the cycle.

A few technical points may be noted. The sedan chair, NIV *carriage* (*miṭṭâ*), is presumed to be synonymous with the carriage of 3:9 (*'appiryôn*). It is guarded by *sixty warriors* (i.e. double the number of David's private bodyguard; 2 Sam. 23:8–39). They are battle-hardened veterans, the elite corps of the royal army. What *the terrors of the night* are is anybody's guess. If they are demonic night hags who want to attack the bride on her wedding night, then the soldiers' swords will offer precious little protection. The *carriage* itself is described in extravagant terms. Incidentally, there is nothing in the passage to suggest that it is actually in motion here. In 1 Kings 10:18–20, we have a description of Solomon's magnificent throne which stood in the throne hall (1 Kgs 7:7). The carriage in the Song here is probably equally splendid, though smaller. A number of the references to its construction are obscure. The reference to love in *its interior inlaid with love* seems rather out of place. Most commentators suggest an Arabic cognate with the same Hebrew consonants as the word for love, meaning 'leather'. Others emend to 'stones', and then *the daughters of Jerusalem* are made to play a parallel role to *the daughters of Zion*. The crowning of the king by the queen mother on his wedding day is otherwise unattested in the Old Testament. *The crown* is more likely to be a laurel wreath of some sort. The whole unit conveys a picture with military, royal and festive connotations. More attention is given to the actual construction of the *carriage* than to the person who is supposed to be riding in it. The thrust of this section is to convey something of the pageantry of a royal wedding. Some have suggested that there is something ironic in all this extravagance; our lovers could never afford so great an affair as this; their love, so simple, so single-minded and faithful, stands in contrast to Solomon's extravagance, Solomon the one who was disloyal to Yahweh's covenant. While that may well be true, I do not think we can necessarily see it here. What we do see here is simply happy celebration.

A wedding is always something to look forward to; a grand social occasion. All the world loves a lover on this day. The lovers' joy is on open display for all to see. Yet different cultures vary in their approach. Some require solemn pomp and heavy formality. Some require their brides to weep, for they are losing the protection of the patriarchal home. Yet underneath it is a time of celebration and of banqueting. Every extravagance is excused; niggardly entertainment is out. There should be no danger of the wine running out, even though it means the couple and their relatives are in debt for the next decade. Improbable in-laws and outlaws attend, ghosts from a long-forgotten past, gatecrashers and those who are there on the flimsiest pretext, matriarchs and patriarchs, the grandees and the man from the shop round the corner; a great social mix, yet people happily and unselfconsciously rub shoulders. People from all walks of life congregate to toast the happy couple. Old animosities are forgotten, long-lost friends reunite, all is forgiven, all eccentricities are tolerated in the pervasive atmosphere of genial bonhomie. Yet it is an occasion for new contacts to be made, new deals to be struck, new friendships to be cemented. A time for sighing, for reminiscing, a time for mutual inspection of old acquaintances, seeing how they have weathered the storms of life, a time for wistful contemplation about might-have-beens, a time of secret jealousies and intolerant criticisms. A microcosm of the world is gathered to see the happy couple off. For the couple themselves it is a day so eagerly awaited, the climax of much agonizing planning. A day of glorying publicly in their love, 'the day of the gladness of [their] heart' (3:11, lit.), full of promise for the future, the formal beginning of a great new adventure. And this is what our young lovers are dreaming about.

Those who are unmarried may sometimes find themselves fantasizing about their own possible wedding day. For some, it may be a daydream of eager expectation. For others, it may be an exercise of the utmost frustration. For still others, it may be the wistful looking back on what might have been. Such longings may be clouded by a haze of self-indulgent romanticism, which may yet be relatively harmless. We all have known of the young person who has the wedding day mentally prepared down to the very last detail: the dresses, the bridesmaids, the decorations, the organ voluntaries, the guest lists, the marquee on the village green, the church bells and the classic wedding car –when as yet there is no bride or groom anywhere in sight. Such dreams are rudely shattered in the waking up, in the morning, cold and alone in our single beds. The sooner we hop out and get breakfast, the better.

However, for our couple in the Song, this happy and very public day puts the seal on their union, and the elated groom is moved to extol the beauty of his bride in the song which follows (4:1–7). His trembling anticipation of their bodily union is reflected in 4:12–15, and at his bride's urgent invitation (4:16) they consummate their marriage (5:1) in the privacy of the bridal chamber.

3. In praise of his beloved (4:1–7)

This is the first occurrence in the Song of what is technically called in Arabic a *wasf*, a poem of praise in which one of the lovers describes metaphorically the other's bodily parts, in a catalogue moving from head to toe or vice versa. This type of poem is one of the characteristics of Arabic love poetry, but the genre occurs in the Old Testament only in the Song of Songs. In this example, the boy praises in turn his beloved's *eyes*, *hair*, *teeth*, *lips*, *temples*, *neck* and *breasts*. It is only a partial *wasf*, moving down her body and stopping at her *breasts*. It is quite probable that the restriction to the upper half of her body is a tantalizing tease, appropriate to this stage of the poem. We are left in a state of suspended excitement, wondering in our imaginations how the rest of her body is to be described.

The only occurrence in the Song of the *girl* describing her lover is in 5:10–16; she moves down from his head, hair, eyes, cheeks and lips, to his hands, stomach, legs and his whole appearance, and then concludes with his 'palate'. In 6:4–10 the lover again describes his beloved – eyes, hair, teeth and forehead. The most daring and explicit description of the girl's physical charms is found in 7:1–10: her feet, thighs, navel(?), belly, breasts, neck, eyes, nose, head and hair. Whether he has intimate access to all those charming secrets is a matter of some debate (see later).

The metaphors used to describe the various parts of the body often seem bizarre, comic, even grotesque to our ears. So much so that it has led some commentators to suggest that these are mocking caricatures of the lovers, parodies of true beauty, like the instinctive reaction we have of revulsion towards an overpainted prostitute. But this is a gross over-reaction in an attempt to come to terms with the strangeness of some of the descriptions. The lovers find each other *beautiful* and attractive, and we must work on that assumption in our study of the metaphors. It has been suggested that some of the descriptions fit more aptly the description of an artist's picture of the beloved, or a statue, or a model. We have mentioned previously the possibility that the girl's eyes are seen as dove-shaped, which is an outstanding characteristic of some Egyptian wall paintings. However, it is much more likely that the metaphors are meant to apply to the living lovers themselves, and not just to portraits of them. Some have suggested that the very form of the *wasf*, a catalogue of descriptions of the body, part by part, freezes the portrayal of the loved ones into statuesque immobility. Yet these same authors insist that the *wasf* of 7:1–10 is a portrayal of a flimsily clad dancing girl, pirouetting and swirling in sensual motion.

Perhaps we should try to think about the nature of these descriptions. They are not identikit pictures. When the daughters of Jerusalem ask the girl in 5:9 what is so special about her lover, her reply in 5:10–16 contains nothing that would help them to identify him in a crowd. Her description of him is more an indication of how she feels about him, creating an atmosphere which borders on fantasy and the surreal; for example, his eyes are (lit.) doves, bathing in milk, sitting by a fullness (5:12). We should not always be looking for precision in every aspect of the metaphor. Perhaps there is only one point of correlation. For example, in *Your hair is like a flock of goats, descending from the hills of Gilead* (4:1), the metaphor seems to take off and have a life of its own, the reference to *Gilead* being redundant in any elaboration of the metaphor, but helping to create an atmosphere of surreality. Also the impact of the description depends very much on how we phrase the translation. For example, 'Your thighs like jewels, the work of a craftsman' (7:1, lit.) does not mean that the girl's thighs glitter and sparkle, but rather that they can be compared to a craftsman's handiwork: 'Your thighs' smooth curves exquisitely turned, as if by craftsmen's skill.' The reference to jewels is marginal; they too are worked by craftsmen. Similarly, the comparison of her *teeth* to *a flock of sheep just shorn* (4:2) is initially shocking. We immediately think of woolly fleeces, which is too jarring. We need to paraphrase as something like 'Your fresh white teeth so clean, so smooth, like skin of sheep so closely shorn, and washed and bleached.'

But the harshness of the dissonance of some of the metaphors cannot be relieved in every case by these verbal and mental acrobatics. In many cases we have to distance ourselves from the immediate visual impact, and allow the metaphors to create a more congenial atmosphere than that which is conjured up by the superficial visual associations. We shall elaborate this in more detail as we progress through the *wasf*.

The poem itself is framed by two similar exclamations of praise: *How beautiful* (4:1); *altogether beautiful* (7). This is how he feels about his beautiful girl, and then he proceeds to the specific aspects of her beauty. *Your eyes behind your veil are doves.* It is possible that fluttering timidity is what is in mind here, especially as she is partly hidden behind her *veil*. The introduction of the *veil* here may be an indication of the marriage aspect of this cycle. Also the veil acts as a barrier; it underlines her inaccessibility, it protects her from too much attention. Yet veils can have exactly the opposite effect. They evoke an aspect of mystery which must be penetrated. The *veil* is a challenge to the lover. He must unveil her if their intimacy is to go deeper; they must meet face to face. Our veils, though, are not only physical. They are emotional, psychological, intellectual, spiritual. We all wear masks to protect our insecurities. We are afraid of appearing weak. We do not want to appear vulnerable. But a progressive unveiling of ourselves to our spouses is an essential prerequisite to deeper relationships. The image we project, the masks we wear, may be totally at odds with our true inner selves. In fact, they are compensatory projections to counterbalance our own deeply felt insufficiencies. But any mask is uncomfortable to wear. The lack of correspondence between the outer image and the underlying unseen reality creates a tension which cannot be endured for long without creating some sort of breakdown. Of course, we are extremely complex personalities and it is only when we develop a relationship of love and trust and mutual acceptance (warts and all) that we can begin to relax and bare our souls to our partners. For it is the essence of love to be able to bear all things, inadequacies, insecurities, fears, failures; all of which we would rather hide behind our veils. But in any relationship there will always be some element of mystery behind the successive unveiling. And that is part of the adventure of knowing each other.

Her *hair is like a flock of goats, descending from the hills of Gilead*. For Western ears, the impact of this metaphor is initially very surprising. Goats are smelly and dirty and their coats are tangled. But surely here, the point of comparison is the flowing and rippling movements of the flock down the grassy slopes. From a distance the jostling flock bobs and weaves in glistening undulation, just as her flowing locks do as she walks and turns. She is like Milton's girl:

Her . . . tresses wore
Dishevell'd, but in wanton ringlets wav'd
As the vine curls her tendrils.[4]

The reference to *the hills of Gilead* in the Transjordan may evoke a picture of distance, inaccessibility, awe; the distant mountains shimmering in the haze of the heat. The woman's glory is her hair (see 1 Cor. 11:15). It crowns her head like a halo or wreath. Her facial beauty is framed by her flowing locks. However wild or unkempt she looks ('My own vineyard I had to neglect', 1:6), her natural beauty shines through. It is

---

4 Milton, *Paradise Lost*, Book 4, lines 305–307.

uncreated, a gift of providence, for all to gaze at and wonder. As H. W. Longfellow put it, 'Not ten yoke of oxen have the power to draw us like a woman's hair!'[5] Its innate attractive power captivates the lover (see later at 7:5). In childish playfulness he wants to ruffle and stroke her crown of glory.

Her *teeth* are white and sparkling, perfectly matched and symmetrical. The smile which lights up her radiant face reveals the perfection of her mouth. The image of the sheep, shorn to their smooth skins, glistening white, and gleaming after their dip, is a metaphor which is comparatively easy to assimilate. As R. Davidson puts it, 'The lady would obviously be a perfect advert for any of the popular brands of toothpaste.'[6]

Her *lips are like a scarlet ribbon*. Obviously she is using cosmetics. Lipstick can be used to change the visible outline of the lips, but it is probably the least successful use of cosmetics. For the natural set of the *mouth* is something that is difficult to mask. We all know the pathetic smile of the poor sad clown with his painted face. Apart from the eyes, the *mouth* and its expressiveness is the most important indicator of our inner state. The mouth can express horror and happiness, meanness and mockery, arrogance, amazement and amorousness, cruelty and contempt. The word used in the Hebrew here for *mouth* (*midbār*) is the one that describes it as an organ of speech. From her *mouth* flow the sweet murmurings of the dove. Her speech is consonant with her beauty. For this is not always true. There are many beauties who betray themselves by coarseness of speech.

Her *temples* behind her veil *are like the halves of a pomegranate*. It is doubtful that we can identify precisely the meaning of the word translated by the NIV as *temples*. It could be 'temple' (through which Jael drove a tent peg in order to kill Sisera; Judg. 4:21), or it could be 'cheeks'. The comparison with the pomegranates indicates either her rosy cheeks, or else the shadow cast by her veil upon her cheeks. (See my paraphrase, 'Your veil's fine web of tracery, its gossamer of lace, their soft fine shadow cast upon the contours of your face.')

Her *neck* is compared to *the tower of David*. This has come in for some harsh words from the critics; for Waterman, the comparison of the lady's neck to the tower of David is 'the earliest recorded description of

---

[5] Longfellow, *Tales of a Wayside Inn*, Part 1, 'The Musician's Tale; the Saga of King Olaf XVI'.
[6] Davidson, p. 127.

goitre'.[7] But this is grotesque. The point of the comparison is not the *size* of the girl's neck, but the fact that it is decorated and built up in layers, with row upon row of beads (as with the Maasai women of East Africa). Some of the details of this verse are obscure, but the general impression is clear. *The tower of David*, built in layers, surrounded by *shields*, gives an impression of uprightness, of defence, of inaccessibility and an intention to repel intruders.

Her *breasts are like two fawns* (5). They are graceful, sprightly and playful. Their texture and softness are invitations to caressing and fondling. Young fawns, like breasts, are tactile. Her breasts *browse among the lilies*. The mixture of metaphors here is remarkable. Since in 5:13 the girl refers to *his* lips as lilies, there is probably the hint here of his very intimate kissing of her breasts. The girl's *breasts* are the most powerful visible expression of her femininity and she wants to share that aspect of herself with her lover. In 8:2 she wants to give the nectar of her pomegranates to her lover. In 8:10 she likens her breasts to 'towers'. These references demonstrate two very different aspects conveyed by the breasts. First, there is the idea of maternal succour. She sees herself as giving wholeness, health, peace, to her lover (see later). But her erect, protruding breasts are also an expression of her assertive and aggressive femininity, a picture of dominance and self-esteem and self-possession. In most countries in the Global South, the breasts are a symbol of fertility, motherhood and succour. Fertility religions always portray the female with grossly exaggerated breasts. But the fertility aspect of the girl barely surfaces here or elsewhere in the Song. The idea of succour occurs later. But in this verse, her breasts represent her sexual attractiveness, her allure for her partner. They are part of her sexual appeal, which she wants to use to great effect.

Perhaps this last thought has so aroused the boy that he expresses his determination (6) to *go to the mountain of myrrh and to the hill of incense*. We have already met at 2:17 the reference to the 'breathing' of the day and the fleeing of the shadows. *The mountain of myrrh* and *the hill of incense* must be in some way equivalent to the mountains of Bether of 2:17. The mountains are singular in this case, but I am not certain that they can be equated with any particular part of the female anatomy, although some have tried to do so (e.g. the mons Veneris). The boy is determined to

---

[7] L. Waterman, *Journal of Biblical Literature*, 44 (1925), p. 179.

embrace the girl in some intimate way and make love to her until the break of day.

The scene closes with the boy's affirmation of the girl's beauty. Indeed *there is no flaw* or blemish on her. She is a flawless beauty. There is nothing to mar her perfection. She is perfect in his eyes, without spot or wrinkle or any such thing. He is amazed at his good fortune, that he has been smitten with love for this amazingly attractive girl and that she, this goddess, should reciprocate his love. Of course, they are walking on air, buoyed up by their mutual passion, energized by the new lease of life that romantic love gives. But of course, love is blind. In its enthusiasm it can exaggerate cheerfully the plain and the ordinary. It draws a veil over the shortcomings and faults of the beloved. The tide of passion takes everything in its flood. And the lovers look down in pity on all those lesser mortals who cannot share this same experience.

Beauty is a very elusive concept. It is something beyond words, indeed indescribable. Yet we instinctively recognize it when we see it. As a French proverb puts it: 'Beauty is silent eloquence.' It speaks, yet without words. We behold and are brought to silence. There is a givenness about beauty, to be accepted freely as a gift. Emily Dickinson wrote, 'Beauty is not caused. It is.' The transcendent nature of beauty has led some to postulate its divine origin. It is like the smile of God. Giovanni Leone has written, 'The strongest evidence to prove that God exists is a beautiful woman.' We instinctively feel that beauty is a bonus. It is a contingent quality – that is the way of things, but it need not necessarily be so; it could have been otherwise. Thus we gratefully receive the radiance of beauty's smile, and so are warmed.

Simone Weil writes, 'Beauty is a fruit which we look at without trying to seize it.' There is always a distancing effect of beauty. We stand apart and admire it from afar. Its intrinsic intangibility gives beauty an aloofness which causes a sadness in the eye of the beholder. Edmund Burke has remarked that 'the passion excited by beauty is nearer to a species of melancholy than to jollity or mirth'.[8]

The metaphors we use to describe the beauty of the female are always the result of our subjective response to her. But how do we identify the criteria by which we judge one girl as beautiful, another as plain? What

---

[8] Burke, *A Philosophical Enquiry into the Origin of Our Ideas of the Sublime and the Beautiful*, Introduction (1757).

makes one pretty, another merely ordinary? To analyse in a more scientific way is to destroy the mystique, and it is the mystique which is so attractive. To build up a verbal identikit picture is extraordinarily difficult, which merely underlines the fact that beauty is for beholding, for feasting our eyes upon, and not for futile classification. For beauty can be approached only through the imprecision of metaphor. The most we can do is to chart out some negatives: her eyes are too far apart, too deeply set or too protruding; her forehead is too high, her nose too angular, her cheeks too hollow, her mouth too wide or lips too pinched, her chin too pointed or receding. But the mysterious combination of the correct proportions that makes for true beauty defies all detached description. We can only stop and gaze in awe, and know that it is so. Alexander Pope has written:

'Tis not a lip, or eye, we beauty call,
But the joint force and full result of all.[9]

Plotinus, writing in the third century AD, also was groping after the mystery that is beauty: 'Beauty is rather a light that plays over the symmetry of things than that symmetry itself.'[10]

The mischievous capriciousness of beauty is well captured by the American journalist Rex Reed in his words describing a certain film star:

What a subject: her nose is too big, her mouth is too big, she has the composites of all the wrong things, but put them all together and pow! All the natural mistakes of beauty fall together to create a magnificent accident.[11]

And so we stand in awe.

For she was beautiful: her beauty made
the bright world dim, and everything beside
seemed like the fleeting image of a shade.[12]

---

9 Pope, 'An Essay on Criticism: Part 2' (1711).

10 Plotinus, *Enneads* V (AD 250).

11 Reed on Sophia Loren in a review of *That Kind of Woman*, 23 October 1968.

12 Shelley, *The Witch of Atlas*.

4. The lover's urgent plea (4:8)

There is a sudden change in atmosphere in this verse from that encountered in 4:5–7. The previous verses conveyed a calm idyllic pastoral scene, of shepherding among the figurative lilies on the mountains of spices. Here in verse 8 we are suddenly confronted with the elements of threat, of hazard and hostility. The mountains are high and far away, they are snow covered and beyond the borders of the land of the covenant people. *The lions* and *leopards* prowl their forested slopes. Their jagged crests are clothed in clouds. There is an awesome magnificence about their beauty. The distant peaks convey an aura of threatening mystique, an almost numinous quality. There is an element of danger and uncertainty associated with them. They make us feel the finitude of our humanity. We cannot take our safety for granted in their presence. They are capricious in their moods. A sudden storm, a lightning bolt, a flash flood, a prowling lion – they all make us feel our vulnerability to the overwhelming forces of nature.

The exact geographical locale of the mountains is irrelevant. They represent a literary motif. The author of the poems is not interested in topography. As M. Fox says: 'The girl is not in Lebanon any more than she is sitting in the clefts of the rock in 2:14.'[13] With this in mind, the questions which immediately spring to view lose their force. We would want to ask, Why is she in *Lebanon?* What is she doing there? Where is her lover at the time of his invitation? Where is he inviting her to go with him? This is by no means the only place in the Song where there is considerable ambiguity as to the comings and goings of the young couple. That it is an invitation is clear from the stark literal Hebrew: 'With me, from Lebanon . . . with me you shall come.' But there is much doubt concerning the Hebrew preposition *min*, normally translated 'from' but which could also bear the meaning 'in', 'at' and even 'to'. The invitation to *come* is clear, but is this paralleled by *descend*, which can also mean 'look down, gaze'? Perhaps the girl is seen by her lover as inhabiting the peaks and crests of the mountains, godlike, awesome and inaccessible, and she is sitting there looking down on the natural order in some sort of aloof contemplation. And he wants her to come down from her lofty throne, to join him in the real world. *The leopards* and *lions* seem to be protecting her and barring his

---

13 Fox, p. 134.

access to her. Perhaps he is frightened by her ethereal presence, and her aloofness makes him scared of initiating any further degree of intimacy, as he is uncertain of her response.

Perhaps he regards her as whimsical and capricious, with sudden and seemingly arbitrary changes in mood and aspect, just like the uncertain weather on the mountains; sometimes sunny, with sparkling rushing streams cascading down, sometimes stern, grey, forbidding, sometimes enshrouded in clouds, mysterious, withdrawn, impenetrable, sometimes erupting with explosive, violent storms, with brilliant lightning flashes and long rolls of rumbling thunder echoing across the valleys. All these moods, characteristic not only of the girl but also of her lover, threaten and disturb a uniform degree of intimacy. But we dress for the weather. We behave appropriately according to our partner's moods. We can be uplifted by those moods when we are down, or be brought down by them when we are up. We can act as counterweights to each other's temperaments and feelings. So long as we recognize them for what they are, we can begin to learn to cope with them. We do not always need to enquire the origin. It may be something totally trivial to us but important to our partner. But it is not always necessary to locate a cause. Just to be there is enough to act as a cushion. Sudden changes of mood can be very unsettling for faint souls. However, our lover overcomes his hesitations and braves his self-doubts and is prepared to take the consequences of being involved with this goddess who has ensnared him and seemingly mastered him. And so he can move ahead with confidence to his union in marriage to his beloved.

The place names and animals, while real, are chosen for their linguistic associations, as well as for their mythological echoes. For *Lebanon* (*lĕbānôn*) is a word that has the same consonants as (and therefore brings to mind) the word for the full moon (at 6:10) (*lĕbānâ*), and also the word for frankincense (*lĕbônâ*). So the girl is ethereal, cosmic and fragrant. The fragrance theme is picked up again at 4:11 where the 'fragrance of Lebanon' is likely to refer to the scent of her famous cedars. Similarly the word for *leopards* (*nĕmērîm*) may arouse associative ideas of myrrh (*mōr*) by assonance.

The girl is here called 'a bride' (not *my bride* as NIV) for the first time in the Song. We shall consider this in more detail in the next section (4:9–11), but would mention here only that it is entirely appropriate for her to be given this appellation in this explicit wedding cycle.

In any relationship, the element of unpredictability can be both stimulating and alarming. Its absence may indicate that we have degenerated into a passive, boring amoeba-like existence. Its presence should be welcomed as part of the unfolding mystery of a growing relationship. Dull, domestic routines may be disrupted and enlivened by a spontaneous outburst of the unconventional, in conversation, social behaviour or new activities. Not that quirkiness and eccentricity should be cultivated as a pose, but rather that room should be made for the mildly shocking, lest we suffocate under the blanket of the solemn conventions of respectability.

5. A lover smitten (4:9–11)

These verses are the beginning of a passage which uses increasingly luscious metaphors to describe our lovers' rapid progress to the consummation of their love in 5:1. The passages are linked by common themes and words: *Lebanon* (4:11, 15); *sister*, *bride* (4:9, 10, 11, 12; 5:1); *wine* (4:10; 5:1); *milk* (4:11; 5:1); *honey* (4:11; 5:1); *fragrance*, *spices* (4:11, 14, 16; 5:1). There is an accelerating theme portrayed in extravagant language which describes their passion almost running out of control, leading to the inevitability of intercourse.

Our lover has been smitten by his girl. The words in the NIV *You have stolen my heart* translate one word in the Hebrew. The verbal form is derived from the noun for *heart*, and can mean either, 'You have captured or taken away my heart' or else, 'You have inflamed, aroused, excited my heart.' It is a rare form in the Hebrew, and can most likely bear both meanings. While in the majority of Old Testament usages the heart is the seat of the mind, the will or the conscience, or more generally the person him- or herself, in this particular case the heart is more evidently the seat of the emotions. Our lover is completely bowled over. *One glance* is enough to slay him, one sparkling shaft reflected from her jewels is sufficient to render him helplessly in love. He is a captive. He cannot help himself. He has been remorselessly drawn to her. His thought process cannot explain it; his love is in a sense irrational. He has been rendered weak and feeble by her beauty, overpowered by her loveliness, yet aroused and made strong by his every thought of her. But it is not mere thoughts that arouse him. Her caresses (*dōdîm*), her stroking and embracing, are more intoxicating than any *wine*. Her *perfume* is heady and sends him reeling. Sight, touch and smell – all these work their magnetic power on her lover. The reference to her *lips* dropping *sweetness* and *the milk and honey . . . under* her *tongue* could be alluding to her speech. Her words are sweet, gentle, mellifluous, even seductive (Prov. 5:3; 16:24). There are many references in the Old Testament to the metaphor of words 'dripping', mainly in regard to the act of prophesying (see AV at Ezek. 20:46; 21:2; Amos 7:16; Mic. 2:11; etc.). But it is much more likely that the reference is to the lovers' deep kissing. Their mouths interpenetrate, their *lips* intermingle in a feast of wet kissing. *Milk* is also a common motif in Egyptian and Mesopotamian love poetry. Of course, *milk and honey* are standard symbols of the land of Palestine. The land to be possessed was a land 'flowing with milk and honey'. It was there to be looked forward to with great anticipation in the arid times of the wilderness. Perhaps this theme of anticipation can be traced in their kissing together. It is a foretaste of things to come, when there will be a much deeper level of interpenetration in the climax of their consummation. The girl's *garments* also add to her allure. Probably they refer to her undergarments or her negligee. The word used is the same as that describing the covering of the wedding bed on which the 'proof of virginity' was found (Deut. 22:17). So there is the possibility of some erotic connotation here. The delicacy and flimsiness of female underwear, sprayed with scent, has an undoubted erotic appeal.

It is only in this cycle of poems that the term *bride* occurs. At 4:8, 11 she is called a *bride*, at 4:9–10, 12 and 5:1 she is called (lit.) 'my sister, a bride'. The Hebrew for the term *bride* (*kallâ*) can very easily mean 'the completed one, the fulfilled one, the consummated one' from its etymology. However, we need to be cautious of trying to force a very common word to bear all the shades of meaning of its linguistic root. Of course, it is only natural to use the word 'bride' in this cycle which begins with a wedding song, includes their own marriage and closes with the consummation of their love in the marriage bed.

6. Moving towards a climax again (4:12 – 5:1)

These verses are a continuation of the theme begun in 4:9–11 and move towards the central climax of the whole book, the consummation of full sexual union at 5:1. As pointed out before, 5:1 represents both the literal centre of the Song, as well as its emotional peak. This passage can be divided up into four natural divisions: anticipation (4:12–15);

invitation (4:16); consummation (5:1); and affirmation (5:1). There is an obvious progression of theme running through these verses. Before considering some of the more general implications of this passage, we need to look at some of the details of the text.

a. Anticipation (4:12–15)

In 4:12–15, the lover describes his girl in terms of a luscious fruity and spicy *garden*. She is an *orchard* of mouth-watering *pomegranates*, with exquisite-tasting fruit. Her *locked garden* contains all sorts of exotic and fragrant perfumes and spices: *henna, nard, saffron*, balsam, *myrrh, cinnamon, incense, aloes* and spikenard. It would perhaps be tedious to catalogue the botanical features of each of these; suffice it to say that this is a fantasy garden, a garden of make-believe. No horticulturalist or herbalist would ever attempt to cultivate all these exotic plants in one patch. It is a 'luscious grove', filled with fruit and plants evocative of love. It is a garden that is watered by its own private spring, *a spring enclosed, a sealed fountain* (12). In 4:15 she is *a garden fountain, a well of flowing water streaming down from Lebanon*. The girl is described in such extravagant terms that the power of the metaphors seems to overwhelm the listener, and the girl herself seems to disappear from view, submerged as it were by the very lusciousness of the flora and fauna.

The *spring enclosed* and the *sealed fountain* are both metaphors for the girl's privacy, her exclusivity, her sole allegiance to her lover. More particularly, they could refer to her sexual exclusiveness, her non-availability to anyone but him. They could also refer to her virginity. She has kept herself reserved for her only love. She has not been profligate or wanton in sharing her favours. The tone of the boy's words is not plaintive as some have suggested. He is not complaining of her inaccessibility (to himself, or to others). Rather he is proud that she is untouched by others, that her greatest self-giving has been reserved for him alone. This sexual exclusiveness is well expressed in Proverbs 5:15–19:

> Drink water from your own cistern,
>> running water from your own well.
> Should your springs overflow in the streets,
>> your streams of water in the public squares?
> Let them be yours alone,
>> never to be shared with strangers.

> May your fountain be blessed,
>> and may you rejoice in the wife of your youth.
> A loving doe, a graceful deer –
>> may her breasts satisfy you always,
>> may you ever be intoxicated with her love.

4:13 mentions *your plants* (lit. 'tendrils'); this is an obscure word and is commonly explained as similar to the 'branches' or 'shoots' of Isaiah 16:8. But it could also mean 'water channels' or 'irrigation conduit'. There is some connection with water in a word from the same root in Nehemiah 3:15 (the Pool of Shelah). But whatever the meaning, the whole picture is one of lusciousness, fragrance and freshly flowing water.

b. Invitation (4:16)

The girl then invites her lover into her *garden*. The word for 'awake' in *Awake, north wind* is the same as that used in the refrain to the daughters of Jerusalem, 'Do not awaken love until it so desires.' There it was a call to avoid premature awakening. But now the time is ripe. There is to be no restraint. What has for so long been held back can now with great abandon be allowed its full expression. With great eagerness the two lovers come together. She is freely giving herself to him, with seductive invitation. She is enticing her lover and making herself so alluring that he becomes mad with desire. She is not merely passive, but ardent and eager. She wants him to feel her attractiveness, her desirability. She wants him to enter her *garden* and taste its exquisite *fruits*. The use of the verb 'to enter' or to *come into* is a standard Hebrew metaphor for sexual intercourse.[14] He is 'entering' his garden, which is *my garden* (i.e. the girl's and also his). The garden is their mutual possession.

c. Consummation (5:1)

This verse describes the boy's response. The tense is perfect, which could describe either his present enjoyment, or his looking back on his imme- diate past pleasure. The verse is full of the first person: *I have come . . . I have gathered . . . I have eaten . . . I have drunk*; four very deliberate and incisive verbal actions. Nine times the strongly possessive *my* occurs:

---

[14] This is seen, for example, in the Hebrew text of Gen. 38:9; Ruth 4:13; Ezek. 23:44, but most modern translations soften the more direct Hebrew 'enter'.

my garden, *my* sister, *my* bride, *my* myrrh, *my* spice, *my* honeycomb, *my* honey, *my* wine, *my* milk. It seems on the surface of it to indicate a strong male triumphalism. 'I came, I saw, I conquered.' But the whole tenor of the Song is against any such interpretation. She has invited him in eagerly; their passion is mutual. Most of the Song is concerned with the girl's feelings; it is only occasionally that the passion of the man is described. His eagerness is described in terms of strong determination in 7:8: 'I said, "I will climb the palm tree; I will take hold of its fruit."'

Here the act itself is referred to obliquely as entering his *garden*, gathering *spices*, eating *honey* and drinking *wine* and *milk*. These are obviously metaphors, not to be taken literally. The drinking metaphor occurs in Proverbs 7:18, where the unfaithful wife invites her lover to come into her marriage bed with the words 'Come, let's drink deeply of love till morning; let's enjoy ourselves with love!' Drinking milk is a metaphor which occurs in Mesopotamian love songs. The usages of the words for 'honey' are interesting. There are three synonyms: *děbaš* (4:11), sweetness, bees' honey removed from the comb; *nōpet* , that which 'drips' from the wild honeycomb; and *ya'ar*, which is normally translated in other parts of the Old Testament as a thicket or brambles. Ancient Near Eastern love poetry often uses the metaphors of honeycomb and of 'thicket' to describe the private parts of the lower female genitalia. There are a number of references in the Old Testament to stolen honey, the taking of the forbidden thing. Samson took the honeycomb from the carcass of the dead lion, thereby violating his Nazirite vow (Judg. 14:8–9). Jonathan dipped his staff into the honeycomb and ate, thus unwittingly violating the command of his father Saul (1 Sam. 14:26–28). Is there here the possible hint of the frisson of delight in doing that which is forbidden? 'Stolen water is sweet; food eaten in secret is delicious!' (Prov. 9:17). However, that is hardly likely to be the case here; what they are doing together is sweet and delicious to them, but there is no trace of any kind of guilt feelings or of a secret furtiveness. They are abandoning themselves unreservedly and unashamedly to each other in an intoxicating orgy of love-making.

d. Affirmation (5:1)

The last line of 5:1 is an affirmation of the lovers' activity. What they are doing is good, wholesome, right and proper. It is the natural physical consummation of their love. Their abandonment in self-giving is thoroughly approved and endorsed. There is to be no reserve, no restraint, but a complete and happy enjoyment of each other in their mutual love. They are to become 'drunk' with love-making, they are to be inebriated, on a physical and emotional high. The last word could be interpreted either as 'with love-making, with caresses' or as 'O lovers', referring to the lovers themselves. These words are spoken by the author of the poems. He intrudes onto the stage, as it were, to pass a comment on the action of the characters whom he has created. It is a literary device to indicate an external approval of the closing scene of intimacy. We do not have to suppose, as some have done, that observers are intruding on their privacy; it is almost grotesque to think that the wedding guests are hovering outside the marriage tent in order to make sure the marriage is consummated appropriately. This is yet another illustration of the misplaced desire to achieve an explicit narrative plot in the sequence of poems.

7. Reflections on themes arising from 4:12 – 5:1

It is time now to distance ourselves from the immediate text and to look at some of its more general implications.

a. Chastity and virginity

First of all, we need to consider the ramifications of the girl as 'a garden locked up . . . a sealed fountain'. At the basic level, this refers to the girl's chastity. She has not made herself available to others. She is not sexually experienced, in the sense of having given herself to any boy previously. In our Western European society, chastity is not considered a virtue. On the contrary, it is mocked and held up to ridicule. Those who are 'sexually inexperienced', both male and female, are either looked down upon with contempt, or else considered to be the objects of pity. The reaction of contempt arises from either guilt feelings or a hostility towards those who do not conform to their own immoral behaviour. The reaction of pathos arises from a misplaced sense of what wholeness means; there is the unspoken assumption that lack of experience at this sexual level somehow is a disqualification from progress in this modern world; that the chaste or the celibate are somehow incomplete or unfulfilled; that they are emotional cripples bound by outmoded religious scruples.

The metaphor of the girl as a garden, watered by an ever-flowing spring, indicates that she is alive, fertile, blossoming in every sense. She has an inner spring that is a source of life, not of barrenness. She herself is the guardian of that fountain, to give or to refrain from giving as she so chooses. Of course, it is entirely possible that she opens her garden in order merely to fulfil some immediate gratification. But that is to separate the physical aspect of our humanity from the wholeness of our persons which enter into any kind of relationship. When a husband and his wife become one flesh (Gen. 2:24), it is much more than a simple physical relationship. The apostle Paul recognizes that to link one's members with those of a prostitute is to become one flesh with her (1 Cor. 6:16). But the sexual act must never be divorced from the context of a permanent total relationship between a man and his wife who are irrevocably committed to each other. The act is but one very small part of the totality of their growing into union together. The writer of Ecclesiastes says '[There is] a time to embrace and a time to refrain from embracing' (Eccl. 3:5). But how then do we know the appropriate time? For the unmarried, the time to refrain is when the physical starts dominating the whole relationship. Things escalate and get out of control, leading to an almost unstoppable desire for full consummation. The sexual instinct that we find implanted in us is so strong that it needs to be handled rigorously. That is why the girl cries to the daughters of Jerusalem not to awaken or arouse love until it so desires (i.e. until there is a legitimate pathway for its full consummation). She fears that she cannot control herself. For, once ignited, it is a fire which is difficult to quench. But within marriage, why, let its passions burn and blaze with no restraint.

b. Laughter and bodies

For the newly-wed couple, this act of intercourse represents the joyful climax of their physical and tactile relationship. Hitherto the lovers have talked, walked and had fun together. They have dined and prayed together. They have held hands, embraced and caressed. They have kissed and fondled each other. And now at last, what they have looked forward to for so long, with such keen anticipation, has become a delightful reality, the consummation of their one-flesh union. It is an act that will be repeated again and again, affirming and consolidating their growing relationship. The continuing expression of their sexual union is both a cause and a result of their growing intimacy and adjustment in other areas of their life together. The initial thrills of self-disclosure and self-discovery will inevitably diminish, but their deep-seated joy at the ever-deepening integration of their lives through their intercourse must surely increase.

The lovers, having tasted the honeypot, having experienced the golden showers, and the shuddering volcanic eruptions, may be tempted to think that these ecstatic heights are attainable every time. But Eros is a mischievous elf, whimsical and capricious, and the sooner we recognize this, the better for our emotional and psychological well-being. We may lay the wood, but on occasion the bonfire fails to ignite. We may be afflicted with a desperately urgent desire at those very times when there is absolutely no possibility of fulfilment, and have to be content with frustrated glances at a distance. But if only we could indulge in a hearty laugh over all this, the tensions and irritations would be dissolved readily. The solemnization of sex with its desperate swoony awe is a consequence of our society's quest for instant total gratification. But we should learn not to treat it with such reverential gravity, as C. S. Lewis put it.[15] Laughter should be an integral part of the marriage bed. For to laugh with each other is to be involved personally; it is an expression of a relationship which is far more than a performance.

The lovers in George Orwell's *1984*, and the hero and heroine of D. H. Lawrence's *Lady Chatterley's Lover*, are so preoccupied with 'it' that they have lost sight of each other as persons. It has become a measurable and quantifiable scientific experiment, an act designed to be honed to the highest possible pitch of self- and mutual gratification. We are even encouraged by the popular psychological sex gurus to chart and rate our own performances in these matters. But we cannot be programmed like computers, to produce guaranteed responses. We are not mechanical toys which puff, quiver and spurt when the correct buttons are pushed. We may try to 'make love' according to page 47 of the manual, but the act is more than technical expertise; the whole chemistry of personal and psychological interaction is involved as well. We may well pick up a few ideas from the experts, but then whoever went to bed with a book? To giggle and romp and play is what makes the day, whether or not the heights of the mountain peaks are scaled.

It has been said that the oldest joke in the world is that we have bodies.[16] To sit and contemplate our modes of locomotion, communication, digestion and reproduction is to invite a smile to play on our lips. We are tempted to think we could have done a better job, and we say to our

---

[15] Lewis, *The Four Loves*, pp. 90ff.

[16] Ibid., p. 94.

Creator, 'Why have you made me thus?' Of course, this reaction arises from our massive pride. We do not like being reminded of our earthiness and of the dependency of our creaturely status. But our very bodies are expressions of the image of our Creator God. What further endorsement do they need? The very bodily incarnation of he who is the flawless image of God conveys further divine approval of the status of our bodies, if that were ever needed. But to emphasize the God-given nature of our embodied existence is not to make an absolute of the flesh. It rather serves as a corrective to those who despise our creatureliness. St Francis of Assisi, in his very robust and down-to-earth way, likened his body to 'Brother Ass'. A donkey is both lovable and frustrating, deserving now the stick and now a carrot.[17] This ambivalent attitude we feel towards our bodies is well expressed by T. Howard:

> This is piquant irony: here we are with all our high notions of ourselves as intellectual and spiritual beings and the most profound form of knowledge for us is the plain business of skin on skin. It is humiliating. When two members of this God-like cerebral species approach the heights of communion between themselves, what do they do? Think? Speculate? Meditate? No, they take off their clothes. Do they want to get their brains together? No, it is the most appalling of ironies; their search for union takes them quite literally in a direction away from where their brains are.[18]

This unabashed revelling in creatureliness must not be cramped by thoughts that it is all somehow beneath our dignity, and that we would be better praying than making love. For this is a false dichotomy that must be banished for ever. We do not need to sanctify an entirely natural act by having simultaneous spiritual thoughts about God in our spouse's arms. Bouncing buttocks, phallic thrusts, heaving bodies, sighs and moans and giggles are all part of the God-given natural order of things.

There are those who by reason of a distorted spirituality despise the body and all its works, and recoil in disgust at the mere thought of sexual relations. This revulsion stems from embracing a false set of categories

---

[17] Ibid., p. 93.

[18] T. Howard, *Hallowed Be This House* (Harold Shaw, 1979), pp. 115ff.; quoted by Carr, *The Song of Solomon*, p. 35.

imported from the worldview of the ancient Greeks, where cerebral and spiritual values are placed on a higher plane than those activities more closely associated with the body. Those of our forebears who felt free to articulate their revulsion at such things are much to be pitied. The great and earthy Martin Luther, who was not usually averse to calling a spade a spade, wrote, 'The reproduction of mankind is a great marvel and mystery. Had God consulted me in the matter, I should have advised him to continue the generation of the species by fashioning them of clay.' Sir Thomas Browne wrote in a similar vein, 'I would be content that we might procreate like trees, without conjunction, or that there were any way to perpetuate the world without this trivial and vulgar way of coition.' He described it as 'the foolishest act a wise man commits in all his life; nor is there anything that will more deject his cool'd imagination, when he shall consider what an odd and unworthy piece of folly he had committed.' Lady Hillingdon, a British aristocrat of the Victorian era, expressed her distaste at her husband's approaches in these words: 'I am happy now that Charles calls on my bedchamber less frequently than of old. As it is, I now endure but two calls a week, and when I hear his steps outside my door, I lie down on my bed, close my eyes, open my legs, and think of England.'

How shall we respond to these pitiful remarks, and how shall we counsel those who find themselves in sympathy with them? We have covered some of the ground already. A proper biblical doctrine of the goodness of creation would need to be expounded, with an emphasis on celebrating the good gifts of the Creator. We would need to clear away many of the popular misconceptions of the teaching of the apostle Paul in the New Testament regarding the body and his use of the term 'flesh', and so on. All this is at an abstract and notional level. But at the personal and psychological levels, the deep fears and anxieties which arise from the human psyche would have to be dealt with gently: fears stemming from the memory of bad experiences in the past; fears of mistrust; fears of being abused and taken advantage of; fears of being manipulated and hurt; fears of allowing another to come too close, both physically and psychologically, because of anxieties about the capacity to respond; fears of mockery, of failure, inadequacy and exposure. When these inhibitions are addressed tenderly, then the pathway may be opened to the gradual self-giving and freedom of joyful physical love; something which far exceeds a duty, but is rather an uninhibited celebration of a joyful oneness, a union which the Song of Songs so beautifully extols. For true love is adventurous, and every adventure involves risk-taking; and this in turn requires the courage to overcome fears and inhibitions. When all this is faced with realism, then glorious and unexpected joys lie at our door.

c. Hang-ups and Augustine

The Western church has long been accused of harbouring shame over the question of sexual relations. The charge is that in some rather unspecified way, sexuality is linked with sin. This is a very complex subject and needs to be treated with care, and we can here only begin to suggest ways in which this theme can be explored. First, we can be certain that sexuality (both male and female) is part of humanity, upon which God, when he had created them, pronounced the verdict 'good'. So just as humankind eats, drinks, sees and walks in a certain way, so also the particular way in which humanity reproduces itself is pronounced good. Humankind's sexuality is part and parcel of their total humanness, which God created. The fall of human beings, representing their disobedience to their Creator, in their desire to be like God and subject to none but themselves, affected every area of their life. Their spiritual eyes became blind, their will became perverted, the image of God in them became warped and twisted, their environment was turned from harmony to hostility, their sexual instinct became perverted with lust. The couple who were previously naked and not ashamed, now became aware of their nakedness and they clothed themselves with fig leaves. The sin of rebellion made them self-conscious as regards their sexual organs. Their nakedness represented their vulner-ability to their Creator's hostile gaze. But why the genital region as the focal point of their embarrassment? Why not their eyes, which looked upon the forbidden tree with great desire? Or their hearts, which decided to flout the commandment? Or their hands, which actually touched the forbidden fruit? It seems that one possible answer to this is that their shame in each other's presence is focused on that area of their bodies which fundamentally differentiates them. They are threatened by the pos-sibility of exploitation. The wilful sin of flouting humanity's creaturely status of dependence on the Creator is shown in the disruption of the relationship of mutual complementarity at the sexual level. The shame arises from the vulnerability to aggression or seduction at the very level where the two were to find their mutual at-one-ness.

Much of the church today is still wallowing in the legacy of the medieval church which inherited a Platonic view of the body. The higher level of the human being was governed by the reason and the intellect. The human body was governed by instinct, by animal appetite. Even the great early church theologian Augustine of Hippo was to some extent influenced by this Greek dualism. He wrestled long and hard with the theological problems of sexuality and original sin. It is somewhat foolhardy to attempt a brief summary of his ideas, but since we have inherited much of his thinking (or have been seen to have inherited it) some attempt must be made. For Augustine, human sexuality was, of course, good. It was part of God's own created order. Adam and Eve were created as sexual beings. The generation of the human species was dependent on the sexual act and Augustine, speaking as a male for males, was of the opinion that the act itself could not take place without the preliminary desires of lust or concupiscence. The main point for Augustine was that these desires that produced the necessary physiological prerequisites for intercourse were totally beyond the control of reason, intellect and will, and therefore sinful. Thus no act of intercourse could take place without sin. However, the guilt of this sin was washed away in the waters of baptism, and while the act of intercourse was not sinful, it used a bad thing (lust, concupiscence) in order to achieve a good end, namely the procreation of children and the propagation of the species. For Augustine, intercourse for the purpose of mere pleasure was a venial sin, as it was indulging in a bad thing (lust) for selfish ends. Of course, Augustine knew nothing about natural nervous reflexes, which have purely physiological and nervous origins. So he speculated (in what to us must seem to be a rather bizarre fashion) on the nature of Adam and Eve's intercourse before the fall, that somehow it was performed without lust, all totally within the control of reason, and not done under the uncontrollable instincts of the flesh. However, rather than trying to excuse Augustine on the grounds of his ignorance of modern neurophysiology, it might be better to say that at this point, he had distorted the full-orbed biblical doctrine of God as Creator.

Augustine's views on the solidarity of the human race with Adam's sin, and of our biological links with him as the progenitor of the human race, forced him to postulate that original sin was propagated through the act of intercourse. While we may agree with him that our very humanness now necessarily implies a sharing of Adam's condition as bearing the infection of sin, we do not have to agree with him that the whole condition is somehow located in the sexual act. This puts too biological a focus on a moral condition. Augustine worked with the standard Greek categories of the higher and lower faculties of human beings. This is at odds with the anthropology of the Old Testament which looks at humanity from a more holistic point of view, rather than analysing human beings into their constituent parts. Human beings are more animated bodies, rather than encapsulated souls. This means that their instincts, appetites, desires, thinking and emotions are all to be considered as part of their corporal being. Of course, all aspects of their nature have been affected by the fall, but there are no intrinsic higher and lower natures which are fundamentally at odds with each other.

d. Sex as sacrament

There are some writers who see the sexual act in sacramental terms. It is difficult to know what to make of this, for the loose usage of religious language can lead so easily to confusion. To speak of intercourse as holy communion, as some have done, needs a great deal of qualification and clarity of definition. What is being hinted at in this usage of language is the fact that intercourse is, or should be, so much more than the physical coupling of bodies. Of course, the act may degenerate into something mechanical, the extreme example of this being the case of prostitution. But the 'one flesh' union is meant to be more than a physical act like eating. Behind the physical there is the relational, the interaction at a psychological, personal level. The two, while retaining their own identities, are striving to be outside of themselves, to become more of the other. It is this mystical union, this absorption into the other, this self-giving which abandons oneself to dissolution in the other, where boundaries seem to be melted in a fusion of personalities, creating one new whole, which lies behind the coupling of bodies. This unselfconscious abandonment in a creative loving act of union is what some have seen to be a religious act. Parallels are drawn between the sexual act and the mystical quest of the spiritual life in which the soul finds its undifferentiated unity with God himself.

However, this is not the place to consider the nature of the mystical union of the believer with God. Suffice it to say that overlap of descriptive language in the two areas surely does not indicate an identity of the types of union. For, in both cases, individuality is always retained. Yet the common element is there in the desire to be changed, to find a new integration in a relationship larger than oneself and be enriched in a larger whole. It is only thus that the act itself may be termed religious. Certainly one should not think that it is in any way sacred, as though we were performing a God-like act. Someone has said that one should never think of God when lying in the arms of one's partner. This simply underscores the fact that it is a very natural act, which does not need to be justified by any spiritual parallels. For even the motivation to find a deeper spiritual meaning behind the act may arise from an underlying sense of aversion to our corporal physical nature and its reproductive process.

e. The language of sex

The language which is used to describe the act of sexual union ranges across a very broad spectrum. It varies from the coarse and vulgar use of four-letter words, through the vast variety of current slang, to the cool and clinical descriptions of a medical manual, and then to the beauty of poetic metaphor and simile. The power of such language to induce desire and stimulate mental images depends not only on the degree of explicitness conveyed, but also on the ability to evoke a mood or feeling into which we can be drawn. Indeed there is the possibility of a distancing effect of the more explicit language, which may cause shock or revulsion. On the other hand, the more oblique metaphors may have a more subtle power of seduction. But the line between erotic sensual language and beautiful metaphor is sometimes very difficult to discern, for pornography can so easily masquerade under the guise of high-class literature. What is good taste for some may be totally unacceptable to others. We have seen that the biblical metaphors are somewhat restrained (knowing, entering, coming into the garden, eating honey and the honeycomb, drinking wine and milk, gathering myrrh and spice) and we are drawn comfortably into their orbit without too much visual stimulation. D. H. Lawrence, in *Lady Chatterley's Lover*, is much more seductive, with his descriptions of dark waves rising and heaving, heavy cumulative rhythms, the depths parting and being rolled asunder, and so on. Chaucer's raunchy bumpkin who 'pricked hard and deep' is at the other end of the spectrum. The high literary reputation of certain authors does not necessarily mean that they will not at times offend the sensibilities of a later age, or that they themselves have not violated universal moral norms of any age.

Our thoughts have meandered a considerable distance away from the actual text of the Song. We have left our lovers enjoying the bliss of the marriage bed, and it seems a pity to have to wrench ourselves away from contemplating their joy. But they cannot stay in bed for ever, and a new scenario presents itself to us in the next cycle of the Song.

Song of Songs 5:2 – 6:3

8. The fourth cycle: lost and found

1. Another dream of frustration (5:2–8)

After the dramatic climax at 5:1, a new cycle of poems begins here at 5:2 with a very sudden change of mood, and carries on through to 6:3. There is an inherent unity to the narrative and dialogue in this sequence. It starts with a sombre poem filled with tension and fear, which ends at 5:8 with the girl's appeal to the daughters of Jerusalem. The flow of the dialogue is carried on by the exclamation of the onlookers in 5:9 which produces the girl's responsive poem in praise of her lover. At 6:1 her friends want to help the girl to find him, but she replies that he's not really lost. They rediscover their love in very intimate ways (6:2–3).

This cycle has some connecting links and parallel themes with the previous cycle: at 4:12 the girl is described as a locked garden; here, access to the girl is barred by a *bolt* (5:5). Similarly, in 4:16 she opens her garden to her lover, while in 5:5 she opens the door to him. At 5:1 the boy enjoys the fruits of love in her garden, and at 6:2 he is again (lit.) 'pasturing among the lilies'.

The girl here is recounting an experience in her past. It is told from her own perspective; the boy's own reactions are not considered at all. In fact, in the whole of this cycle the boy does not speak once (except for her reporting of his words in 5:2). The time at which the incident took place is not recorded. It is impossible to place it in any narrative sequence; for that would be foreign to the whole tenor of the poem, which is to portray feelings and emotions against a bare minimum of supportive narrative framework. It would be unnecessarily pedantic to insist that any actual incident underlying this poem should have taken place *after* the marriage of the previous cycle.

The girl is probably half asleep, half awake, lying in bed alone. She obviously has not succumbed to the total oblivion of deep slumber where all her anxieties and tensions are momentarily submerged in the unconscious. No, her churnings are very much at the surface level of her consciousness. And her lover is *knocking* at the door late at *night*. He is evidently in some degree of physical discomfort (his hair dripping with the droplets of the cold night mist). But what has he been doing? We can only assume that it is a sudden romantic impulse that has driven him to seek his beloved at this late hour. How long he intended to stay is yet another unanswerable question. (Surely it is perverse to insist that the couple here are married.) He addresses her in the tones of delicate affection: *my sister, my darling, my dove, my flawless one.* He is knocking on the door and wants to come in.

But what is the girl's reaction? How does she respond? She seems to be playing hard to get; by gentle (or is it not-so-gentle?) teasing she wants him to know that she is in control. She is not at the mercy of his every whim. She is not going to be at his beck and call every moment of the day. Perhaps this display of coquetry is a desire to assert her independence and her freedom. Or perhaps it is a deliberate seductive ploy; knowing her own desirability to her lover, she plays on this to taunt him and rouse his urgency. Perhaps it is all part of an innocent game. Or perhaps it runs deeper than that, and her behaviour masks an underlying insecurity about their relationship. Her excuses are patently transparent and very flimsy and unconvincing. She has taken off her clothes and is lying in bed. 'Her gentle limbs did she undress, and lay down in her loveliness.'[1] Perhaps she is driving him wild with excitement at the suggestion of her unclothed body between the sheets. She has washed her feet; it would be too much trouble to have to get up and dirty them again, just to open up for her lover at the door.

Her lover loses patience and rattles the door lock, trying to get in. The girl suddenly seems to change her mind. She skips out of bed and rushes to the door, all of a tither. Her 'innards' (lit.) are seething or becoming hot because of him. This is most likely a reference to some sort of sexual arousal. The Hebrew word, *mēʿîm*, can refer to the womb, the bowels, the intestines or the inner parts generally. It could mean that she is in a general state of excitement at her lover's arrival. She flings open the door,

---

[1] Coleridge, 'Christabel'.

but alas, her lover has clean gone away (for that is the force of the repeated Hebrew verbs). She meets his absence, she opens the door, but nothing there, 'nothing but the midnight air' (see paraphrase). And her heart sinks at his flight (the word translated *departure* by the NIV normally means 'word', but this usage is established by cognate Arabic parallels). This may mean that she swooned when she realized her stupidity. She had overplayed her hand and was reaping the consequences (cf. 'I nearly died when I found that he was gone').[2]

She then begins her panic-stricken search. Seeking, seeking, but never finding. Calling, calling, but never an answering reply. She flits around the empty streets and squares in desperation, and bumps into the city *watchmen*. They obviously take her for a loose woman, and begin to beat her up and strip her of her clothes. The public judgment of a prostitute was the ritual exposure of her nakedness (Ezek. 16:37; Hos. 2:3). But it is unlikely that there was any formal judicial act here. In her struggle to free herself, her flimsy garments were torn from her, leaving her battered, *bruised*, shivering and half naked. This is a picture of her defencelessness, without her clothing as a covering, without her lover as a protection.

She then appeals to the *daughters of Jerusalem* not to expose her even further. She is painfully aware already of her own stupidity. And she appeals to the *daughters of Jerusalem* not to aggravate her pain by telling her lover of this mad escapade. Different translations of this verse (8) put a different interpretation on her request. What exactly is the girl requesting? The Hebrew here is slightly problematic. The question is to determine whether the girl is asking the *daughters of Jerusalem* to tell her lover something, or asking them *not* to tell him. Other adjurations to the daughters of Jerusalem occur at 2:7; 3:5; 8:4. Those at 2:7 and 3:5 are identical negative requests. The one at 8:4 has a slightly different form, which literally reads, 'I adjure you, daughters of Jerusalem, how will you excite love . . .' The word translated 'how' (*mah*) occurs here in 5:8. Thus, if in 8:4 *mah* means 'not', to make it parallel in meaning to 2:7 and 3:5, then it also perhaps means 'not' in 5:8. So the request may be her demand that they will not tell her lover that she is sick with love. The latter idea occurs at 2:5. There are two possible interpretations of this. First, it could mean that she is already sated with love and cannot take any more. This is hardly likely as she was seething for him in 5:4. More probable is the idea that she is so distraught with love that it makes her do irrational things like running out scantily dressed into the city streets at night, and she is embarrassed by her behaviour, and doesn't want her lover to know about it.

There are a number of parallels between this scene and 3:1–5. In both, the girl is alone in bed at night; in both, there is the motif of seeking and finding; in both, she goes out into the city streets and squares; in both, she encounters the watchmen on patrol. However, there are also different emphases. In the first, she seeks him upon her bed; in the second, he seeks her by coming to her house. In the first, the girl goes out and finds her lover; in the second, her search is futile and her plight is brought about by her own stupidity. In the first, the watchmen are silent and passive; while in the second, they are hostile and aggressive. The first has a clear climax when she finds her lover. The second has the searching theme spread out until the end of the cycle. It is quite clear that the second passage is more tension-filled than the first. The drama is heightened by the various reactions to her behaviour. The boy departs, leaving her soul-stricken. The watchmen beat her. The dream (or is it a nightmare?) has recurring themes – the fear of loss, the fear of his permanent absence, and the desire to recover his presence.

Perhaps it should be mentioned that many commentators have seen in this passage a number of double entendres, of sexual innuendos, creating a secret frisson of sensuality to the poems. The problem about this is that once we begin to see them, we start looking for more hidden meanings until we see them everywhere. For once the point is mentioned, we become disorientated and lose track of the main theme of the poem, and we become sidetracked down a blind alley which gets us nowhere. It puts an explicit genital focus on the whole of the Song which is just not there. For the Song is a celebration of love, beauty and mutual devotion, which does also include a physical sexual element. However, we must not allow that element to take over our interpretation of the Song. The verses which have been interpreted in this way are 5:4–5 (literal translations): 'he thrust forth his hand through the hole', 'I arose to open for my lover', 'My hands dropped flowing myrrh upon the bolt.' References to holes, opening doors and bolts carry their primary literal meaning here. Any sexual meaning exists purely in the mind of the reader, as the secondary meaning is too distanced from the actuality of the narrative description. In other words, the phrases are not being used metaphorically as in the example of 'the mountains of Bether', where there is a clear meaningful transfer of ideas from the context as a whole. If we start looking for references to intercourse and private parts everywhere, we lose track of the main theme of the Song and begin to sink into a quagmire of eroticism.

This poem raises a number of different themes, which we should consider briefly. First, there is the fear of loss, the tension between his presence and his absence. This is well brought out in the two dream-like sequences. In the first, she is on her bed absolutely tormented with longing, when he is absent. In the second, she is on her bed, and when her lover comes, she wants to be alone and her responses drive him away. While this may seem like arbitrary capriciousness, it reflects an underlying deeper tension within the human personality. The girl in our Song needs space to be alone. She wants to cultivate that private space around her, so that she can be truly herself, and not concerned with how others will be reacting to her. She wants to preserve a core of her inner being untouched by another. This is not just temperamental reserve or shyness, but the preservation of her own mystique which runs deep in her personality. There is that element within each one of us which wants to be accountable only to ourselves and not to another. She wants to be alone with her own thoughts and does not want her privacy to be invaded. For any invasion represents a threat, a meeting of the unknown. It also represents the potential for vulnerability, for we do not know how we ourselves are going to react. And sometimes in our fear we withdraw, because the risks of interaction seem too painful. On the other hand, our girl longs for the presence of her lover. She wants to know the security of his presence, and fears his absence. Her heart has gone out to him, her whole life is now suffused with his presence, in mind if not in body, and she wants to give herself completely to him. It is this existential paradox which lies at the heart of any relationship. To withdraw is to wither and die. To surrender and risk interaction is to grow and receive life through pain and accommodation.

Second, the girl is being deliberately coquettish – she is playing on her lover's emotions. She is deliberately withdrawing her affection, perhaps as a punishment for some supposed slight or lack of appreciation. In everyday relationships it may be an eloquent signal that something is wrong. We may not feel able to articulate our complaint or sense of griev- ance with our partner, so we withdraw, hoping to provoke a reaction. Sometimes it works, sometimes it may backfire. But it is hardly a solid foundation for building up an enduring relationship. The verbal articulation, however painful, however much courage it takes, is in the end much more productive than mute withdrawal. But if in our Song the girl is merely being playful, then that is another matter altogether. Being seductive in a growing relationship is all part of the fun.

Third, we can see something of the irrationality of love. We all know, I suspect, something of this. Our boy is doing something on impulse in coming to his girl's house in the middle of the night. Can he be sure he won't disturb the other members of the family? Similarly, the girl takes risks, the flouting of conventions. She charges out into the city squares heedless of what others might think. They are both driven by a force which storms all barriers, flouts all reproaches, violates all codes. She seems hemmed in by the guardians of morality, the disapproving watchmen of the city walls, and her brothers who forced her to work under their close supervision in the vineyard (1:6), who are also responsible for their budding little sister (8:8). She chafes at their being unable to kiss and show their affection in public (8:1). The social and public conventions force the lovers to seek a place away from the disapproving eyes of the moral censors; they seek the shady bower (1:16–17), the country hideaway (7:11–13), the shepherds' huts (1:8). The desire for the secret place does not arise from any illegal or immoral intentions. But they fear the disapproval of the guardians of public convention, whom they regard as colourless killjoys. Yet we need to insist that the fullness of love can and ought to blossom within the boundaries of religious and social convention. The conventional need never be drab and dull. Joy, exuberance and fulfilment are to be found within its walls.

2. The daughters of Jerusalem reply (5:9)

The tone of this request of the girl's companions is difficult to determine with precision. Perhaps it is a slightly mocking exclamation: 'Who do you think your lover is? What's so special about him?' The use of the term *most beautiful of women* may be the girls' sneering repetition of the lover's (or their own?) words at 1:8, which they throw back in her face with the mocking contempt deriving from their pathetic jealousy. They envy the girl's beauty. They envy the girl's lover. How else can they vent their spleen except by words of disparagement? The friends' question reads literally, 'What is your love more than a love?' There is a slight ambiguity here. The

169

Hebrew word for love (*dôd*) is used here in the singular, thus most probably referring to the boy himself. But as we have already seen (see on 1:2), in the plural form the word is used for the various acts of intimacy in love-making. The actual thrust of the question depends on how it can be regarded as an appropriate response to the girl's somewhat ambiguous adjuration of 5:8. Are they asking after the distinguishing marks of her lover in general terms, or are they questioning his sexual prowess, that is, his capacity to satisfy his girl's lovesickness? In view of the girl's response in 5:10–16, it seems clear that the reference is to her lover's general character and stature. If he is as outstanding and as exceptional as she thinks he is, then they might accede to her request to refrain from betraying her stupidity to her lover. But they need to be thoroughly convinced; hence this girl's extravagant praise in the following verses.

3. In praise of her lover (5:10–16)

The girl sings this song in response to the query of the daughters of Jerusalem in 5:9. It is a defiant hymn in praise of her lover, extravagant and lush in its metaphorical description. It is full of poetic hyperbole and again we must emphasize that it is not an identikit picture. The girls would not be able to recognize the lover from this description; it would not help them to recognize him in the crowd. It is rather an expression of how the girl feels about him. If it borders on the realm of fantasy, well, that is the way of love. After her detailed itemization of the various parts of his body, she triumphantly concludes, *This is my beloved, this is my friend*, daring anyone to have the audacity to contradict her.

Of course, the whole picture is a literary stylization. It is the poetic creation of the author of the Song, put on the lips of the girl. A realization of this distances us slightly from the extravagances of the power of the metaphors. But we must appreciate that this is but one way in which the ideal of beauty may be articulated, and we must make some attempt to get into the emotional frame of mind of the poet and his girl. Like any work of art, the poem seeks to create an illusion, an atmosphere. Any painting, sculpture or poem sets out to do this. The actual physical reality as perceived by us is far different. Yet we want to identify ourselves with that illusion. Greek statues, impressionist paintings, Hebrew poetry, all are creating their own special ambience which invites us to taste and see through the eyes of the artist. The pathway to that level of appreciation is never straightforward. We have to shed our own cultural, psychological and philosophical prejudices, our own private perceptions of reality, and immerse ourselves in the private world of the creative artist. We must be prepared to suspend judgment, to refrain from dismissing the artist's work as grotesque, just because our initial reactions are those of shock or disgust. What is important in the perception of these poems is that this is the way the girl feels about her lover, and we must try to empathize.

The description moves from *head* to *legs* with an overall impression of his appearance. He is *radiant and ruddy*, that is, he is in rude good health, glowing with the full flush of his youthful prime energized by love. His inner contentment radiates through his shining face. His *ruddy* face may be his natural complexion or part of a windswept tan. The young David was described in similar terms: 'He was glowing with health and had a fine appearance and handsome features' (1 Sam. 16:12). The word for *ruddy* (*'ādām*) could also imply the idea of manliness. His head is described as *purest gold*, again extravagant use of language, probably referring to her perception of him as being beyond price, or his regal stature, or simply his bronzed appearance. He is distinguished beyond all others. The word could imply that he is conspicuous, easily visible, identifiable among a crowd, either in handsomeness or stature. The NIV's *outstanding* captures it well. Two of Israel's well-known leaders were of this category. As well as David noted above (1 Sam. 16:12), Saul stood head and shoulders above all others (1 Sam. 9:2). And our lover is certainly a hero to the girl, an idealized superman.

His curly locks are as *black* and glistening as a *raven*, framing his golden appearance. *His eyes are like doves.* This metaphor is very fluid. It is hardly likely that she has the same qualities in mind as he perceived when he described her eyes as 'doves' in 1:15. Many attempts have been made to unravel the very obscure words, translated literally as 'by the channels of water, bathing in milk, sitting upon a fullness'. Surely the whole metaphor grinds to a halt if we try to locate all the references to the eye (i.e. the eye ducts, the whites of the eye, a brimming watery pool). It is perhaps better to make these references apply to the dove itself rather than to her lover's eyes. The metaphor takes off and has a life of its own, becoming more and more developed and fantastic, so that the original point of comparison is lost to view. The NIV links the word for 'fullness' with a similar word used at Exodus 28:17 for the setting of jewels on the high priest's breastpiece.

His cheeks are garden plots of spices, with (literally) 'towers of perfumes'. *His arms* are like rolled gold, his body (perhaps torso or belly) a plaque of ivory. The *lapis lazuli* and the *topaz*, both costly gems, heighten the extravagance of the description; they add nothing to the visualization of the description and are visually redundant. He has lovely *legs*, smooth as alabaster columns. His whole *appearance* is solid, immovable, firm and steadfast, like the range of the *Lebanon* mountains, imposing in their permanence. He is a *choice* specimen of his type, like the cedars of Lebanon. His palate, the taste of his *mouth*, is like sweet wine, obviously referring to her estimate of his kissing. This harks back to 5:13, where his *lips* are referred to as *lilies*. *Lilies* are always metaphors in the Song with some undertone of sexual activity. Here his *lips* drip with liquid *myrrh*. Nothing is too exotic or extravagant to describe this incomparable young man. His magnificence, his splendour, is almost out of this world. Her triumphant verbal description has overwhelmed both herself and her sceptical companions. If she has gone overboard in her poetic metaphors, well, that is excusable. After all, she is totally and irrevocably over-whelmed with her lover.

4. An offer of help (6:1)

Presumably now the girl's companions are convinced that this paragon of masculine beauty, this almost godlike figure, is worth finding, and they want to catch a glimpse of him. So they offer to help the girl. Perhaps even they have been carried away and melted by her extravagant eloquence.

The role of an outside third party in any romantic relationship is often very ambiguous. There are those who, under the guise of 'wanting to help', are nothing more than interfering busybodies. Such interference may take many forms. It may be a kind of possessiveness which refuses to let go. The proverbial mother-in-law jokes have often a solid basis in practical experience. There are the incorrigible matchmakers, both male and female, who are anxious to line up any two singles within sight of each other. But sometimes we need true friends, who will tell us the truth as they see it from their own wisdom and experience, and cause us to face truths which we otherwise would have missed. They can help us to work our way forwards, or backwards, through tangled difficulties, so that we can come to a more objective assessment of our own situations. Or perhaps we just need our own 'daughters of Jerusalem', those mute sounding boards who stimulate us to articulate our deeply hidden emotions. We hear the echoes of our own voices, and may perhaps become alarmed at the sound of alien strains. But we are always free to evaluate and accept or reject the advice of our friends. And so the responsibility for decisions is ours and ours alone. For under God we all chart our own destinies in these matters, and with our hands on the helm we sail into the uncharted waters of unknown seas.

5. Not really lost (6:2–3)

The girl's response here is curious and enigmatic. It is as though her lover is not now lost. Not that he has been found, but rather, he has found her; as if her extravagant praise has brought him to her very presence; her powerful imagination has brought about the reality of his presence, and she relaxes in the knowledge that she really does belong to him, and he to her. Of course, all this seems illogical. But then love and dreams of love are often beyond the realm of analytical reason. In 6:3 the girl reverses the previous order of the expression of their mutual possession. In 2:16 she said, 'My beloved is mine and I am his.' This is surely a mere legitimate poetic variation, but some have seen a sort of progression in the lovers' relationship here. The girl's dream of loss has now culminated in a happy reunion. The whole cycle has been an expression of her fears, which have proved ultimately groundless.

The lovers' togetherness is secure, not just emotionally and psychologically, but physically. Her dreams here are sexual and physically very intimate. For her lover has gone down to *his garden . . . to browse in the gardens and to gather lilies.* We have already met in 4:12 – 5:1 the theme of the garden as a metaphor for the girl in all her femininity. This overlaps to a large degree with the similar metaphor of the vineyard. Some commentators have stumbled over the plural reference to *gardens* in 6:2b. But the plural here is a plural of composition or a plural of extension. The girl is both a garden and gardens. The boy is not here, as some suppose, being unfaithful to his girl, and tasting the fruit of other gardens. Neither is he Solomon, plucking wantonly from the flowers of his harem. For this would produce a radical disjunction between 6:2 and 6:3. No, she is a luscious extensive garden, with a dazzling variety of flora and fauna.

The metaphor of the garden can be developed in a number of ways. A garden is a source of pleasurable fruit. In 4:13 the girl is described as an 'orchard' whose fruit is there to be plucked and tasted. In 5:1 the lover has entered his garden and tasted its fruit. The fruit in the garden is always a source of pleasure. It is never an indication of fertility. For our Song has very little interest in conception and procreation. The act of sexual union is an act of pleasure which is an expression of their mutual love. Children, offspring, the preservation of the family name, are mentioned only very obliquely. The lover is never seen as sowing seed in his garden. That is a concept totally alien to the Song. This 'agricultural' concept of the garden, which is a common metaphor for the type of marriage often envisaged by men in traditional-type societies in various parts of the world, has no justification from the Song. For this concept of the garden reduces the woman to a possession to be bought or sold. Her price is an indication of her potential for bearing fruit. If she doesn't bear fruit, another garden can be purchased. But these are ideas totally foreign to the thought-world of the Song, even though they were prevalent in the indigenous Canaanite population among whom the Israelite people dwelt. Of course, this concept gradually infiltrated the stream of Israel's social consciousness, but it was never theologically sanctioned by the prophets or priests of the religious establishment.

A garden is a private exclusive world, a place for retreat, relaxation and meditation. It gives hints of the invisible gardener, the cultivator of this paradise. It is natural, yet not natural. It is a place of order, of the primal wildness of nature tamed and brought under control. It represents a halfway house between the uncontrolled riot and profusion of the natural order, and the cultivating influence of the civilization of the city. The garden has to be tended to look its best, and needs constant attention.

We all know the seductiveness of a garden. We enter a beautifully maintained garden with tenderly manicured lawns, immaculate rose beds, magnificently flowering shrubs, and the bowers of overhanging firs or willows, and we enter coyly, shyly, almost with reverence, as if we were on holy ground. We feel as though we were trespassers, with no right to be there. P. G. Wodehouse has a magnificent description of such a stately grove, into which foolhardy snails momentarily penetrate and then 'retire abashed'. It is all so natural, yet the product of human horticultural artistry and imagination. The civilizing influence is not obtrusive, yet it is always there; the pruning, weeding, staking, potting, bedding of seedlings, watering, manuring. The final result is overwhelming, and produces in us a sense of awe. It would be a wanton act of mischief to pick the flowers, or swing on the branches, even to tread on the grass. Its inherent privacy is both forbidding and inviting.

The notices 'Private', 'Keep out', 'Trespassers will be prosecuted', tempt us to intrude on their privacy. The sense of peace and quietness is something which enfolds and embraces us. The noisy outside world is but a faint memory. The distant roar of traffic beyond the high stone walls and cloistered walks and wrought iron gates creates a sanctified world in which we tread slowly and with awe. We are privileged to enter into this private exotic world.

This is the garden into which the lovers enter. She is the garden into which her beloved comes, and yet they are both enfolded in it. She envelops him in her embrace, and creates a new world for him, a new dimension, in which he lives and moves and has his being. It is all too easy to develop the garden imagery into an asymmetrical metaphor, in which the man 'enters' his garden and eats its fruit. Our Song itself lends credence to this. The physical asymmetry of the act of sexual union, a biological and anatomical inevitability, also underscores this aspect. But the emotional, psychological and mental reciprocity is something that is a mutual two-way interaction. Her garden waters the man, gives him succour and wholeness. She is equally a shade to him, as he is to her (2:3). They taste the sweetness of each other's fruit.

A number of writers[3] have recently sought to draw parallels between the garden motif in the Song, and the Garden of Eden before the fall, in Genesis 2. Various parallels have been pointed out. Both gardens are lush and fruitful. They are beautiful to look at and their fruit is mouth-wateringly sweet. The gardens are watered by springs, fountains or the mist. There is no sense of shame or guilt. They are gardens of delight, a paradise to be explored and enjoyed. There is complementarity and union between the man and his wife; neither embarrassment nor restraint; only a sense of fun. However, once these parallels have been drawn, the important question is how to proceed further. And it is here that the problems start to arise. For comparisons are made under titles such as 'Paradise lost, Paradise regained', and 'Love's lyrics redeemed'. While there may well be literary motifs in common between the Song and Genesis 2, and while the reading of the Song may induce a wistful backward glance to Eden in the longing to recapture the primal innocence and freedom experienced

---

[3] Among others, see Landy, p. 183, and Trible, *God and the Rhetoric of Sexuality*, p. 144.

there, in fact there can be no going back, theologically or morally. Man and woman were expelled from the garden for their rebellion, for their insubordination in refusing to accept their creaturely status as dependent upon their Creator. This rebellion against their Maker not only fractured their relationship with him, but their relationship to each other and to their environment was also irreversibly disrupted. They became self-conscious: pain and labour were multiplied; and the created order itself was convulsed and became hostile to humankind. This moral disaster resulted in the couple's expulsion from the garden, with the cherubim wielding their flaming swords to prevent re-entry. Their expulsion was a one-way street. The idyllic conditions of paradise can never be recaptured. Any attempt to do that can only be illusory. Sexuality, nudism or openness therapy can never provide a re-entry path. This is simply because our sexuality, our wills, our minds, have all been affected by the fall. To pretend that they have not been is to live in a fool's paradise of self-delusion. But for the Christian, with the hope of a new heaven and a new earth, the restoration of all things will not be a replay or re-enactment of Eden, but something far more glorious. Humanity in Christ will not be stripped naked, but clothed with garments of glory. Any other hope of a transformed experience, however it may be induced – by drugs, music, art, therapies of whatever sort – will ultimately be exposed for what it is: a human attempt to walk back into Eden. Those who attempt that way have only themselves to blame if they are lacerated and wounded by the cherubim's whirling swords. The only way is forward, out of the death of Eden, to the spiritual rebirth of the kingdom of God, leading finally to the reconciliation of all things in the consummation of Christ.

Song of Songs 6:4 – 8:4

9. The fifth cycle: beauty kindles desire

1. Her awesome and terrifying beauty (6:4–7)

The fifth cycle of the Song begins here with the lover's exclamation of awe at the beauty of his girl. Verses 6:4–10 probably constitute a unit, framed by the identical phrases, literally translated as 'awesome as the bannered ones', at verses 4 and 10. The NIV obscures this with its two different paraphrases (*majestic as troops with banners* and *majestic as the stars in procession*) of the same Hebrew phrase. It continues with some sort of dream experience, containing the very obscure verses from 6:11. The comings and goings of the girl in this section are very uncertain. However, her actual (or assumed) departure at 6:12 (whether real or imagined) gives the excuse for the boy's descriptive praise poem in 7:1–5. It is usually assumed that he is visualizing the girl as dancing in front of him in this scene. There follows a duet in which the two lovers express a strong desire for physical intimacy, culminating in the girl's invitation to him to come out into the countryside, there to make love together (7:11–13). There seems to be a break at 8:1, where the girl is expressing a renewed longing for intimacy, which sets her off again on a new flight of sexual fantasy, culminating in her adjuration to the daughters of Jerusalem not to arouse love until it please (8:4).

In 6:4 the lover appears from nowhere. He had been the object of her futile search until he was dreamed upon by the girl's reverie. These words are now his response to the girl's affirmation in 6:3 of their mutual possession. His words are parallel and similar to his poem of praise in 4:1–3, except that here, the reference to her eyes as doves has been omitted, as also the mention of her lips. The initial acclamation of her beauty has been expanded by comparisons to *Jerusalem* and *Tirzah*. Again the *wasf* is only partial, leaving the reader to speculate as to what he might have said about the rest of her body. Our curiosity is satisfied in 7:1–5 where he describes her from the feet upwards.

The comparison of the beautiful girl to capital cities falls somewhat strangely upon our modern ears. But the resemblance is not so much in physical beauty (who would these days think of likening a girl to a city?), but in royalty, power and stature. *Tirzah* and *Jerusalem* are obviously mentioned in poetic parallelism. *Tirzah* was an ancient Canaanite city, mentioned in Joshua 12:24. Jeroboam I moved his capital there at the time of the schismatic breakaway of Israel from the Solomonic dynasty which ruled Judah. Omri later established Samaria as the capital of the Northern Kingdom (1 Kgs 14:1–20; 16:8–26). The site of *Tirzah* has been described as one of great natural and rustic beauty. *Jerusalem* of course was the capital of the Davidic kingdom of Judah. It is possible that we are meant to perceive connotations from the etymologies of these names. *Tirzah* comes from a root meaning 'to be pleasant' (hence: Mount Pleasant). *Jerusalem* means something like 'a foundation of well-being'. Later, in 8:10, the girl describes herself as the one who brings *šālôm*, that is, well-being, peace and security. We say that a city in a prominent position has a certain 'aspect'. So also our girl 'looks out' with grandeur, dignity and loftiness. Her aspect is awesome, yet pleasing. *Tirzah* may be regarded as the archetype of the delightful garden city, while *Jerusalem*, perched on its fortified rocky outcrop, represents imposing royal impregnability. *Jerusalem* is described elsewhere in the Old Testament as 'perfect in beauty' (Ps. 50:2; Lam. 2:15). Samaria was described by Isaiah as a 'wreath', 'his glorious beauty, set on the head of a fertile valley' (Isa. 28:1).

The girl is described as literally 'awesome'. She inspires admiration mixed with dread. We have already mentioned this in our discussion of 4:8. The NIV's *troops with banners* is somewhat problematical. There is no mention in the Hebrew of troops or military units. The Hebrew *nidgālôt* is a plural (abstract) passive participle from the root *dāgal*. We have already come across this same root in the noun *degel*, usually translated as 'banner', at 2:4. The NIV's *troops* presumably derive from the military units which assembled according to their *degel* as the camps of Israel set out on their wilderness journey. It is more likely that the meaning there should be associated with an Akkadian verbal root *dāgal*, meaning 'to see'. So then the word just means something like 'spectacle', a sight to behold in solemn awe. The same expression occurs again at 6:10 (NIV 'stars in procession'). She is splendid to look upon. We might say 'she is terrific', not that she is necessarily terrifying – we often use the word in this weakened sense without regard to its root meaning. However, our lover is overwhelmed by her beauty; he begs her to turn her eyes away from him, so great is their power to unsettle him and churn him up inside. I have paraphrased this as:

> Avert your tantalizing eyes,
> your gaze which threatens danger.
> Your awesome beauty has the power
> to churn the depths of deep desire,
> to light the fire of yearning strong
> that drains me of all strength.
> A helpless victim I am left,
> a slave at beauty's mercy,
> weak captive of magnificence.

This terrifying aspect of beauty is what Marcabru, a French poet of the twelfth century, conveys in the lines:

> Fountain of beauty, perfect love
> You light up all the world;
> And I, for all us wretches,
> plead for mercy.

The girl's awesome beauty is then elaborated on in detail: her waving glistening *hair*; her magnificent display of *teeth* revealed by her dazzling smile; her cheeks or forehead outlined behind her *veil*. We have met these before at 4:1–3. We should not be surprised at repetition in the Song. It is part of the very nature of a song to be cyclic and repetitive. The repeated refrains help to sustain the ambience of the Song, like the strands or threads, the warp and woof of a fabric, holding it together. At a more homely level, the language of love bears repeating.[1] Relationships are oiled and progress more smoothly with a little bit of praise. It is not self-serving flattery, but a genuine desire to compliment the other. And it is

---

[1] Davidson, p. 141.

often surprising how a small word of praise goes such a long way in energizing and establishing a relationship. If someone praises you, you are not likely to forget it readily. A certain amount of self-esteem, corroborated by a partner, does wonders for the system.

2. She is utterly unique (6:8–9)

The boy continues his lavish praise of his beloved. She is unique, incomparable. She is not only the special subject of her beloved's adoration, but she is also praised by *queens, concubines, virgins* and *young women*; she is also the favourite of her mother. As R. Davidson puts it, 'With that conceit born of love, he depicts all other women coming to congratulate her and to praise her beauty.'[2] The *queens, concubines* and *virgins* are mentioned in order of decreasing rank, but their numbers increase in the ascending scale – *sixty, eighty, beyond number*. The numbers must not be taken literally; it is merely a literary device to indicate an indefinitely large number (see Amos 1:3 etc., 'For three sins . . . even for four . . .'). All these gorgeous females are usually considered to be members of Solomon's harem. But the reference is more general. There is no mention of the king at all. Many have tried to reconcile these numbers with the seven hundred wives and three hundred concubines of Solomon's harem mentioned in 1 Kings 11:3, by assuming that the Song was composed in the king's early years as monarch, before he was corrupted by his increasing number of consorts who led him astray. But we do not need to be concerned with such matters. The reference is non-specific. However many royal beauties, consorts or young women there may be, our girl outshines them all in the radiance of her dazzling splendour. Twice she is mentioned as being 'one', meaning unique; she is the special favourite of her mother (not an only child). Like Isaac, the 'only son' of Abraham (see Gen. 22:2), she is the object of special parental affection. She is blessed because she has been so well endowed with natural beauty (she is 'flawless', so RSV), so that heads turn to admire her wherever she goes, and she is the subject of so much admiring comment.

Happy is this girl who receives so much extravagant praise. She is the *favourite* of her mother, she is called *blessed* by the *young women*, she is *praised* by *queens and concubines*. She is indeed fortunate in receiving the

[2] Ibid., p. 142.

undiluted feminine approval of those who are perhaps not so naturally well endowed with the ornaments of nature as she is. The capacity to delight in and to give unqualified praise of those whose gifts of nature and of skill far exceed our own, and to be able to do so without the slightest tinge of envy or desire to denigrate, is indeed the gift of a gracious Creator. For the plank in the eye of the natural person has never inhibited him or her from pointing out the specks in others' (Matt. 7:3–5). Similarly, the capacity to receive the gracious approval of others without our heads being turned is also a gift not to be despised. For what have we got which we did not first receive (cf. 1 Cor. 4:7)?

Unselfconscious beauty possesses a purity whose innocence shines forth to illuminate the drabbest of circumstances. Like the sun breaking through on a mist-enshrouded autumn day, so does nature's gift of beauty warm our hearts and lift our spirits. Bathed in beauty's translucent light, we are subdued into awe, and impelled to match its purity by rejecting all unbecoming coarseness of responding thought. For beauty is a bonus that makes our world a better place.

But beauty is not to be aesthetically appreciated merely as an abstract concept. The girl in our Song is not a cold, lifeless statue, with a remote untouchable beauty. There is a real-life warm-blooded person behind the radiant exterior. Her beauty is a gift, a possession, which, like all such qualities, may be exploited for good or ill, by herself or by others. She may be conscious of her power to attract admirers, and could easily become conceited and vain, or manipulative and selfish. On the other hand, her outer beauty could well become a vehicle for reflecting an outgoing selfless spirit, renewed and nurtured by the Creator himself.

Beauty is a gift on loan to us, as it were, to be received and cultivated with joy. To recognize its transitory and ephemeral nature is not to denigrate it, however. It is merely to acknowledge the all-too-obvious fact that we all possess things that we cannot keep. Beauty withers and fades like a flower, and not all the cosmetic lotions of the beautician's parlour can stem the inevitable ravages of time. We all get wrinkled and lined, our skin loses its glow, and we begin to sag and bulge in all the wrong places. And how we wish it were not so. But the quest for eternal youth is a fool's errand, and the sooner we recognize it as such, the better for our mental and psychological health. Yet the harsh realities of the cosmic laws of entropy and disintegration evoke from the deepest levels of our being a longing for renewal and transformation, where decay and corruption are a thing of the past, and where we are being remade in the image of our Creator. We will each then uniquely reflect the perfection of our individual personalities with all the freedom and liberty of the children of God (see Phil. 3:20–21 and Rom. 8:20–23).

In these verses, our lover describes his girl as being *unique*. It is the extravagance of the language of love; that is the way he feels about her, for she is beyond all comparison; there is absolutely no-one else who can fill his life as she does. But in any real-life relationship, as opposed to the literary fiction of our Song, we know that we need others beside our partners to fill out our needs at different levels. The close relationship we form with a member of the opposite sex is unique only in the sense that the claims we make on each other give a signal to any third party to keep his or her distance. But this does not mean that our girlfriends, boyfriends or spouses are themselves alone capable of stimulating or satisfying us at every different level, be it psychological, social or intellectual. It surely is very rare that our partners are able to give satisfaction in all these areas. Recognition of this will then allow us to give our partners the freedom to interact with others at levels which we ourselves are unable to satisfy. Of course, a certain amount of trust has to operate for this to be the case. I may not be able to fulfil my wife's capacity for conversation about gardening, so I must, without jealousy, be able to let her fulfil that lack elsewhere. A unique relationship must allow for rugby club talk and mums' groups, however much they might pour scorn on each other. We must always be aware that however close our union, we still remain individuals. We do not always think as one; the 'otherness' of the 'other' will always remain, enshrouded in perpetual mystery. Differences of opinion can lead to a sharpening of perspectives. 'Iron sharpens iron', and we strike sparks off each other. Yet thought patterns may coincide on occasion in a myriad of details and cause us to exclaim in delighted astonishment, 'So you see it that way too!' And so we are comforted and affirmed in our questionings. For there is someone very close travelling along the same road with us. So our uniqueness is a sparkling jewel, a multifaceted gem. We cannot see all the varied splendours of a unique relationship all at once. But from many different perspectives, through circumstances rough and smooth, we can begin to appreciate the infinite value of the one we hold so dear.

We may often say of a young couple starting off in life together, 'I hope they'll make each other very happy.' A capacity to fill each other's cup of happiness to overflowing is a very blessed condition. To bask in each other's presence, to find supreme fulfilment in the complementarity of their union, is a prize which many find elusive. The richness deriving from mutual self-surrender, from self-giving creative expressions of love in the wider community, can lead to a deeper-seated contentment that is true happiness. Yet even in those moments of deepest happiness together, we may become aware of an inner loneliness, an unutterable existential longing, which no earthly union can ever assuage. We realize the ephemerality of all our deepest unions, and stretch out longingly for another world which is our true home. We sense that there must be something more, some truer, more solid and enduring happiness, of which our present joyous experiences are but a very pale reflection. C. S. Lewis is a most eloquent exponent of this theme of eternal longing. 'If I find in myself a desire which no experience in this world can satisfy, the most probable explanation is that I was made for another world.'[3] As he points out, this is not mere escapism, for this yearning is most intense in the moment of our highest joys. And as the great North African theologian Augustine put it, 'Thou hast made us for Thyself, and our hearts are restless until they find their rest in Thee.' So let us never be deceived into thinking that our most profound happiness can ever reside in any human partnership. We are made in the image of our Creator, and it is in him alone that we find our true rest.

3. Her cosmic beauty (6:10)

It is most likely that these words should be in quotation marks; that is, they are the exclamation of praise uttered by the queens and concubines of 6:9. Again it is a rhetorical question, similar to 3:6 and 8:5. It is the girl herself who is the subject of their praise. This verse ends the unit beginning at 6:4 with a closing reference to 'the bannered ones'. The beauty of the girl rivals any other natural phenomenon. She is compared to *the dawn, the moon, the sun* and the 'bannered ones'. This last expression is the one we have met before with the meaning of 'spectacle' or 'sight' or 'apparition'. The other references in this verse to natural phenomena have led the NIV translators to particularize the 'spectacle' as the cosmic canopy of *the stars in procession*. The use of the terms *the dawn, the moon, the sun* and *the*

---

[3] C. S. Lewis, *Mere Christianity*, Book 3, ch. 10, p. 118.

stars gives an impression of the transcendental nature of the girl's beauty. She is indeed a natural phenomenon, but almost out of this world. In fact, those commentators who espouse the pagan cultic view of the Song say that these verses referred originally to the dangerous love goddesses Anath and Ishtar, both violent, beautiful and sensuous women of the mythological fertility cult. Even if we do not embrace this view, it is still possible to perceive godlike undertones in this verse. For the sun and the awesome manifestation of God himself are compared in Job 37:21–22:

> Now no one can look at the sun,
>> bright as it is in the skies,
>> after the wind has swept them clean.
> Out of the north he comes in golden splendour;
>> God comes in awesome majesty.

The sun and the moon are so ethereal that they are always a temptation to the superstitious. Job himself recognized the possibility of such idolatry:

> If I have regarded the sun in its radiance
>> or the moon moving in splendour,
> so that my heart was secretly enticed
>> and my hand offered them a kiss of homage,
> then these also would be sins to be judged.
> (Job 31:26–28)

The girl *appears like the dawn*. The verb in other Old Testament contexts means 'to look down on something' or 'overhang'. While this meaning might be appropriate for *the sun, the moon* and *the stars*, it hardly fits with the appearing of the dawn. But the general idea is clear. We are observing the manifestation of the girl, her epiphany. There is a sense of anticipation at the first light of *dawn*. One waits in patient expectation for the first rays of the rising sun to illuminate the grey outline of the mountain slopes. So with the girl; if the hints of her initial appearing are so enticing, what will the full manifestation reveal?

The poetic Hebrew word for moon is *lĕbānâ*, meaning whiteness. This plays on the word for Lebanon (*lĕbānôn*) and for incense (*lĕbônâ*). The full moon, ethereal in its pale whiteness, seems aloof, remote, yet infinitely enticing. So also our girl possesses these seductive qualities. There is a longing to reach out and touch such an entrancing vision, yet there is always the strange fear that in doing so, one might contaminate her purity. This is one of the strange paradoxes of beauty. If the desire to possess is fulfilled, one loses the entrancement of beauty aloof in its isolation.

Her presence is also likened to the blazing *sun*: a source of light and life and heat for all who gaze upon her. Sometimes just to see a glimpse of a radiant face can fuel a person's energy for an entire day. Our girl appears like *the sun*. She has 'presence' which no-one can fail to observe. She makes an impression on all who come within her attractive orbit.

She is as awesome as the starry canopy of night. To gaze out upon the stars on a clear night is an awesome experience. One feels one's existential loneliness, one's total insignificance in the cosmic order of things, a sense of aloneness which is profoundly unsettling.

Of course, all these metaphors are to some extent mutually exclusive at a surface level. But they all contain an element of awe, of majesty, of remoteness. The very distance of these natural manifestations has a tendency to produce in us a feeling of reverence. When this is applied to the girl, it may very well summarize momentary feelings. But those feelings of awe prevent any degree of intimacy. If we put someone on a pedestal, then we are condemned always to view him or her from afar. The person becomes an idol, to be served and worshipped at a distance. Of course, the further away we place an idol, the less we are able to see its flaws and cracks. We begin to worship something that is unreal, or else that is the creation of our own imagination. But reality always involves the pain of interaction. For a cold dose of reality always disabuses us of our fantasies. But that is part of the pain of intimacy, of facing and accepting the reality as it is and of working within the constraints of those limitations.

The poet Lord Byron has superbly captured the ethereal nature of beauty, in lines which echo the sentiments of our Song:

> She walks in beauty, like the night
> Of cloudless climes and starry skies;
> And all that's best of dark and bright
> Meet in her aspect and her eyes:
> Thus mellow'd to that tender light
> Which heaven to gaudy day denies.[4]

---

4 Byron, 'She Walks in Beauty'.

4. Dreaming in the walnut garden (6:11–12)

The boy's song in praise of his beloved clearly ends at 6:10 with his quotation of the words of the queens and concubines. A new section begins here at 6:11, but the meaning and context of the next few verses are very obscure. It is not at all clear who is speaking these words. The NIV puts these words on the lips of the boy. However, I take it that the girl is speaking, since the words of 6:13 are obviously addressed to her, where she is bidden to return from the place to which she had gone. So 6:11 most naturally describes the girl's own departure to the walnut grove, and 6:13 represents a request that she return from there. But there are no linguistic pointers in the Hebrew which would enable us to decide the gender of the speakers. Some link this verse with 6:2 where the lover went down to his garden, the assumption being that the girl has now followed her lover and is there in the garden with him. In 6:2 we interpreted the garden metaphorically; here in 6:11, the garden seems to be a literal one. The theme again is love in the springtime (cf. 2:10–13); but here the girl is inspecting *the new growth* in the horticultural gardens, rather than in the open countryside. The vineyard may have been irrigated in the rainy season by a wadi (Heb. *naḥal*) (not *valley* as in NIV) which ran through it. A wadi is a water channel which is normally just a dried-up river bed except in the rainy season. Walnut trees have many erotic, cultic and mythological associations, but we do not need to concern ourselves with the details here. The girl is wandering alone, dreamily inspecting the budding trees and vines, when she is suddenly transported in her thoughts into the presence of the lover.

6:12 is probably the most obscure verse in the Song. The Hebrew text as it stands hardly makes any sense at all. All the words are well known, but the syntax is problematical, and the overall meaning is very puzzling. There have been numerous attempts to unravel the mystery by postulating slight emendations to the Hebrew text, but this is just inspired guesswork. Literally the Hebrew reads:

	I did not know
	My soul (f)
(She)	Set me
	Chariots (of)
	My people
	A prince

It is uncertain whether 'my soul' is the object of the verb 'to know' or the subject of 'set me'. Is there a preposition missing in front of 'chariots'? What is the relation of 'my people' to 'a prince'? The Hebrew for 'my people a prince' is *'ammî nādîb*. This has been emended by some to read the proper name Amminadab. Here is a selection of what some English versions make of the verse:

AV	Or ever I was aware, my soul made me like the chariots of Ammi-nadib.
JB	Before I knew . . . My desire hurled me on the chariots of my people, as their prince.
NJPSV	Before I knew it, my desire set me mid the chariots of Ammi-nadib.
NEB	I did not know myself; she made me feel more than a prince reigning over the myriads of his people.
GNB	I am trembling; you have made me as eager for love as a chariot driver is for battle.
RSV	Before I was aware, my fancy set me in a chariot beside my prince.

The general sense seems to be something like this: before the girl knows what is happening, she finds herself in some heightened ecstatic state, as though she is out of the body. She has lost her balance or normal sense of composure, because of the great joy and excitement her lover instils in her. Overwhelmed with ecstasy, she is transported dream-like into the presence of her lover; she imagines she is alongside him, being taken away in his royal chariot. (Those who espouse the shepherd hypothesis make this scene describe the girl's abduction by King Solomon.)

The scene itself conveys connotations of nobility, royalty, glamour and splendour. The girl is literally swept off her feet. She is being publicly acclaimed by the crowds as the acknowledged consort of her royal hero, as she is taken off to be with him.

It is most likely that all this is a fantasy. The Hebrew word *nepeš* (soul) can sometimes be translated as desire, or longing. Her dreamings may not have any point of contact with reality, but no matter; she is in love. At some time or other, she will have to come down to earth. But for now she is far away, lost in her own thoughts.

It is all too possible to be in love with the idea of being in love. The private fantasy world we inhabit may be fuelled by excessive longing for intimacy or by disappointment over previous relationships. These fantasies are not harmful in general, so long as we recognize them for what they are. We may dream of our future spouses as being wonderful actresses or successful managers, brilliant doctors or well-known politicians. But when Eros's fiery dart smites us, the manager may have become an unemployed market gardener, or the actress a community relations officer. For Eros is no respecter of persons, and the fire of love is often ignited between the most unlikely candidates. And yet the diverse realities of mutual adjustment must be encountered with patience, hope and humour. This is where our fantasies have to be abandoned. We accept our spouses as they actually are and not as we would perhaps like them to be. Entering a relationship with a programme for the reformation of the other partner is a recipe for disaster. Yet the mutual accommodation, with its yielding, deferment, tolerance and love, opens up the pathways to hitherto unexpected discoveries, which never cease to amaze, however far one travels along this road of adventure together.

5. A sight for tired eyes (6:13)

The girl is far away, lost in her dreams, and she is being called back to reality by her friends, who want to gaze on her beauty. The second half of the verse could be uttered by either the boy or the girl. I take the latter view, so that the girl uses the term *Shulammite* in the second part of 6:13 as a means of self-designation. The tone of 6:13b seems to be somewhat petulant, hostile or defensive. The girl seems to be suggesting that the motives the girls have in gazing at her are not in the least honourable. The request *Come back, come back* is an urgent appeal. Some have emended the Hebrew text to read 'leap, leap', so making it into a command to the girl to begin dancing. But such an expedient is based only on the presupposition of the interpreter, who wants to make the whole of the *wasf* in 7:1–5 to read as a description of the girl dancing in diaphanous veils before the onlookers. However, there is no indication that the girl is here or elsewhere actually dancing. She rebukes the onlookers for gazing at her as if she were a camp dancer; but we do not have to suppose that that is what she actually is.

The girl here is called the *Shulammite*. This has exercised the commentators to no small degree. There are a number of possibilities. First, it could be referring to a female inhabitant of the village Shunem. The fact that the middle 'l' has been replaced by an 'n' is not too much of a problem for the Hebrew. Shunem is a village mentioned in Joshua 19:18 as part of the allocation of Israel to the tribe of Issachar. Abishag, the beautiful maiden assigned to act as a hot-water bottle for the ageing King David, is described as a Shunammite (1 Kgs 1:3). However, we must leave it there and agree with H. H. Rowley 'that it is high time Abishag was banished from commentaries on the Song of Songs, into which she has been imported on such slender grounds'. Second, *šulammît* (Hebrew) has been explained as the feminine form of the name Solomon (*šĕlōmōh*), as if Solomon were the title given to the groom, and *šulammît* the title given to his bride. However, a feminine form 'Shelomith' occurs in Leviticus 24:11 and 1 Chronicles 3:19, although we cannot be certain that there was not a variety of feminine forms. The Greek form of this word is Salome. Those who espouse the pagan-cultic view of the origin of the Song regard the term *Shulammite* as a conflation of the term Shunammite (female inhabitant of Shunem) with Shulmanitu (Ishtar), the war goddess of the fertility cults. However, it is probably least controversial to see the word as deriving from the Hebrew noun *šālôm*, meaning peace, wholeness or well-being. Since the girl describes herself in 8:10 as one who 'brings shalom', this seems an appropriate guess even if its exact etymology is uncertain.

At the very least, *šĕlōmōh* and *šulammît* are linked by a very strong assonance; and the word pair gives more than a hint of the mutual fulfilment of the two lovers. Each one finds *šālôm* in the complementarity of the other. This seems to be yet another reflection of the Garden of Eden narrative of Genesis 2, where the primal pair, man (*ʾîš*) and woman (*ʾiššâ*), find their mutual complementarity in the one-flesh relationship. *ʾîš* and *ʾiššâ* are linked by assonance (though most probably not by etymology); the woman was originally taken out of the flesh of the man, and they are reunited in the bodily one-flesh union of their marriage (Gen. 2:22–25). For man in his solitariness had found no suitable helper in the rest of the created order. His joyful exuberance at his recognition that the creation of the woman has brought the possibility of the gift of peace is shown in his triumphant cry, 'This at last is bone of my bones . . .' (Gen. 2:23, RSV).[5]

---

[5] See also on 6:2–3 for other parallels between the Song and the Garden of Eden narrative.

The dance of Mahanaim is also a puzzle. The word appears as a proper noun, as a place name in the Transjordan, in Genesis 32:2 and elsewhere. The Hebrew *maḥneh* means an army camp and *Mahanaim* has the dualized ending, giving the meaning 'two camps'. It is doubtful whether this throws any light on the verse. Some have seen the dance as a typical Middle Eastern dance where the girl dances between two long lines of men who are clapping and stamping and singing to the rhythm of the girl's movements.

This reference to a dance here has led some commentators to see as the background of the Song the seven-day-long festivities surrounding a wedding. The man who popularized this view was J. G. Wetzstein, who studied Syrian wedding customs from Damascus at the end of the nineteenth century AD. Those customs of village weddings to which he found parallels in the Song were a seven-day cycle of feasting, the honouring of the couple as royalty, the extravagant praising of the physical charms of the bride and groom in song (the *wasf*) and the performance by the bride of a war-like sword dance. However, Syrian wedding customs of the nineteenth century AD are a rather insecure basis for extrapolating backwards to several centuries BC to find a suitable background for the Song. Also the division of the Song into seven components is somewhat arbitrary, as also is the suggestion that an actual dance is taking place here at 6:13.

However, it is probable that the girl here is protesting against being leered at *as if* she were a common dancer entertaining the troops. Others have suggested that the girl senses a rival here: that she is being upstaged by a Shunammite who is being recalled by her companions. But it is all too easy to explain away awkward verses by positing yet another intruding character, and thus adding to the complexity of the story.

The sight of a beautiful girl dancing can be very alluring and absolutely riveting. The athleticism, the grace, the whirling movements of her limbs, the motion of the torso, the wild flinging of her legs and arms, give rise to a seductive scenario. A public dancer is an untouchable entertainer. She always remains at a distance, leaving her audience in a state of high tension. Of course, differing styles of dancing may be more or less provocative. From the posturing of modern rock artists to the traditional rhythmic tribal dancing of Africa, there is often a deliberately calculated element of sexual provocation. The provocation is always the greater because of the movement. A dance is always more alluring than a static pose. To watch such displays may be at worst a feeding of the lust of the eyes, at best an 'arousing of love' before 'it pleases'. But some find pleasure in observing the graceful movement of ice skaters without the least suggestion of sexual enticement. Beauty, grace, form and movement can be observed with much appreciation without being tarnished with lust.

But a girl who is dancing is not merely entertaining others, she is not just providing a spectacle for others to feast their eyes on. She is enjoying the exhilaration of physical self-expression. That there is a thrill in un-hampered bodily movement is one of the joys of having a body. To dance, to climb a mountain, to swim, to run on a beach – all these promote physical and mental well-being. But even here we experience the limitations of our corporate nature, and long to be free of them. We envy the birds, so effortlessly gliding and soaring in the three-dimensional sky, while we are so pedestrian. Underwater swimming is the nearest we can get to this multidimensional experience; not all of us can have the experience of the weightlessness of astronauts in orbit round the earth. A dancing girl may become so engrossed with her own whirling movements that she may induce within herself a trance-like state, where she is barely conscious of her body, and is transported into another world, like the whirling dervishes of Turkish Islam. This self-intoxication may be yet another form of escapism from reality, the futile attempt to recapture the bliss of Eden.

However, not everyone is able to find pleasure in the observation of or the participation in physical movement. Their joys are more cerebral or aesthetic, musical or gastronomic, requiring the minimum of motion.

We have strayed rather far from the *dance of Mahanaim*. But in whatever way we choose to link the girl with this dance, she is still the object of the onlookers' gaze, more particularly that of her beloved, who again begins to sing her praises (7:1).

6. Her graceful form (7:1–5)

The boy now responds to the gaze of the onlookers and affirms his beloved in her beauty in this *wasf* which merges into the duet of 7:6–10.

Extravagant in his praise, he regards her as royalty, *a prince's daughter*, her hair like the purple royal tapestry. But the others regard her as nothing more than a common camp dancer, entertaining the soldiers. Another view is that these verses are uttered by the onlookers who are observing the dancing girl. The fact that parts of the girl's body are described which normally would not be visible – her thighs, *navel*, *waist*, *breasts* and *neck* – has led some to believe that the girl here is either naked or else dancing in the flimsiest of see-through veils. The suggestion is not really necessary, as the powers of imagination are sufficient to enable the onlooker to describe the various unseen parts. I take it that here the boy is speaking; the words are of genuine praise, not a mocking sensuous description, even though there may be erotic connotations in parts of the *wasf*. Again we should issue the caution that the poem is not primarily visually descriptive, but rather the emotive response of the lover towards the beauty of his girl. He first sees her feet and then allows his eyes to travel to her thighs and thence upwards, finally beholding her wondrous tresses. What he sees produces within him a train of fanciful metaphors illustrative of his own inner feelings. A few comments on this list are in order before looking at the unit as a whole.

Her *feet* and ankles are delicate and dainty. The Hebrew word used for *feet* (pa'am) can also mean a step, a pace, an interval of distance. This would lend support to the dancing scenario. So her movements are swift and light and well coordinated. Like the ladies of Jerusalem of Isaiah, she is 'strutting along with swaying hips, with ornaments jingling on their ankles' (Isa. 3:16). Her ankles are slender and finely formed.

> Grace was in all her steps,
> Heav'n in her eye,
> In every gesture dignity and love.[6]

She is a *prince's daughter*. This evokes an atmosphere of royalty and nobility. We are under no obligation to take it literally, as some have, thinking her to be Pharaoh's daughter.

The NIV's *your graceful legs* is too general. The Hebrew is much more specific – 'your rounded thighs'. They are so exquisitely smoothly turned as if by a craftsman's skill, just as *jewels* are. The mention of *jewels* sends us careering up a blind alley. We are not to suppose that her attractive legs glitter and sparkle; rather, their smooth polished curves seem like the handiwork of a meticulous artisan. A woman's thighs may present a very alluring impression. A girl with her skirt tucked up, wading through water,

---

6 Milton, *Paradise Lost*, Book 8, line 488.

can be a rather sensuous picture; the roundness of her thighs is amplified by the concealment of the rest of her submerged legs.

Her *navel* has been the cause of much mirth. The word is usually translated as 'umbilical cord' or 'navel string' at Ezekiel 16:4. The only other occurrence of the word is at Proverbs 3:8 where it is translated as 'body' (NIV) in poetic parallelism with 'bones' ('health to your body and nourishment to your bones'). Here in the Song it would seem to have a much more specific location. The movement of description is upwards: thighs, navel, belly. It has been pointed out that some ancient Egyptian paintings of women emphasize the navel, so that it was considered an object of beauty by some ancient cultures. However, it seems that the Hebrew word is etymologically associated with the Arabic word meaning 'secret', so it is possible that the meaning refers to her secret part, her 'valley'. The *rounded goblet that never lacks blended wine* is an obvious reference to drinking, which we have already seen to be a metaphor for sexual activity. So the boy looks at her body and is filled rather naturally with erotic thoughts.

Her 'belly' (not *waist* as NIV) is *a mound of wheat*. The Hebrew word is normally translated as 'wombs', but here it is obviously something that is visible. Her stomach is gently curved (she is *not* pot-bellied) and of a tawny hue, inviting to his touch. Mounds of wheat on the threshing floor at harvest time may have been protected from straying livestock by an encircling thorn hedge. This may lead to the extension of the metaphor to the girl's lower abdomen, encircled by a garland of flowers hanging down from her hips, but it may possibly be a delicate reference to the secret garden of her 'valley'. *Lilies* are found in various contexts of intimacy in the Song (5:13; 6:3), and thus may give a hint of secret sources of pleasure.

Her *breasts are like two fawns*, highly tactile, inviting to the touch. Perhaps we should see pictures of shyness and gentleness here.

We have met the description of her *neck* as a *tower* before at 4:4, but this time the emphasis is not on the beauty of her beaded decorations, but rather on her stateliness. Her swept-up hair would reveal the stature of her 'smooth pale neck, erect, a tower of ivory tall' (see paraphrase).

The pools of Heshbon are not natural reservoirs; rather they are deep cisterns hewn out of solid rock. The images conjured up here are those of calmness, stillness, tranquillity, profundity. To gaze into a deep, clear pool is an invitation to contemplation, to immersion. The lover wants to penetrate the mysterious depths of his beloved's personality. *The gate of*

Bath Rabbim was presumably the name of the gate of the city of *Heshbon* nearest the cisterns. But there may be an oblique flashback to the *prince's daughter* (1) since *Bath Rabbim* means 'daughter of many' or 'daughter of noble people'.

Your nose is like the tower of Lebanon has been thought a bit of a joke. Has she really such a prominent *nose*? Is not the description just too grotesque? Perhaps the seeming initial harshness can be alleviated by realizing that in comparison with other metaphors describing other parts of her body, the *nose* is not at all out of proportion. Her *neck* is *an ivory tower*, her head is like *Mount Carmel*, her *eyes* are huge cisterns. Elsewhere (2:17) her breasts are mountains and hills. But we are not looking at some female giant. We would be nearer the mark by realizing that the link is linguistic and not visual; for the Hebrew root *lābēn* means 'to be white', and from this root are derived the words *Lebanon* and *lĕbônâ* (meaning frankincense). So her *nose* may be straight like the *tower of Lebanon*, but it also may be pale and fragrant. I have paraphrased it thus:

> Your nose, its bridge a ridge so straight,
> so white and fragrant as
> the distant mountain ranges.

This is rather different from the imagery of Tennyson:

> And lightly was her slender nose
> Tip-tilted like the petal of a flower.[7]

Her whole aspect is crowned by her glorious face and head, as majestic as the huge promontory of *Mount Carmel*, jutting out by the Mediterranean Sea. It is also possible that Carmel brings to mind the Hebrew *karmîl*, meaning 'crimson', in poetic parallelism with 'purple' in the second half of verse 5 (see the literal translation). It can be paraphrased as follows:

> Your flowing locks, so black,
> with purple sheen and oily lustre
> gleam. A royal queen!

---

[7] Tennyson, 'Gareth and Lynette', line 577.

The king is held captive by its tresses is playfully humorous. Imagine a mighty potentate reduced to abject slavery and weakness by a woman's beautiful hair! I have tried to put something of this idea in the paraphrase:

How are the mighty fallen!
My fearsome warrior king
brought low, hemmed in,
entrapped by trailing tresses.
By maiden's hair ensnared,
made captive by her locks.

The reference is to *a* king, not *the* king as NIV. The royal motif is carried right through to this last verse. In previous times the mighty rulers Samson (Judg. 16:13) and Absalom (2 Sam. 14:26; 18:9) were ensnared by their own locks. Here the downfall of the boy in the guise of a king is brought about by the locks of a simple beautiful maiden!

The captivating allure of a woman's hair is a common theme in the literature of love. Listen to Alexander Pope:

Fair tresses man's imperial race ensnare,
and beauty draws us with a single hair.

And Thomas Carew:

Those curious locks so aptly twin'd,
Whose every hair a soul doth bind.

This is probably the most sensual portrayal of the girl in the Song. The mental images evoked by the verbal descriptions of the poem depend not only on our ability to filter out the redundancies of the overweighted metaphors, but also on our own culturally determined criteria of beauty. Western European beauties tend to be severe, slim and unsmiling, so delicate that they might be blown away like twigs in the breeze. Other cultures like their women to be more fleshed out. The wall paintings of ancient Egypt portray their women as very slim and scantily dressed. These stand in stark contrast to the buxom roly-poly nudes of the medieval Renaissance period of European art. It is more than ever clear that beauty is in the eye of the beholder.

Our images of beauty are nearly always idealizations, somewhat distanced from the actual harsh realities. For example, the naked girl posing in front of a class of art students will often present a pathetic, vulnerable figure. But this will all disappear in the artist's portrayal. All blemishes will be erased, all wrinkles smoothed out. We see what we want to see, not what is actually there. We filter out that which inconveniently obtrudes. The same happens in photography, as well as in drawings and paintings. There is always some distancing from reality in the photos of the beauties in the glossy fashion magazines. The tricks of angled illumination, of tinting and shading, all create an atmosphere of fantasy. But this is the goal of all art forms: to soften the harsh realities of the life we live and to project us into a safer, more secure world of escape.

But however coolly seductive the artificially created images of beauty in various art forms may be, they are totally eclipsed by the warm pulsating reality of beauty in the flesh. And our lover, confronted with the radiance of his beloved, can only cry out in ecstasy and extol her beauty in the verses which follow.

7. A duet of desire (7:6–10)

The boy's poem of praise quickly arouses his desire for complete union with his beloved, and she is equally ready to reciprocate. The tempo seems to quicken throughout these verses, leading to the girl's invitation to him in 7:11–13 to make love in the countryside, and concluding with perhaps an imagined act of union at 8:3.

With the slightest of emendations 7:6b can be made to read, 'O love, daughter of delights.' The *delights*, or 'exquisite things', to which the boy is referring may very well be both general and specific, just as we say that a girl is charming and also that she possesses 'charms'. Her whole appearance, her *stature*, he likens to a tall, stately *palm* tree with leafy fronds sprouting from its top. There is some debate whether the word *sansinnîm* means leafy fronds or clusters of dates. Her *breasts* are twice described as *clusters* of the vine, and this metaphor is mixed in with the imagery of the *palm* tree. But does he seize her dates, or her fronds? It hardly matters. Here is the violent urgency of aroused desire. It is not a male chauvinistic triumphalism. He articulates (*I said . . .*) a passionate intention to climb the tree; this is his 'conquest'. But it is a willing and eager surrender on the part of the girl. Her *breasts* are taut and juicy, grapes ready to be plucked, the object of great desire. *The fragrance* of her nose is *like apples* (or apricots). The NIV translates the Hebrew *'ap* as *breath*. The word normally means 'nose' or 'nostrils', and by extension, flaring anger, a heavy snorting through flared nostrils. Nose-kissing may have been part of love-making practised by the couples of ancient Israel. Some commentators have sought to get rid of the troublesome nose by interpreting *'ap* as nipple or, as Pope says, 'some more distinctly feminine zone'.[8] The taste of her *mouth* is like the *best* vintage *wine*. They taste each other in their deep intimate kissing. At 7:9 it seems that the girl takes up the refrain of wine introduced by the boy and she responds, *May the wine go straight to my beloved*. The latter can only refer to the boy. The NIV's *go straight* we have met before in 1:4; the meaning is probably something like 'flowing smoothly'. The NIV's *lips and teeth* assume a slight emendation of the Hebrew 'lips of sleepers'. Another very minor emendation yields 'scarlet lips'. Whatever the precise meaning, the picture is of smooth, silky, erotic kissing.

In verse 10a the girl reaffirms that she is her beloved's. She gives herself to him eagerly, willingly and with gladness. She is aware of her own attractiveness in his sight; she is the object of his desire. The word translated *desire* occurs elsewhere in the Old Testament only in Genesis 3:16 and 4:7: 'Your desire will be for your husband, and he will rule over you'; 'Sin is crouching at your door; it desires to have you.' In our present context, the word has a strongly sexual element. Here it is the boy's strong desire for his beloved. In Genesis 3:16 it is the woman's desire for her husband. In the Genesis context, the word has been much debated. Some have hotly disputed the sexual element and the suggestion has been made that the woman's desire is actually to dominate her husband, as sin's urge is to dominate Cain in Genesis 4:7. So then the result of the fall is the disruption of mutual complementarity into a desire for mutual domination, the one over the other. Be that as it may, our lovers here in the Song are not trying to dominate each other. She is giving herself to him as his willing partner or opposite number (Gen. 2:18). If the language of the boy seems domineering, that is only because of the strong natural urge for fulfilment once desire has been aroused. The urge for consummation is violent for both the girl and the boy.

---

[8] Pope, p. 636.

The imagery of the vine with its clusters is used by Milton to portray the union of man and wife in marriage:

> . . . Or they led the vine
> To wed her Elm; she spoused about him twines
> Her marriageable arms, and with her brings
> Her dow'r th'adopted clusters, to adorn
> His barren leaves.[9]

8. Love in the countryside (7:11–13)

The girl wants now to do something about their mutually aroused desire and erotic excitement. It would appear that the lovers in these verses are not yet married, since the reason for their adventurous escapade into the countryside is presumably because they could not be alone together in any other place. If they were already married, there would be no need for this. But perhaps it is all a flight of fancy on the girl's part, an expression of her deepest yearnings. Here the girl is taking the initiative, she makes the invitation, she makes the promise to give him her love in the countryside. Again the theme is love in the open country (literally, in the Hebrew, 'field'). She is inviting him to spend the night in the *kĕpārîm* with her. This can mean either *villages* or 'henna bushes'. It is most likely that the latter is the meaning here. They want to be far away from human habitations, they are seeking the solitude of the rustic bower. They are to go on a tour of inspection of the springtime, to see whether *the vines have budded* and *the pomegranates are in bloom*. There, in the *early* morning, in the fragrance of the misty countryside, among the blossom and budding fruit, she will give herself totally and unreservedly to her beloved. We have met this theme of love in the countryside before (2:8–13). The whole of nature seems to be sprouting and blossoming, and the two lovers want to be part of that. Their love has blossomed and become fragrant; they are ripe for love. Love in the springtime is a common literary motif. It seems to suggest that powers and urges that have long lain dormant can now burst forth unhindered and without restraint. The imagery seems to indicate that there is a time and a season for everything. There were times when restraint was necessary, but now it is a time to embrace (Eccl. 3:1, 5).

---

[9] Milton, *Paradise Lost*, Book 5, line 215.

Romance in the great outdoors is also a picture of untrammelled freedom and of closeness to nature. The literary fiction reminds us of our creatureliness and of our unashamed delight in participating in the natural order of things. Of course, the fantasy of the lovers' love-making is an illusion, which must not be punctured by a crudely literal interpretation, where all such romantic notions are too rapidly frustrated by the intrusions of nettle rash, soldier ants, bumble bees and stony ground, to say nothing of ragged urchins peeping through the undergrowth. The fertility and reproductive aspects of springtime do not surface at all in the Song in any explicit way. The mention of *mandrakes* in 7:13 is not part of this motif of spring, and in any case it is their property as a sexual stimulant that is in view here, and not their aid to reproduction.

Verse 13 seems to describe the very heights of fevered anticipation and stimulation. The girl hardly seems to be in need of the mandrakes[10] as an aphrodisiac. It would appear that she is already aroused to a very high pitch of excitement. The tangential mention of the *mandrakes* is a literary device to give a sexual frisson to the poetry. They are mentioned in Genesis 30:14–16 where Rachel and Leah, the rival wives, are competing to produce offspring for Jacob.

Many have tried to envisage a scenario for the *door* over which there is *stored up* every kind of rare fruit, delicacies old and new. But surely we are not meant to take it all literally. She has reserved herself exclusively for her lover. She has often dreamed of the moments of intimacy and rehearsed them in her mind. But it is not just a dull routine. Together, they explore new ways of stimulating and pleasing each other in their physical relationship. I have tried to express some of this in the paraphrase:

> With ardour's pent-up passions,
> by ancient roots aroused,
> with eager love I'll give myself,
> I'll share with you my secret store
> in awe and expectation held and hallowed long,
> a den of new delights;
> the novelties of love, its ancient paths as well,
> are at our door, and trembling entering in,

---

[10] The Hebrew for the word *mandrakes* is etymologically related to the word *dōdîm* ('love, caresses') encountered earlier in the Song (1:2).

we shall explore
the intimacies of love.

The girl in these verses is again taking the initiative in furthering the progress of their love life. She is being very suggestive and seductive. She cannot wait for her lover to make the next approach, and so prepares a feast for him. No Lady Hillingdon this, suffering in ungracious passivity! Supremely confident of her capacity to satisfy him, she articulates all the delights she has in store for him, and describes the circumstances in which she will give him her love. This kind of advance planning must drive her lover wild with frenzied anticipation. Such psychological ploys are part of the game of love. She is creating a mental and physical environment in which their union may be consummated with the maximum intensity and minimum of inhibition. She even hints that she is able to teach him a thing or two. All is fair play in the desire for a happy release of sexual tension.

So what has this to teach us today? Perhaps it may act as a stimulus to revive a flagging physical relationship by being more adventurous, more romantic and less mechanical. Manuals of technique can give the mechanics. But the human dynamics, the relaxed, playful fun of un-inhibited romping with each other, are the essential ingredients. How we overcome our inhibitions is for us as couples to work out. How to articulate our desires verbally is yet another matter. We cannot all be acrobatic nymphs, and not all our fantasies may be realizable. But what really matters is that it is her or him that we are concerned for in our mutual enjoyment, and not just 'it'. If the sparks fly and the earth moves, then well and good. If they don't, the tension may be released by dissolving into laughter. For even some of the most carefully laid plans designed to lead to the giddy heights may on occasion fall flat. Of course, we should try again and be more relaxed about the whole thing, breaking up dull routines with spontaneous outbursts of tenderness. So shall we make room for the serendipitous enjoyment of our whimsical passions.

9. A longing for intimacy (8:1–4)

We do not know whether the girl's invitation in 7:11–13 has been taken up or not. However, the language is so graphic that we see ourselves with her in spirit. But perhaps it is all in the future. These verses too in 8:1–4 express a longing for intimacy that does not yet seem fulfilled. *If only . . . if I found you . . . I would kiss you . . . I would lead you . . . bring you . . . give you . . .* The girl has probably worked herself up into a frenzy of desire, so that she imagines she is lying with him (8:3) in fond embrace. Again her fantasies and dreamings have run far ahead of any possibility of fulfilment. So she cries out to the *daughters of Jerusalem*, her alter ego, her conscience, not to get her aroused before there is adequate and appropriate opportunity for the consummation of their love. It is with this (supposedly) imagined scene of intimacy that the curtain falls on the fifth cycle.

The lovers so far in this particular sequence have had very much a private relationship. Her beauty has been publicly acclaimed by queens and concubines, but their relationship is still secret. They long to get away from the prying eyes of curious onlookers and to fulfil their love in the remote countryside. It is most likely that in this cycle of poems, the lovers are neither betrothed nor married. Their behaviour in the last unit (7:11–13) is hardly characteristic of an engaged or newly-wed couple. Although their love is very private, they long for public recognition of their relationship. They want all the world to know that they are in love. This is a theme that recurs in 8:5–6 in the next cycle. Yet paradoxically, she longs that he might be as *a brother* to her, in order that she might be more than a sister to him. She wants their intimacy to be seen and demonstrated publicly. The reason behind her strange request is that a brother and sister could openly display affection towards each other without public social disapproval, whereas if they were already married, such public intimacy would be frowned upon. However, the girl has not shown any concern for public approval or disapproval of her behaviour in previous cases where she might have been concerned about it (i.e. dashing out into the city squares alone, late at night, and spending the night together among the henna bushes). Also we cannot be certain as to the social mores of the time. In Genesis 26:8 Abimelek 'looked down from a window and saw Isaac caressing his wife Rebekah'. Our ignorance of the particular circumstances of this public display of marital affection make it difficult for us to draw any general conclusions. Social mores in the area of what is acceptable public behaviour between the sexes are very much a matter of cultural preference and convention. For example, in many Western countries, romantic kissing and fondling in public is becoming the norm, whereas in more conservative non-Western countries, even holding hands in public is frowned upon. In conservative Islamic nations there is often no public social intercourse between the sexes. In Palestine at the time of Jesus, in the traditional Jewish society of the day, public interaction between unacquainted members of the opposite sex was not considered proper. (See how Jesus broke this taboo when talking to the Samaritan woman at Jacob's Well; John 4:27.) In African countries, young men may often be seen walking hand in hand down the street; this perfectly acceptable behaviour sends all sorts of wrong signals to a Western observer. Similarly, the degree of public exposure of the naked body is often a sensitive issue. Customs vary from almost total exposure to almost total covering.

The girl's yearning for a public recognition of their love (1) very quickly leads on to a desire for intimacy in private (2). The movement through verses 2–3 is one of increasing intimacy. Again the initiative is with the girl: *I would lead you . . . I would give you . . .* We have met 'the house of my mother' before at 3:4, where it is further elaborated as (lit.) 'the chamber of her who conceived me'. A literal *mother's house* is hardly an appropriate venue for courtship or love-making, for which privacy and seclusion are needed. For, in her *mother's house*, the boy has to be on his best behaviour; he is being inspected to see if he meets with her approval. But the boy must find this atmosphere rather suffocating and inhibiting, even irritating and frustrating. For it acts as a brake to his amorous intentions. And yet it does actually encourage the polite and less intimate conventions of social intercourse. It may even enable the two lovebirds to see each other in a slightly different light. For it is all too easy for them to be so self-absorbed and engrossed in each other that they fail to see how they behave before friends, relatives and more distant acquaintances. The intensity of their amorous relationship needs to be diluted by the conventions of the normal social round. However, as previously, I take 'the house of my mother' to mean the place where motherhood originates, that is, the womb. That is the intimate place to which she wants to bring her lover.

The next phrase is ambiguous (8:2). The syntax as well as the verbal form is awkward. The NIV introduces the relative pronoun *who* which is absent in the Hebrew. It could mean either 'you [masculine singular] would teach me' or 'she would teach me'. It is very problematical. Who would teach the girl what and in what context? If it is the mother, then she would be teaching her daughter the ways of public behaviour between an unmarried pair of lovers. It hardly seems likely that the mother would be teaching her daughter the facts of life, for she seems to be so very experienced already. If it is the boy, then he would be instructing the girl in the delicate techniques of love. But does she need such instruction? For she has already promised that she would bring to her lover's door all sorts of delicacies, new things as well as old (7:13). Since both of these contexts seem somewhat forced, perhaps the best expedient is to realize that the troublesome *tĕlammĕdēnî* can easily revert to *tĕladēnî* by the dropping of the 'm', thus meaning, 'she gave me birth'. This emendation is not an arbitrary alteration, for it does in fact bring the thought into line with the other references to the mother or mother's house, which are elaborated with the phrase 'she conceived me' (or 'she bore me') at 3:4; 6:9; and 8:5.

The girl, in bringing her lover to 'the house of my mother', also wishes to give him some exotic, heady *spiced wine* and the pressed-out juice from her *pomegranates*. We have already seen the close association with wine and kissing in the Song at 1:2. *I would kiss you* (8:1) and *I would give you . . . to drink* (2) are almost identical in sound in the Hebrew. The unit as a whole is held together by other examples of assonance. *Pomegranate* (*rimmōnî*) and *right* [*hand*] (*wîmînô*) have similar sounds, as also do *under* (*taḥat*) and *spiced wine* (*hāreqaḥ*).

So the girl has now dreamed herself up into a passionate embrace with her lover (3) and she makes her now customary appeal to the *daughters of Jerusalem* (4). But this time there are two slight variations. First, she does not invoke the gazelles or does of the field, as previously in 2:7 and 3:5. Second, the literal translation of the Hebrew reads 'How' or 'Why will you excite love . . . ?' There is linguistic evidence that the Hebrew *mah* can mean 'not', thus bringing the phrase into line with the other adjurations. Davidson, taking the word 'excite' to mean 'disturb', suggests that since the girl has now publicly brought her boy home and their relationship is there for all to see, she is defiantly challenging anyone to hold them apart and interfere with the consummation of their love-making.

The whole unit of 8:1–4 is somewhat ambiguous. At the surface level, there is a strong movement from the public social realm to the privacy of loving intimacy. Yet hovering in the background are her *mother*, a *brother* and the *daughters of Jerusalem*. These public figures seem to act as a brake on the amorous activities of the young lovers, so they are in constant tension. They want to be free of the restraints of society, yet they want to possess that public recognition of their love. It is like driving a car with the brakes on; a lot of unproductive heat is generated. The solution to this impasse is either to step off the accelerator and allow things to cool down (*do not arouse . . . love . . .*), or else to be recognized publicly, then take off the brakes and forge ahead. Such public recognition by society is a valuable cement. The marriage certificate is not 'just a piece of paper' which transforms an immoral cohabitation into an acceptable relationship. It is a public exchange of vows that the couple will support and edify each other 'for better, for worse, in sickness and in health, till death us do part'.

Song of Songs 8:5–14

10. The sixth cycle: the security of love

1. The happy couple (8:5a)

The previous cycle ended with the familiar adjuration to the daughters of Jerusalem, providing a clear break at 8:4. This final cycle begins, as did the third cycle at 3:6, with an exclamatory cry of admiration. It continues with the theme of arousal, followed by the yearning for public affirmation (8:6). Then follows the great hymn of love (8:6–7) which closes with the thought that love cannot be bought with money. 8:8–10 introduces the theme of the little sister, to whom our girl compares herself in 8:10. The theme of love-not-for-hire is reintroduced in 8:11–12, and the cycle closes with the two rather enigmatic verses, 8:13–14.

Of all the six cycles of poems in the Song, this final cycle is the most difficult in which to identify a coherent progression of theme; so much so that many commentators view 8:5–14 as a series of unrelated appendices of isolated fragments. R. E. Murphy writes, 'If the word "anthology" is used for any part of the work, it is particularly suitable for 8:5–14.'[1] If that is the case, the main Song ends at 8:4. This has the advantage of making the cycle 3:6 – 5:1 the centre of a five-cycle Song. This centre contains the most explicit reference to consummation, within the context of an assumed marriage. However, as has already been pointed out, 5:1 represents the exact centre of the whole poem (chapters 1–8) on a line count. So it is probably best to include 8:5–14 within the main Song. All the participants in the Song reappear here: the companions, the brothers, King Solomon, the mother, the two lovers. As R. Davidson writes,

---

[1] Murphy, p. 195.

We are witnessing something like the curtain call at the end of a play or musical. One by one the leading characters come forward, take a bow, and through a characteristic action or by a few well chosen words, recall what has gone before.[2]

The rhetorical question of 8:5 is really an exclamation: 'Look who's coming up . . .!' We already know who it is. The girl is appearing from the freedom of the open countryside, *coming up* (possibly to Jerusalem), proudly displaying her beloved on her arm. She wants the approval of civilized society for their match. She is thrilled, yet slightly apprehensive, for she is eager for their blessing. She is bringing him 'home', wherever that might be, for public inspection. The girl is *leaning on her beloved*. This may indicate a sense of dependence, in that he is a tower of strength to her. More likely it conveys a sense of possession. 'I want you to know that this is the one who is mine, whom I have chosen.' We should notice that the focus of attention in this verse is the girl, not her lover. The boy here seems to be a rather shadowy appendage.

Of course, we do not know exactly how the girl will respond to the comments of her brothers, friends, onlookers and mother. But we have seen that she is a girl of spirit, and is sure of her own mind. So it seems likely that she would be influenced only marginally by their opinions. If adverse comment were forthcoming, her reaction would most likely be one of defiant independence, and of petulant defence. Surely she is old enough now to look after herself and form her own mind and choose her own pathway? She wants to break free from the constraining ties of family and friends, and wants to launch out on her own voyage of discovery with her chosen lover. For this is no arranged marriage, but rather a love match. And love is usually very impatient with the rumbling of old greyheads. We hear their questions: Whose son is he? What clan is he from? How many cows and servants has the family? What are his prospects? All questions arising from the corporate solidarity of the society of which they are an integral part. The lovers' own feelings towards each other are irrelevant, as also are their individual identities and desires. The question is, will their union cement the relationships of family, clan and tribe? Or will it be a source of contentious rivalry, condemning their lives to perpetual animosity? Their questions have their modern-day equivalent: What kind

---

[2] Davidson, p. 151.

of degree has he got? What are his career prospects? Does he stand to inherit a fortune? Does he own property, and a good car? How does his bank balance stand? True love can brave the disapproval of those whose criteria are not met. But equally, the beginnings of love can be polluted by consideration of the worldly standards imposed by society.

This verse is concerned with whether the boy receives the approval of society when the girl presents him publicly. But there is also the opposite consideration to take into account. Will the girl herself meet the approval of society? One portrayal of the ideal wife is found in Proverbs 31:10–31. Doubtless this is couched in very patriarchal terms. She is praised primarily because of her power to enhance the reputation of her husband. She is of noble character, and her husband has full confidence in her. She brings him good and not harm. She is a merchant, a trader, a tireless businesswoman. She looks after her family, instructs her children with 'wisdom', and is generous to the poor. 'Her husband is respected at the city gate, where he takes his seat among the elders of the land', because of her. She gets up before first light, manages her household affairs well, and 'does not eat the bread of idleness'. Her husband praises her: 'Many women do noble things, but you surpass them all.' 'Charm is deceptive, and beauty is fleeting; but a woman who fears the Lord is to be praised.' While many of these values may be culturally nuanced, similar questions are asked today by prospective in-laws hovering around. Will she be a good mother? Is she too bossy? Will she be able to look after my son? Is she a practical manager of affairs? How much is she a career woman? Will she be good for him?

We may well ask ourselves these questions of our potential partners. But they are not likely to be the most pressing ones. For the questions which affect us most deeply are the ones which society does not impose upon us. We are much more likely to be concerned with matters of temperament, of the personal chemistry of interaction, of mutual interests which draw together, of mutual goals and aspirations. We all laugh at the couple who were drawn together by their common love for horses; for we ask the question, surely there must be a more durable cement to a relationship than love for racing thoroughbreds? Of course, common interests are essential. But there must be room for the development of divergent interests. In our modern generation, we are dominated by the question of mutual compatibility. This has had a deleterious effect on our attitudes in entering a relationship. Trial marriages, cohabiting, easy divorces, all stem predominantly from dilution of the determination and willingness to make a relationship work right from the beginning. Arranged marriages were and are often successful. Not that there is any suggestion that these should be the norm. But at least in these there is the constraint that society imposes on them of the expectation that they should work. They may start off cold, but the warmth of romance may blossom as the relationship of the couple grows with their determination to make a go of it.

Of course, we may choose our partners for many differing sets of reasons. And it is important that we should be conscious of some of them. Our partners may be exact opposites of ourselves temperamentally. We may choose to be attracted by them, to counterbalance our own temperaments. For example, a quiet person may feel the need to be stimulated by a noisy extrovert. The happy socialite may be challenged to think more deeply by a thoughtful reflective partner. We may choose a partner in order to dominate him or her, or be dominated by him or her. We may wish to manipulate, or simply to serve. We may wish to mother and smother, or simply to be pampered. It would be good if we were able to clarify our own expectations in these matters before choosing a spouse. For we may be influenced by considerations which are often subconscious. We may choose partners who are as like or as unlike our parents, depending on what kind of relationship we had with them. The role models (or anti-models) of our parents often deeply influence us in our choices.

We have all along in our exposition been assuming that our lovers are possessed by a love which may be described by the adjective 'romantic', and that this is a worthy and honourable state in which to find oneself. But not every age and not every culture has assumed this to be so. Listen to the Rev. George Whitefield, writing a letter of proposal to an eligible young lady in mid-eighteenth-century England: 'For I bless God I am free from that foolish passion which the world calls love.' (The fact that his proposal was turned down was nothing to do with his rejection of the romantic view of marriage.) His own view of love led him to perceive marriage as an exalted spiritual vocation, where physical and romantic attraction were considered to be an irrelevance as a solid foundation for a stable relationship. To the minds of modern Western culture, marriages of convenience and arranged marriages are considered to be a fundamental denial of the individual's rights of freedom of choice and freedom of self-fulfilment. In other cultures, the right of society to cement relationships between family, clans or tribes by means of arranged marriages is seen to override any priorities which an individual may have. There is very strong pressure from society to make such an arrangement work, far more so than in the cases of 'romantic' Western-type unions. The marriage has been made, and it must work.

In the culture of the ancient Hebrews, we hear of a number of arranged marriages. Abraham sent his aged retainer back to Haran to find a wife for his son, Isaac, from among his own clan (Gen. 24:1–67). Solomon concluded a political and trading alliance with Egypt by marrying the daughter of the pharaoh (1 Kgs 3:1). Naomi schemed to get her widowed daughter-in-law hitched up to the eligible Boaz (Ruth 3:1–2). Samson, outrageously choosing a Philistine bride, had to twist his parents' arm to initiate the marriage negotiations (Judg. 14:1–3). It seems that even Yahweh, the covenant God of Israel, was in the business of arranging marriages, for his command to Hosea to marry Gomer, a woman of dubious moral character, was hardly, by any stretch of the imagination, a love match (Hos. 1:2–3). However, we do have a number of occasions when romantic love is implied. Jacob was in love with Rachel, but he had to serve Laban seven years for her; however, 'they seemed like only a few days to him because of his love for her' (Gen. 29:20). Abimelek, king of the Philistines, spied Isaac caressing his wife Rebekah, a sure sign of romantic affection (Gen. 26:8). Michal, the daughter of Saul, was in love with David, an occasion which the king used to his own advantage against David (1 Sam. 18:20–21). When David had later dealt with Nabal, he sent word to Abigail, asking her to become his wife. He surely must have been stirred in his heart concerning her, at the same time recognizing in her a very strong and sensible woman. However, Abigail's response was more conventional: 'I am your servant and am ready to serve you and wash the feet of my lord's servants' (1 Sam. 25:41; see 25:39–41).

So, even in a severely patriarchal age, romantic love keeps breaking through. Yet the practical necessity for security in a harsh subsistence economy led to a view of marriage which put the claims of survival at a higher level than romantic attachment. This was hardly a devaluation of romance, but a pragmatic facing of practical realities. And it was the pressure of those realities which acted as the impetus to make the marriage work. Our present-day society has perhaps an exaggerated view of the importance of romantic love. It becomes the touchstone for the survival of a relationship. But as we have seen, romance comes and goes and comes again; it is a delicate plant that needs to be sensitively nurtured;

a flickering flame that constantly needs to be fuelled. The will to refuel and nurture is the true love that makes for survival. We need to fan the flames by little acts of kindness, springing thoughtful surprises that break the patterns of dull routine.

2. Love's arousal (8:5b)

This verse rivals 6:12 in obscurity. A number of its words and themes have appeared elsewhere in the Song: *the apple tree* (2:3, 5), 'awakening' (NIV, *roused*; 2:7; 3:5; 4:16; 8:4), *mother* (as conceiver; 3:4; 8:2[?]). These themes coalesce in this verse, but it is difficult to unravel the sense. There is no clearly defined context, except perhaps that of public approval of their union. Perhaps 8:6 speaks of security, the desire for a public seal; 8:5 also speaks of a desire for public approval. There may be the slightest of hints here that public approval of their relationship depends on their obligations to society (the family, the clan) to reproduce and provide for the continuity of the generations. This is a very tentative proposal. While in Old Testament times it was of the utmost importance for a marriage to produce offspring (particularly males), to carry on the name of the father's house, in the Song itself there seems to be virtually no interest in procreation, children and fertility. In ancient Israel, as in many countries today, the family, the clan, the tribe, were more important than the particular individual. In modern Western society, we find this difficult to comprehend, with our strong emphasis on the individual (individual rights, individual freedoms, individual self-expression and self-fulfilment). But in the majority of cultures, the individual is subservient to the society. The individual's identity is defined by his or her place in society. When Boaz enquired of the overseer of the harvesters about the identity of the young woman gleaning in his fields, he asked the question, 'Who does that young woman belong to?' In other words, he was seeking to locate the identity of Ruth in the wider context of her immediate family, whether brothers, father or husband. Her real identity was defined in terms of her family relationships. She was not a solitary individual in her own right (Ruth 2:5). Similarly, in modern Africa, as John Mbiti said, 'I am, because we are.' So it is possible that our young couple (or perhaps the author of the Song) are seeing their union, particularly their sexual union, as their contribution to that primal urge to maintain and regenerate society. They are re-enacting the conception and travail of their mothers. It looks backwards through their mothers to generations gone by. The future is made secure by their own participation in this act of union. They are expressing solidarity with the generations past and the generations yet to come. They see themselves participating in the flow of history, a history which is so importantly catalogued in the endless genealogies of the Old Testament. I have tried to convey something of this in the paraphrase:

> Underneath the fruit tree's bowers,
> heavy, ripe with golden showers,
> 'neath the shades of family tree,
> branches of maternal pedigree,
> there I stirred your sleeping form,
> where your mother brought new birth
> in agony of ecstasy writhing.

The verse is spoken by the girl. Her beloved is *under the apple tree* asleep. And she takes the initiative to wake him up. In 2:3 it was the girl herself who was lying in the shade of the fruit tree, a symbol of her beloved. Here, the tree probably represents an erotic symbol of fertility. There are indications from pagan mythology that the gods gave birth under an apple tree. Some commentators have seen in this verse a reference to previous escapades of the lovers to make love in the countryside, but it is much more likely that the verse is a literary device, representing the lovers' solidarity with the past and the future. Again, we have the problem of whether arousal means sexual awakening, or arousal from sleep. The repeated emphatic *there* presumably means 'underneath the apple tree', which is where the boy's mother conceived him. If the boy's mother had made love in the countryside, so also may the son, with his own beloved, reproduce the act in which he himself was *conceived*. The word translated as *conceived* may equally well be translated as 'writhed in the birth pangs'. The imagery of giving birth under the tree is somewhat grotesque. Perhaps the act in which conception occurs is seen as one involving an agony of ecstasy, an almost delirious state of exquisite pain. However, the metaphors in this verse appear to be very fluid, and perhaps it would be wiser not to insist on any specific concrete reality underlying the overall meaning, the picture being wholly symbolic.

Another possible slant on this verse may arise from a consideration of a superstition prevalent in the ancient world. Some people believed that the actual location at which copulation occurred determined the charac-teristics of the offspring conceived. Thus, in Genesis 30:31–43, where Jacob was trying to outwit Laban by selectively breeding a strong strain of sheep and goats, he not only segregated the stronger from the weaker breeding animals, but also made the sheep mate in front of peeled branches of trees, thus causing the offspring so conceived to be striped. Whatever we may think of this ancient superstition, it is possible that it may have some relevance to these verses. The boy himself was conceived underneath the apple tree, and thus was considered to bear some of its characteristics. Just like the apple tree, he offers shady protection, and is himself a bearer of refreshing tasty fruit.

If we are correct in recognizing in these verses reference to the con-tinuity of the species over the generations, we must beware of thinking that our lovers are coupling with that primary intention consciously in mind. Here, as before, the literary motif is at variance with the reality. For few real lovers would ever describe their act of union primarily as a means of reproduction. For then, the deed would become a merely mechanical act of procreation. While the sexual instinct that is so strong and urgent gives rise to the propagation of the species, it is surely more than an expedient for the survival of the human race. Emerson has written: 'The preservation of the species was a point of such necessity that Nature has secured it at all hazards by immensely overloading the passion, at the risk of perpetual crime and disorder.' But the non-seasonal nature of our human mating-urges may perhaps suggest that more than reproduction is in view. For the giving and receiving of sexual pleasure is one of the several means of binding and strengthening an ever-growing relationship of love. Indeed, in the Garden of Eden account of the creation of man and woman, the emphasis lies squarely on the mutual companionship of the couple. There is no mention of offspring as the intention or result of the one-flesh relationship. The complementarity of the pair is com-plete in the dual relationship alone. It would appear that in Genesis 1 the issue of fruitfulness is relegated to the status of an extra blessing/commandment, *after* the creation of the sexual pair (Gen. 1:28).

Of course, in the Old Testament the gift of children was considered to be one of the outstanding blessings of God (Pss 127:3–5; 128:3; Prov. 17:6), and it was an essential part of the fulfilment of the promises to the patriarchs (Gen. 15:5; 22:17; 26:4). So barrenness and infertility were matters of great individual and social concern (Gen. 16:2; 30:2; 1 Sam. 1:5).

It is in the light of this theological and communal background that the Old Testament nearly always describes the sexual act as issuing in conception. But the procreation aspect of the act is only a by-product of its primary recreational function. With this in mind, we should cast aside any hesitations about the use of contraceptives in planned parenthood within marriage. Since the act itself should be a means of pleasurable mutual self-giving and bonding, its primary benefits will always be less than fully appropriated if there is always in the background the fear of an unwanted pregnancy. So we should not think that the use of contraceptives within the marriage relationship is somehow thwarting the primary purpose of the act. For this represents a distorted understanding of God's purposes for the husband–wife union, as revealed in the Bible.

It might be worth mentioning in this connection another type of misconception which the apostle Paul was counteracting in the Corinthian church (1 Cor. 7). It would appear that some of the Corinthian believers held an overspiritualized view of marriage, in which sexual intercourse was devalued and prolonged sexual abstinence in marriage was considered a virtue. However, there are some complex arguments involved in the interpretation of the Pauline correspondence here, and the issue is still the subject of much debate.[3]

3. Love, strong as death (8:6–7)

We have already suggested that the link between 8:5a, b and 8:6 is the theme of public approval of the lovers' union. For in 8:6 the girl, under the metaphor of the *seal*, is seen to be seeking the security of that public affirmation of their intimacy. The gender of the Hebrew suffixes makes it clear that it is the girl and not the boy who is speaking in 8:6 and following. But from line 3 of 8:6 to the end of 8:7 she seems to fade from view. It appears that here, the author of the poems is himself intruding into his own creation and meditating on the nature of love itself. No longer is it the particular love of our young lovers, but love in its most abstract guise.

This unit also introduces new themes which have not previously arisen in the Song: *death*, Sheol (*the grave*), *jealousy* and the *many waters*. There is a new element of hostility here, dangerous forces which threaten the

---

[3] G. Fee, *1 Corinthians* (New International Commentary on the New Testament, Eerdmans, 1987), pp. 266ff.

very existence of love. For many, this unit represents a high point in the Song. If 5:1 represents a climax in the lovers' physical relationship, then these verses represent a climax in praise of the unconquerability of love in the face of all its foes.

We need to look at the various aspects of this unit in detail before considering its more general implications for us. The girl is requesting that she might be placed *like a seal* over her beloved's *heart*, and *like a seal* on his *arm*. The *arm* here may be a poetic synonym for 'finger'. Hebrew poetry is somewhat imprecise in its use of anatomical terms (cf. 5:14: are his hands, or his arms, or his fingers, compared to cylinders of gold?). So rather than trying to imagine a bracelet on his *arm*, it is better to see a ring on his finger. There are a number of possible connotations of the *seal* which are applicable in this metaphorical usage. There is the idea of a publicly visible mark of identity or possession, peculiarly one's own. In former days in Europe it might have been one's own coat of arms or heraldic crest and motto. In the times of the Ancient Near East, it would have been a ring on the finger, as with Pharaoh's signet which he gave to Joseph (Gen. 41:42), or it may have been some sort of metal cylinder suspended round the neck of its wearer by a cord.[4] It may also bear the connotations of preciousness, for some seals in the ancient world were made of precious metals or gems with ornately carved inscriptions or decorations.[5]

The ideas of delegated authority (Pharaoh's ring) and of authentication[6] seem inappropriate in this context. The primary metaphorical usage here in the Song must be the indication of closeness and intimacy.[7] The girl wants to have such close access to her beloved that all the world will see that he has taken her into his confidence. She longs for their union to be more than one of physical closeness: a union that is secure and firm and indissoluble even when they are separated from each other. The seal could thus be interpreted as a keepsake or memento. But she herself is that seal, indelibly stamped upon his heart. She wants their union to be intimate (*over your heart*) and public (*on your arm*). In 8:5, she is leaning physically

---

[4] See Judah's seal, Gen. 38:18.

[5] See Hag. 2:23, 'I will take you, my servant Zerubbabel . . . and I will make you like my signet ring, for I have chosen you.'

[6] See Jeremiah's sealing of the property deeds, Jer. 32:10–11, and Jezebel's use of Ahab's seal to authenticate forged documents, 1 Kgs 21:8.

[7] See Jer. 22:24, 'Even if you, Jehoiachin . . . were a signet ring on my right hand, I would still pull you off.'

on his arm, but she wants to be securely impressed upon his heart. In an entirely different context, this link between symbol and intimacy is graphically illustrated in Deuteronomy 6:6, 8 where God's commandments are to be 'on your hearts . . . Tie them as symbols on your hands and bind them on your foreheads.' Perhaps the girl's urgent desire, *Place me like a seal . . .*, gives a slight hint of an element of insecurity on her part. She is not quite sure whether he will forget her when she is absent from him. That is why she wants to be emblazoned on his *heart*. She wants, perhaps not unreasonably, to be the very centre of his existence. For she knows without a shadow of doubt that he is the centre of her life. But is it true that *she* is the centre of *his* life? Perhaps she has a lingering doubt, for she needs constant reassurance and affirmation. She knows that she has already captured him (7:5, '[a] king . . . held captive by . . . tresses'), but will he escape? Will she lose him to someone or something else? Germaine de Staël said, 'Love is the whole history of a woman's life; it is but an episode in a man's.' This, as a generalization, probably polarizes too strongly the differences between the psychology of the male and the female. It is sometimes said that a woman is seldom at the centre of a man's life to the same degree as a man is to his beloved, and that she is but one aspect of his broad spectrum of interests. For a man may have his job, his hobbies, his club, his companions, as well as his wife. But it may just be the simple fact that a man may often compartmentalize his life so that he devotes his full attention to each of his interests in turn, and seldom allows one area to overlap with another; whereas for a woman her equally varied interests spill over and enrich one another, and her life becomes a more integrated whole. Thus her love relationship suffuses every part of her existence, whatever job, career or vocation she pursues.

Also it is the publicly recognized aspect of their relationship which brings added security. The social pressure of public recognition is an added stimulus to the determination to make their relationship work, even when external circumstances threaten to rend them asunder. An engagement ring or a wedding ring is more than a mere sign that some form of ceremony has been enacted. It is the significance of what lies behind the seal that is important. It is obviously the public sharing of private joy. But more profoundly, it is the public pledge of mutual vows, a pledge of willingness to work at their relationship, to persevere throughout all the ups and downs of life, that constitutes the solemnization of marriage.

It is this central theme of security that links the girl's words to her lover to the theme of the following lines, namely the strength and enduring nature of true love. In order to explore this theme more thoroughly, we need to enquire in some detail into the usage of the Hebrew word for love, 'āhab. This root, in its various forms, occurs in the Song some seventeen times. It is almost always used to describe the passionate ardour of the two lovers, who seem to inhabit the timelessness of eternal youth (for them it is always springtime). But here in these verses we have a more philosophical reflection on the nature of love. The word is used in a more general and abstract sense, apart from the actual experience of the two lovers. In the Old Testament, the Hebrew root 'āhab has a wide variety of meanings. It is used to describe the friendship and devotion that exists between members of the same sex – for example, between David and Jonathan (1 Sam. 18:1–3); Isaac and Esau (Gen. 25:28); Ruth and Naomi (Ruth 4:15). It is the common word used to describe the love of a married relationship – for example, that of Isaac and Rebekah (Gen. 24:67). The relationship between Yahweh and his covenant people is also described by this term (e.g. Deut. 10:15). It is used to describe relationships where the primary motivating force is physical desire – for example, Solomon loved many foreign women (1 Kgs 11:1); Amnon loved Tamar (2 Sam. 13:1); and Samson loved Delilah (Judg. 16:4, 15). So 'āhab is a general-purpose word.

Just because the one word can be used in a large variety of contexts does not mean that the Hebrews were incapable of making fine distinctions between various forms of love. The gracious covenant loyalty which Yahweh shows to (and expects from) his people is described by the Hebrew word ḥesed. Friendship, companionability, affection, even romantic love, are conveyed by the Hebrew root rāʿâ, which we have met before in 1:9 as 'my darling'. Bawdy, lascivious 'love songs' are mentioned in Ezekiel 33:32 using the root 'āgab, which means 'to lust after'. Psalm 45 is a wedding song, a song 'of loves', yĕdîdōt. The Septuagint (LXX; a pre-Christian Greek translation of the Hebrew Scriptures) generally used the verb agapaō and the noun agapē to translate the Hebrew root 'āhab. However, in the New Testament, the agapaō word group has come to bear predominantly the connotations of love that is modelled on the divine love, that is, a self-giving gift love that serves freely without expecting any reward, or without any consideration of the worthiness or otherwise of the recipient. The specifically sexual love, the erotic impulse that demands such urgent physical expression and fulfilment, is generally termed in

Greek literature as *erōs*, though it does sometimes bear the connotations of a more mystical desire. C. S. Lewis has written popularizing this distinction.[8] This differentiation is a useful categorization to make, but it can be pressed too far, and is probably a gross oversimplification. For it is somewhat theoretical and academic and does not take into account the complexity of human experience. For the antithesis of *agapē* and *erōs* depends on very precise definitions which do not do justice to the very mixed nature of human love. All this leads to the devaluation of *erōs* in comparison with *agapē*. For *erōs* is then always seen as appetitive and self-seeking, while *agapē* is the unselfish product of the will. As such the two are irreconcilable. *Erōs* on this view will always be on the lower moral plane, *agapē* on the higher. For *erōs* is instinctual, compulsive, uncontrollable, sensual, even irrational. It is part of our corporeal nature, a consequence of our nervous, biological, anatomical and psychological nature. But to reduce *erōs* to a mere necessary consequence of our bodily existence is to demean the body. We are caught once again in the trap of dividing ourselves up analytically into higher and lower natures, where the will, the mind and the spirit are set on a higher plane than the body, the emotions, desires and instincts. For even though some of our desires appear to be more closely associated with our physical and biological functions, that does not thereby require us to put a lower value on them.

It is essential to recognize that, in the fall of humanity, every faculty of a human being's existence has become disordered and contaminated through rebellion against the Creator. The mind, the will and the spirit have become blinded, enslaved and dead. Our bodily functions have become degenerate in their desires of greed and lust of various kinds. So in Christ, the whole person is brought into the sphere of redemption; therefore we must not seek to deny any part as a valid function in our redeemed lives.

So an action which gives pleasure to another is not to be devalued if that act is itself a source of pleasure to the donor. For mutual self-fulfilment is part of the pleasure of love. Yet this is not selfishness multiplied by two. For there will be many times in a relationship of love when giving pleasure to the other will be very costly to the partner. But of course, love is far more than giving pleasure. Our capacity for pleasure may diminish with increasing age, but love remains. The desire to see the other enriched, the

---

8 Lewis, *The Four Loves*, ch. 5.

loyalty that serves even should physical pleasures decrease, are part of an enduring selfless love which lasts to eternity (as in 1 Cor. 13:13).

Thus, the love in our Song is all-embracing. It embraces pleasure, it embraces pain. It is passionate, yet fearful. It possesses, yet lets go. It liberates, yet binds. It empowers, it weakens. It brings turmoil, it brings peace. It is solemn, yet playful. It is lofty in conception, yet earthy in expression. It is self-centred, it is totally other-centred. It gives, it receives. It longs to give pleasure, it hopes to receive pleasure. It is cautious and timorous, yet extravagant and brave. Such a union of opposites, such a conflicting array of incompatibles, alone can do justice to the immensely complex phenomenon of the love between a man and a woman. It transcends logic, rationality, definition and even sense. Yet this whole thing called love is there to be experienced in all its agony and ecstasy. It is this love about which our Song sings.

> For love is as strong as death,
>> its jealousy unyielding as the grave.

The lines are in synonymous parallelism. *Death* is paralleled by *the grave*, *love* by *jealousy*, *strong* by *unyielding*. Yet the two lines are not saying exactly the same thing. For the first line is much more violent than the second. *Death* is an active power, holding its victims in its irresistible sway, and none can escape. *Death* claims those under its power, and draws them into its grip. The strength of *love* is like the strength of *death*. Not that the two forces are here seen to be in conflict. There is no battle being waged. It is simply (at this stage) a comparison. *Love is as strong as death*. It is not the case here that love survives death, that love is stronger than death, but rather that love holds its victims under its sway in exactly the same way as death does. Once smitten, there is no escape. The process is one-way and irreversible. Love binds those under its sway with a permanent bond. Love, like death, is here almost personified: an external force which hunts, overpowers and masters its victims. And once smitten, the victim can never be the same again. The second line, in a literal translation from the Hebrew, reads: 'Jealousy unyielding as Sheol.'

The NIV translators have a stated policy[9] of translating the Hebrew word 'Sheol' by *the grave*. Their understanding of the contexts in which

---

[9] See R. Laird Harris, 'Why Hebrew "Sheol" Was Translated "Grave"', in *The NIV: The Making of a Contemporary Translation*, ed. Dr Kenneth Barker (Hodder & Stoughton, 1987, 1991).

the word occurs leads them to regard Sheol as nothing more than the literal grave, the place in which the corpse is sealed. However, most commentators regard Sheol as the realm of the dead, the subterranean netherworld, the general domain inhabited by the shades (the *rĕpâ'îm*). Because of the wide variety of contexts in which the word is used in the Old Testament, it is not easy to make accurate generalizations about its precise nature. It would appear that all men and women, both good and wicked, lived on in Sheol after death, in a dark phantom-like existence, in the lower parts of the cosmic ocean (Job 26:5), beneath the roots of the mountains (Jon. 2:6). It was a place where people lingered on, a 'land of oblivion' (Ps. 88:11–12), a place of solitude and isolation, the complete negation of life and wholeness, barely one step up from non-existence; where those who had toiled and laboured in this life found rest and ease (Job 3:17–19). Yet the domain of the sovereign power of God extended even over Sheol (Ps. 139:8), from whose power he would deliver the righteous, and vindicate them over the injustices they had suffered in this life (Pss 16:10; 86:13).

Sheol is sometimes characterized as a monster with an insatiable appetite, with a wide-open throat or gaping jaws (Prov. 1:12; 30:16; Isa. 5:14; Hab. 2:5). Its throat is a one-way channel, its hunger is never assuaged. Such is the *jealousy* of love. It is the emotion of single-minded devotion which, when turned away from self, produces overpowering zeal to promote the undivided glory of the person who is loved. The negative connotations of jealousy must surely be absent here. So perhaps it may best be translated by 'single-minded passion'. There is virtually no hint in the Song of the self-destructive envy that arises from frustrated love due to the intrusion of a rival party. The morbid gratification of endless introspection, the intolerance of another's happiness or good fortune, the ceaseless self-destructive desire to inflict pain on the one whose happiness is denied to oneself – this too is as unyielding as Sheol. But the Song is singing of the all-embracing *jealousy* of *love*, its zeal, its passion, its ardour which will brook no rivals.

Death may be regarded as a personification of the life-denying force. In the Canaanite legends from Ugarit, *Death* (Hebrew and Ugaritic *Môt*) is in cyclical conflict with the god of fertility, Baal, the Canaanite weather god. When Baal prevails, then the rains fall, the crops germinate, the flocks are fertile. But when Mot prevails, then barrenness, infertility, drought and famine reign supreme. So with this mythological background, Death and Sheol may be regarded as personifications of warring monsters.

Death and Sheol are often paired together in the Old Testament, as in Hosea 13:14, 'Where, O death, are your plagues? Where, O [Sheol], is your destruction?' and Psalm 18:5, 'The cords of [Sheol] coiled around me; the snares of death confronted me.' Death and Sheol are both seen as hostile to humanity, and they are often associated with the raging torrents of the watery deep (see 8:7a–b).

But the metaphors suddenly change. The Hebrew literally reads 'Her darts are darts of fire, a flame of Yah.' From the cold negative destructive forces of death we are transported to flaming darts of fire, or lightning flashes of love. A lightning bolt (*rešep*) is the same word as the proper noun Reshep, the Canaanite god of war and pestilence. But the point of the metaphor is to underline the sudden inflammation which occurs when the arrows of love strike. Cupid's arrows strike in the most unexpected places, at the most inconvenient times; the victim is never consulted in advance, but is struck suddenly, forcibly, from without. The victim is injected with a divine intoxicating fluid which transforms life, overwhelms the senses and radically alters perspectives. Such is the perturbation of love. Those who are smitten are engulfed in its conflagration, helpless in the baptism of love. It is not at all cold and calculating or manipulative or worked up. It is a happening beyond all control. Love is a 'flame of Yah'. This translates the rather obscure Hebrew *šalhebetyah*. It is possible that the *-yah* ending is a contraction of Yahweh, the covenant God of Israel, but this is debatable. 'Yah' occurs in the proper names Isaiah (*Yĕša'yah*, meaning 'Yahweh is salvation') and Jeremiah (*Yirmĕyah*, meaning 'Yahweh is exalted'). So it is possible that the meaning here is that love is a flame of Yahweh. But it may just express a superlative: as we might say, it is an almighty great flame. There are other instances of this usage of the divine name as a superlative in the Old Testament.[10]

Whatever the resolution of this particular linguistic debate, however, it is beyond question that the flame of ardent love is the good gift of a beneficent Creator. Robert Browning has expressed this thought in 'Any Wife to Any Husband'.

---

[10] E.g. Jer. 2:31, 'great darkness' ('gloom of Yah'); Ps. 118:5, 'a spacious place' ('wideness of Yah'); Jon. 3:3, AV, 'an exceeding great city' ('Great with respect to God'); Ps. 80:10, 'mighty cedars' ('Cedars of God').

It would not be because my eye grew dim
Thou couldst not find the love there, thanks to Him
Who never is dishonoured in the spark
He gave us from his fire of fires, and bade
Remember whence it sprang, nor be afraid
While that burns on, though all the rest grow dark.

Marcia Falk, in her literary study of the Song, has translated the phrase *šalhebetyah* as 'a fierce and holy blaze'.[11] Of course, the Song in its canonical role as wisdom literature affirms this dimension, which also receives further substantiation from the wider context of the Bible. The God-givenness of marital love is affirmed not only in the creation narratives, where God brings the woman whom he has created to the man, to be one flesh with him, but also in the other biblical wisdom literature books, Proverbs and Ecclesiastes. The exhortations to 'enjoy life with your wife, whom you love' (Eccl. 9:9), to 'rejoice in the wife of your youth, a loving doe, a graceful deer' and to be ever 'intoxicated with her love' (Prov. 5:18–19) are all made on the unspoken assumption that marriage is an honourable estate, the gift of a loving Creator. Pursuing this thought a little further, we may note that the Bible indicates that the very capacity to enjoy God's gifts is itself a gift from God (Eccl. 5:19). Also the rabbis said that God would bring into judgment all those who could have enjoyed his gifts but did not. The divine origin of human love is also made plain in the formation of humanity in the image of God. All human love is to some degree a reflection of the love of God, whose image we bear. But we need to sound a note of caution here lest we begin to think that every passionate affair of the heart necessarily has divine approval. 'God is love' can so easily be misconstrued as 'love is God', where anything goes, and we lose contact with all our moral bearings.

The *many waters* of verse 7 (*mayyîm rabbîm*) occur several times in the Old Testament, especially in the Psalms (e.g. Pss 29:3; 32:6; 77:19; 93:4; 107:23; 144:7). They may echo the restless chaotic waters of the primal flood, which are a dominant theme in the creation mythologies in the Ancient Near East. These threatening forces of chaos had to be subdued and brought into order before the creation of the dry land could take place. There may be hints of this mythology underlying the account of

---

[11] Falk, *Love Lyrics from the Bible*, p. 131.

Genesis 1. But the raging torrents may well represent the forces of death, as in Psalm 18:4, 'The cords of death entangled me, the torrents of destruction overwhelmed me', and Jonah 2:3, 6, 'You hurled me into the depths, into the very heart of the seas, and the currents swirled about me; all your waves and breakers swept over me . . . But you, LORD my God, brought my life up from the pit.' The juxtaposition of the images of fire and water, together with the usage of the verb 'to quench', now give a powerful illustration of the indestructibility of *love*. For though water can quench any flame, there are no hostile forces which can quench the flame of love. It is inevitable that love will always be tested and tried, will always encounter forces that threaten to undermine and destroy it. These may be the outward circumstances that may erode love's power: the pain of separation, the uncertainty of the present or future, the loss of health or means of livelihood. But the love which is fuelled by the energy of God will triumph and overcome all these adversities, and will emerge purer and stronger and more precious through the testing.

This supreme quality in human experience is not something that can be traded; it cannot be bought or sold as though it were a commercial transaction. One cannot buy allegiance or faithfulness by gifts or flattery. Those who attempt such commerce will be *utterly scorned*, along with their wealth. (It is uncertain whether what is scorned in verse 7 is the *wealth* itself or the person who tries to use it in this degrading way.) As this theme recurs in 8:12b–c, it will be explored in more detail there.

The similarity of vocabulary between 8:6–7 and Isaiah 43:2 is remarkable. Both passages contain the words 'waters', 'rivers', 'fire', 'flame' and 'sweep away/over'. The peace and security of the new eschatological era, brought about by the birth pangs of the new age, are mirrored in the individual experience of new love, in all its overwhelming disruption.

> When you pass through the waters,
>> I will be with you;
> and when you pass through the rivers,
>> they will not sweep over you.
> When you walk through the fire,
>> you will not be burned;
>> the flames will not set you ablaze.
> (Isa. 43:2)

4. The little sister (8:8–10)

This little poem seems to spring out of nowhere. But in fact, its themes are a recapitulation, in a happier frame, of those first met in 1:5–6. The two motifs which the passages have in common are the brothers' sense of duty in protecting their *little sister*, and the girl's proud self-assertion of her own value. In the first chapter, the brothers put their erring sister in quarantine, to keep her out of trouble, while she for her part petulantly and defiantly protests her own beauty. Here, in these verses, the brothers hover around her defensively while she is growing up, while in 8:10 she asserts (from a later perspective), with great self-confidence and aplomb, her self-possession and power to please. That, at least, is my view, for there is much debate as to who is speaking in verses 8–9. I take it that the girl is remembering what her brothers had said about her when she was younger and that she is comparing herself now to the person she was then. So the *little sister* of verse 8 is the same person as the girl in verse 10. Now she is mature (*my breasts are like towers*); then she had not yet reached puberty (*her breasts are not yet grown*). The Hebrew of verse 8 makes it clear that the sister is a 'minor' (under the age of twelve). *Little* ('young') is not an adjective qualifying *sister*, but a separate noun, 'minor', in apposition to the noun *sister*. The brothers were watching their developing young sister protectively. As in the allegory of Ezekiel 16, they watched her grow up and develop and become the most beautiful of jewels. Her 'breasts had formed and [her] hair had grown' (Ezek. 16:7). In Ezekiel 16:8 we read, 'Later I passed by, and when I looked at you and saw that you were old enough for love, I spread the corner of my garment over you.'

So the brothers are debating their future responsibilities towards their younger sister 'on the day when it shall be spoken about her' (literal translation). This has usually been taken to refer to the time when she is to be betrothed, since the same expression is used when David took Abigail for his wife after the death of Nabal (1 Sam. 25:39). However, it may refer more generally to the time when she starts getting noticed, and the rest of the family start wondering what sort of girl she will turn out to be and what sort of match they can make for her. For she still belongs to the family. She remains under the domain of her brothers' authority until she actually gets married. As an eligible young girl, she is fussed over, cossetted, decorated and beautified as one of the family's most important assets. As such, with the potential for earning a large dowry for the family, she must be preserved and protected in all her purity and splendour. However verse 9 is interpreted, the brothers are performing their duty of protection, preservation and public presentation towards their sister.

The next point at issue is to decide whether the metaphors of the *wall* and the *door* are saying the same thing, or the opposite. For a *door* can be either open or shut, a means of entry or a barring of access. Are the two halves of the verse in synonymous or antithetic parallelism? It is impossible to be certain and it is probably best to leave the matter open. In any case, the question of the brothers is one of self-deliberation, of speculating about her potential for chaste or unchaste behaviour. Nothing has yet occurred which may precipitate a protective action. (But there are hints of this in 1:6, where she is put to work in the vineyard for having offended her brothers in some unspecified way.) In any case, the girl herself asserts that she is a *wall* (10), and about the meaning of this metaphor there is little doubt. The *wall* (the Hebrew word signifies a fortified city wall, not the wall of a house) then suggests defence, impregnability, repulsion of intruders. Metaphorically it represents chastity, unavailability, self-protection and preservation. She is then adorned and beautified by her brothers with turrets or battlements of silver to celebrate her chastity and her purity, for not having cultivated her 'vineyard' in a sexual sense. Alternatively, and less likely in view of verse 10, the wall could mean that she is flat-chested and needs some extra power of attraction.

Concerning the *door*, let us consider first the case of synonymous parallelism. The *door* bars entry, it prevents access to all undesirables. So just as the picture of the wall led to her being decorated with turrets of silver, so here the girl will be adorned (for such is a possible meaning of the Hebrew word translated by the NIV as *enclose*) with panels of cedar. Both silver and cedar are luxury items. Jeremiah regarded Jehoiakim's use of cedar panelling in his palace as the outrageous extravagance of profligate luxury (Jer. 22:14–15). So we have a picture of the door being decorated with expensively carved ornate cedar panels.

However, in the case of antithetic parallelism, the *door* stands for access, entry, an open passageway for all and sundry to go through. Metaphorically speaking, this refers to the girl's potential unchastity, that she is free with her favours and her body is a passageway for every lustful youth. That being the case, the protective brothers would board her up with wooden *panels*, preventing access, putting her in quarantine as it were, as did Hosea his wife (Hos. 3:3). However, in whichever way we are to interpret it, the girl in verse 10 proudly and confidently asserts her maturity, both morally and sexually: she is a *wall* and her *breasts are like towers*. The reference to her breasts as towers is somewhat ambiguous. They, like the *silver* battlements, are decorative and attractive; she is not flat-chested, but full, mature and ripe for love. Yet they are symbols of her self-confident self-possession. She will give her 'consoling breasts' only to the one to whom she is committed. All others will be repelled. She no longer needs her brothers' protection. She can look after herself now, thank you very much. Thus she has become in her lover's estimation like one bringing peace. The lover has not been mentioned in this unit, but he is the only one who can possibly be meant. It is rather unlikely that she will be bringing *contentment* to her brothers, however proud of her they may be. Her virginity, her chastity, her maturity, her strength, are all a source of shalom to her beloved. It is most likely that here we have a deliberate play on the words peace, Solomon and Shulammite (*šālôm*, *šĕlōmōh*, *šulammît*). She, the Shulammite, brings shalom to her king, her lover, her Shelomoh. In what sense does the girl give shalom to her beloved? He will be proud of her self-possession, that she has reserved herself solely for him. He will feel a whole person, now he is in love with her. He will be glad that the family of brothers and mother have finally accepted their relationship.

Perhaps it should be noted that the phrase *one bringing contentment* is ambiguous in the Hebrew. It could be an active participle of the root *māṣā'*, meaning 'one finding'. Or it could equally be a causative participle of the root *yāṣā'*, meaning 'causing to go forth' ('bringing forth'). Those who espouse the shepherd hypothesis believe that what is being described here is Solomon's facing the inevitable fact that he is not now going to win over the Shulammite, and that he is now seeking 'peace' – in other words, he has surrendered his claims over her, and is surrendering her over into the keeping of her shepherd lover.

5. A vineyard not for hire (8:11–12)

This fascinating little unit has been the subject of endless speculation. The two verses have the common themes of vineyards, money and fruit. What is being compared and contrasted here is the administration of two different vineyards and the disposal of their fruit. On the one hand, we have King Solomon's literal *vineyard in Baal Hamon*, which he lets out to tenant farmers. On the other hand (12), we have the girl's own metaphorical vineyard which unlike Solomon's is not to be let out for hire. Her person, her body, her sexuality, are not to be made an object of a commercial transaction; she cannot be wooed with money. She herself is in sole charge of her future destiny, and she will give herself freely only to the man of her choice.

We need to attend to a number of details in the two verses before looking at their general implications. The appearance of *Solomon* here in the Song is a literary device; he is not one of the participating actors in the poem, but appears as a character foil to the girl. He is being 'set up' as a bad example, as the archetypal lecherous plutocrat who thinks that his money has the power to obtain anything he wants. This interpretation hinges on the nature of the girl's words in verse 12, *the thousand shekels are for you, Solomon*. The view taken here is that they are negative in tone: that she is telling *Solomon*, and all those similar types of men he represents, that money is powerless to buy love and allegiance. She can have nothing to do with such commerce; she cannot be bribed, seduced or hired. Her message is identical to that of 8:7: 'If one were to give all the wealth of one's house for love, it would be utterly scorned.' Of course, in the shepherd hypothesis, Solomon is here being addressed directly as one personally involved in a love triangle. On both of these views, Solomon can hardly be seen as the author of the Song. (Some commentators give undue weight to the fact that Solomon is here referred to in the past tense, thus lending support to a late dating of the Song. However, since this is such a peripheral issue, we need not consider it further.)

It is curious that the first line of 8:11 bears a marked similarity to the Song of the Vineyard in Isaiah 5:1, literally 'My beloved had a vineyard in Qeren-ben-Shemen.' That song too is a love song and the singer sings to his beloved about his 'vineyard'. We might be led to think that the vineyard is to be his girl, but right from the start, the vineyard (which has been so painstakingly cultivated) stands for the house of Israel. So in our Song, we might begin to suspect that Solomon's *vineyard* operates at two different levels. His literal vineyards were of legendary fame (Eccl. 2:4). One of them was planted at a place called *Baal Hamon*. This is otherwise unknown in the Old Testament, and is most likely a fictitious name, just as in Isaiah 5:1 Qeren-ben-Shemen (meaning 'Horn of Olive Oil') is obviously an invention. *Baal Hamon* means either 'owner of wealth' or 'owner of a crowd'. Solomon was both: he was sumptuously wealthy – '[Everything was made of gold]. Nothing was made of silver, because silver was considered of little value in Solomon's days' (1 Kgs 10:21) – and he was the owner of a large harem – 'He had seven hundred wives of royal birth and three hundred concubines' (1 Kgs 11:3); 'I amassed silver and gold for myself . . . I acquired male and female singers, and a harem as well – the delights of a man's heart' (Eccl. 2:8). So there are hints here that Solomon's vineyard may be considered as more than just a source of grapes, but as a source of sensual pleasure.

The details of how Solomon sublet his vineyard to the *tenant* farmers are obscure. Isaiah mentions a plot of one thousand vines being worth one thousand silver pieces in Ahaz's day (Isa. 7:23). Since Solomon had several plots, presumably let out to different *tenants*, his vineyard must have been worth a considerable sum. But do the verses mean that the *tenants* each pay Solomon the *thousand shekels* for the right to cultivate a plot, and then they keep what they can make from selling the grapes to the owners of the winepress? Or do they make the *thousand shekels* from selling the produce, and keep *two hundred* for themselves, the remaining eight hundred then going into Solomon's coffers? We do not know, and it is unimportant. For the verses are not meant to convey to us the details of the economics of viniculture. All that is meant is that the cultivation of the vineyard is part of a commercial and financial enterprise. But the girl has not stooped to this in the cultivation of her own *vineyard*. These verses recall the time when the girl was set to cultivate her brothers' vineyards, but 'my own vineyard I had to neglect' (1:6). In 8:12, the girl is emphasizing her own rights over how to govern or dispose of her own vineyard. The Hebrew reads literally, 'My vineyard which is mine is before me.' There is a strong emphasis on the personal possession ('my very own vineyard'). The usual interpretation of the phrase 'before me' is that she alone has the sole right of disposition, a right that she is guarding jealously and is not going to surrender. So she is telling all those who might be tempted to exploit her *vineyard* to keep their distance.

We have been assuming all along that it is the girl who is speaking here. It is evident that the speech in 8:10 comes from her lips, and we naturally have assumed a continuity in the speaker. However, there are no linguistic markers in the Hebrew text which would enable us to identify the gender of the speaker in 8:11–12. Some have taken the words to be those of the lover. The boy then looks on Solomon's vineyard, his harem, and sees how other noblemen of the court take advantage of the women there. But his own 'vineyard', that is, his own girl, is not to be taken advantage of by others. He alone has the right to *its fruit*. M. Pope points out, 'If the groom speaks, declaring dominion over his spouse's body, it is classic male chauvinism. If the female here asserts autonomy, this verse becomes the golden text for women's liberation.'[12] But this may be an overstatement of the case; the groom could be speaking in tones of wonder and love.

The basic message of these two verses is that love is not a commodity that can be bought or sold as though it were the subject of some kind of commercial transaction. Of course, the attempt may be made to win loyalty, allegiance or favours by a grandiose display of pseudo-generosity, but this is sheer manipulation. A man who is constantly showering gifts upon a girl in order to win her affections is a rather pathetic figure. He is giving his gifts, rather than himself. His one end in view is to gain some immediate gratification, and once that is achieved, the means of gratification may very well be ruthlessly discarded, like an empty packet of cigarettes, useless when its original purpose has been fulfilled. He may indeed have nothing of himself to give, a shallow character, uninterested in forming any permanent personal relationship. The girl who is subject to all his attentions must surely keep her eyes open to what is going on. She may very well string him along and wear his gifts like decorations on a Christmas tree. But if the girl has any perception of personal worth and dignity she would utterly scorn such gifts and the person who gives them (8:7). For such attempts at exploitation do not deserve to be dignified by the name of 'love'. For love senses the worth and dignity of the other, and wants to enhance it, even at the cost of self-denial.

Love cannot be coerced; the response of love is given freely. Awakening love is the dawning realization of the worth and dignity of the other, which blossoms into the desire for mutual self-surrender and self-giving and is not merely a relationship of convenience, for mutual self-gratification.

This exploitation can work both ways. While it is most often the male who is the guilty party in the commercialization of sexual relationships, it is not always so. A woman can be equally exploitative on occasion. She can 'sell' her favours to her lover in order to extort from him a greater prize, of security or material advantage or marriage. The sight of a woman brazenly chasing an unwilling man is as grotesque as that of a man

---

12 Pope, p. 690.

flattering an uninterested woman. See Isaiah 4:1: 'In that day seven women will take hold of one man and say, "We will eat our own food and provide our own clothes; only let us be called by your name."'

Commercialization of sex stems from a loss of a sense of personhood. Sex becomes a thing to be experienced apart from the dimension of a committed personal relationship. It assumes a genital focus totally divorced from the wider dimensions of human intercourse. The extreme case of this thinking is the trade of prostitution. The degradation of prostitution is that a mechanical act is being sold for money, totally apart from the only proper context of an enduring binding contract of marriage. There is a meeting of bodies, but not of persons. As such, it is as degrading for the man as it is for the woman.

Another consequence of this impersonal mechanical attitude to sex is the trade in pornography. This exploits the tragic loneliness of modern men and women, and lures them into the trap of solitary sexual gratification; desires are aroused which can only be satisfied illegitimately. It is a revolting trade whose victims end up not only in self-disgust, but also under the judgment of God. Yet none of us is immune from its snares, and we all have to be on our guard. Again, it is a question of plucking out the eye, and not walking into temptation (Matt. 5:27–30). Yet it is one of the glories of the Christian gospel that there is always the liberating, transforming and forgiving power of Jesus Christ available to everyone who falls. The heartfelt prayer of David, 'Create in me a pure heart, O God, and renew a steadfast spirit within me' (Ps. 51:10), is one which can never fail to be answered.

Yet even within the framework of an established marital relationship, the sheer urgency of sexual desire may make it vulnerable to exploitation, a trading counter to be bargained with; a sort of 'I'll give you this if only you'll buy me that', a mutual trade-off in selfishness. This toffees-for-good-behaviour mentality is a cheapening of the sexual instinct and a devaluation of its currency. A relationship based on this type of bartering has not yet discovered the fundamental meaning of love, the self-surrender for the good of the other, without expecting or demanding any reward. This unselfish abandonment to the other will bring its own happy and unsought compensations.

Love seeketh not itself to please,
Nor for itself hath any care,

But for another gives its ease,
And builds a Heaven in Hell's despair.[13]

6. The continuing cycle of desire (8:13–14)

The Song ends on what appears to be an anticlimax with these two obscure and enigmatic verses. It seems a rather peculiar way in which to conclude a beautiful love song, and leaves us hanging in mid-air with a number of unresolved questions: What is the girl doing *in the gardens*? Who are the *friends in attendance*? What is the nature of the lover's request? And what kind of a response does she make? Is it an invitation to an intimate meeting? Or is she telling him to flee away? There is much uncertainty here, but at least the identity of the speakers is relatively clear. In 8:13 the boy is addressing the girl, for the participle translated by *You who dwell* is feminine singular, as also is the possessive suffix attached to *your voice*. The *friends* (masculine plural) are her companions, possibly suitors. The word is the same as that used in 1:7 in the phrase 'flocks of your friends'. The friends are *in attendance*, hanging on to her every word, straining to catch every utterance that drops from her lips. The invitation in 8:14 (or is it a command?) is the speech of the girl. Whether it is her direct reply in response to his request in 8:13, or whether it is the invitation which the boy himself is dreaming up and wishes to hear from her lips, is a moot point. If the latter is the case, the whole of verses 13 and 14 are the boy's speech; the words in verse 14 should then be in inverted commas and the two verses linked by the introductory word 'saying'. So we would have, 'Let me hear your voice, saying, "Come away, my beloved . . ."' However, I take it that 8:14 is the direct speech of the girl, and not an imagined response.

But what is the context, and what is the girl commanding her lover to do? In 8:13 the garden theme is reintroduced. The girl seems to be sitting (or staying) there, surrounded by other men. However, the garden in this case seems to be in the public domain, not a private secret grove. One senses an element of competition (the 'foxes' of 2:15?) and the boy seems to be outside, excluded from what he had previously regarded as his own personal property, the locked garden of 4:12. Is he being crowded out by others wanting to muscle their way in? If that is the case, then he presents

---

13 Blake, 'The Clod and the Pebble'.

rather a pathetic figure. He plaintively begs his girl to pay him some attention (*let me hear your voice!*). He wants her to speak to him, and him alone. There seems to be some rupture in their relationship, or at least a misunderstanding on his part. Has the girl left him? Does she find her lover's ardour insufficient, and want the public applause and flattery of a host of suitors? Or is she deliberately trying to provoke him to jealousy, the true jealousy of love? There is no certain answer to any of these questions. The verses tease us, as perhaps the girl is teasing her lover.

The girl's response is equally ambiguous, perhaps deliberately so. The NIV's *Come away* is an interpretation of the straightforward Hebrew word translated 'flee'. To flee is normally to take a flight away from someone or something. But where is our lover supposed to be fleeing to? To the mountains of spices? But where and what are they? We have already met something similar elsewhere: the mountains of Bether (2:17), the mountain of myrrh and the hill of frankincense (4:6), and the towers of perfume (5:13). As we have already seen, there are strongly erotic connotations in these contexts; so perhaps here something similar is going on. She invites him to be like a gazelle or a young stag on the mountains of spices. This sounds very much like an invitation to intimacy. There may also possibly be a subtle double entendre hidden here. For the Hebrew word 'to flee' (*bāraḥ*) has the same consonants as the word for 'bolt' (*bĕrîaḥ*), the sliding shaft described in Exodus 36:33 for linking together the frames of the tabernacle. But the invitation is couched in such oblique language that it could be taken to mean the exact opposite. It is not the first time we have observed some imprecision about the movements of the lovers (see on 6:2). She could be telling him to assert his independence and fly away, skipping over the mountains with untrammelled freedom, in language reminiscent of Habakkuk 3:19. But perhaps we are trying to be oversubtle. The girl may simply be telling her lover to flee away to a secret hideaway, to which she will follow him when her 'companions' have finished paying attention to her. There they will make love together. Hence the Song (on this view) ends on an anticipation of love yet to be fulfilled.

In most love stories, the young lovers overcome mountainous obstacles in order that they might achieve their goal of finally being united together; after which they live happily ever after. But that happens only in fairy stories. Real life is often very different. And perhaps it is the function of these closing verses to mirror something of that reality – the endless cycle of love, its restless ebb and flow and fluctuating moods. For in any developing relationship, we never 'arrive'. There are always new lessons to learn and old lessons to relearn. We may sometimes play 'hide-and-seek', as these two lovers do on occasion. But there is always the coming back and starting anew, the making of fresh beginnings. How foolish to think that we ever become experts in the realm of human relationships. Here, as elsewhere, it is a case of 'Let any one who thinks that he stands take heed lest he fall' (1 Cor. 10:12, RSV). A casual word here, a shrugging gesture there, an innocent silence totally misinterpreted, and the whole fragile house of cards comes tumbling down, and we have to start rebuilding again, slowly, painfully, honestly, clearing the air through mutual forgiveness, and a determination to get on an even keel again. All this can be emotionally and nervously exhausting. We nurse our grievances; we mentally catalogue the faults, real or imagined, of our partners; we prefer the hostility of stony silence rather than be the first to take the initiative in reconciliation. But the sharp recriminations and counter-accusations of the lovers' violent quarrel can open the way towards a calmer mutual acceptance. But it is only when the tension has dissolved and the atmosphere has lightened that the real issues can be addressed. Compromises have to be made; each has to defer to the other in different ways. Only then can a modus vivendi be reached, with a greater degree of tolerance of each other as we really are, warts and all, with our idiosyncrasies, our volatile temperaments and stubborn wills. The see-saw goes backwards and forwards, the changes in motion being often sickeningly jarring and violent; and what we fear most of all is being totally thrown. But perhaps that is not the happiest of illustrations. For we spiral around each other, sometimes drawing closer in deepening intimacies of intercourse, physical, emotional, psychological, intellectual and spiritual; sometimes withdrawing, letting each other find our own separate pathways, yet always secure in the knowledge of our ultimate mutual acceptance and attraction. Each cycle of movement towards and away from each other must bring a deeper sense of that underlying commitment which is the true bond of freedom.

The linguistic ambiguity (does she invite him to make love to her, or is she telling him to go away?) may at a deeper level reflect a fundamental existential tension, even a paradox. As Cervantes has said, 'Love is a power too strong to be overcome by anything but flight.' We desire our freedom and independence, yet we have an urge for intimacy. However, the very fulfilment of that urge destroys that which we so deeply prize: our independence.

The paradox lies in the fact that we only find our true selves in our self-surrender; in order to live, we must die. For that is a fundamental truth of human relationships as well as of relationships in the spiritual realm. We can't live with our partners, we can't live without them. It is this tension between freedom and dependence which we all experience and have to come to terms with, which is hinted at in these verses. It is a mystery, beyond the capacity of humankind to understand.

> There are three things that are too amazing for me,
>> four that I do not understand:
> the way of an eagle in the sky,
>> the way of a snake on a rock,
> the way of a ship on the high seas,
>> and the way of a man with a young woman.
> (Prov. 30:18–19)

For further thought

It has already been mentioned that the Song has a somewhat untidy structure with many repetitions and sudden changes of mood. The various themes with their colourful images jostle each other to form a beautiful complex fabric. It may be helpful in our study of the Song to disentangle a few of these strands which are tightly interwoven in the poetry. This is not to suggest that there is a progressive plot in the poem; it is merely a device to help our appreciation of the Song. The strands I have selected do in fact appear to have some sort of sequence, but this is not something to be imposed on the text as a whole. After the delineation of each theme, a number of questions are posed to stimulate discussion and to apply the message of the Song.

Many of the questions could be discussed in marriage-preparation classes. For a wider use in a mixed-group discussion, it is recommended that the material is used selectively, bearing in mind the needs of a particular group and cultural sensitivities.

Themes

1. The attraction and articulation of beauty
2. Joys and tensions
3. Erotic arousal
4. Betrothal and marriage
5. Consummation
6. The permanency of love

1. The attraction and articulation of beauty

Dark am I, yet lovely (1:5)
I liken you, my darling, to a mare (1:9)
Your cheeks are beautiful with earrings (1:10)
How beautiful you are, my darling! (1:15)
How handsome you are, my beloved! (1:16)
I am a rose of Sharon, a lily of the valleys (2:1)
... show me your face ... (2:14)
How beautiful you are, my darling! (4:1)
Your eyes behind your veil are doves (4:1)
Your hair is like a flock of goats (4:1)
Your teeth are like a flock of sheep just shorn (4:2)
Your lips are like a scarlet ribbon (4:3)
Your mouth is lovely (4:3)
Your temples ... are like the halves of a pomegranate (4:3)
Your neck is like the tower of David (4:4)
Your breasts are like two fawns (4:5)
... there is no flaw in you (4:7)
My beloved is radiant and ruddy (5:10)
His head is purest gold (5:11)
His hair is wavy (5:11)
His eyes are like doves (5:12)
His cheeks are like beds of spice (5:13)
His lips are like lilies (5:13)
His arms are rods of gold (5:14)
His body is like polished ivory (5:14)
His legs are pillars of marble (5:15)
His appearance is like Lebanon (5:15)
His mouth is sweetness itself (5:16)
You are as beautiful as Tirzah, my darling (6:4)
... as lovely as Jerusalem (6:4)
... as majestic as troops with banners (6:4)
Who is this that appears like the dawn? (6:10)
Your graceful legs are like jewels (7:1)
Your navel is a rounded goblet (7:2)
Your waist is a mound of wheat (7:2)
Your breasts are like two fawns (7:3)

Your neck is like an ivory tower (7:4)
Your eyes are the pools of Heshbon (7:4)
Your nose is like the tower of Lebanon (7:4)
Your head crowns you like Mount Carmel (7:5)
Your hair is like royal tapestry (7:5)
Your stature is like that of the palm (7:7)
. . . your breasts like clusters of fruit (7:7)

Discussion questions

1. Physical attraction is only one factor to be considered in a man–woman relationship. How important do you think this is? What other factors need to be taken into account, about which the Song says absolutely nothing?
2. Read Proverbs 31:30 and 1 Peter 3:3–6. Do you think these verses downplay the importance of physical beauty?
3. Do you think it a mark of vanity that we should desire to enhance our physical attractiveness?
4. How would you define physical beauty or attractiveness?
5. In what ways can beauty be seen as threatening?
6. How far do you think norms of beauty are culturally determined?
7. How much of our self-image is determined by the consideration of our external appearance?
8. How can we learn to live with our own limitations or with how we think others perceive us in the area of physical attraction?
9. How easy do you find it to articulate your praise of the one you love? Is it important that those who feel inhibited in these matters should overcome their inhibitions, or is the praise of the lovers in the Song purely an artistic device, with no correspondence to real relationships?
10. In what ways do you think it appropriate to enhance our physical appearance by dressing, hairstyle, cosmetics, and so on?

2. Joys and tensions

Togetherness

My beloved is to me a sachet of myrrh resting between my breasts (1:13)
I delight to sit in his shade (2:3)

My beloved is mine and I am his (2:16)
I belong to my beloved, and his desire is for me (7:10)
Take me away with you – let us hurry! (1:4)
Our bed is verdant (1:16)
Let him lead me to the banquet hall (2:4)
Arise, my darling . . . come with me (2:10)
. . . in the hiding-places on the mountainside, show me your face (2:14)
Come with me from Lebanon (4:8)
Come, my beloved, let us go to the countryside (7:11)

Aloneness

I went down to the grove of nut trees (6:11)
All night long on my bed I looked for the one my heart loves (3:1)
I slept but my heart was awake (5:2)

Fears of loss

I opened for my beloved, but my beloved had left; he was gone (5:6)
I charge you – if you find my beloved, what will you tell him? (5:8)
Which way did your beloved turn, that we may look for him with you? (6:1)
I looked for him but did not find him (3:1)
I called him but he did not answer (5:6)

Hostility

My mother's sons were angry with me (1:6)
They beat me, they bruised me (5:7)

Barriers of separation

There he stands behind our wall, gazing through the windows, peering
   through the lattice (2:9)
My dove in the clefts of the rock (2:14)
. . . the rugged hills (2:17)

Teasing

I have taken off my robe – must I put it on again? I have washed my
   feet – must I soil them again? (5:3)
Catch for us the foxes (2:15)
Tell me . . . where you graze your flock . . . If you do not know . . . follow
   the tracks of the sheep (1:7–8)

Frustration

If only you were to me like a brother . . . I would kiss you . . . (8:1)

Discussion questions

1. In any relationship there has to be a compromise between togetherness and aloneness. How should courting couples apportion time spent alone as compared with time, for example, in wider Christian fellowship? How should married couples preserve their private moments from being lost in the busyness of life – working life, family life, church life?
2. Does absence always make the heart grow fonder?
3. How far are we able to tease each other in an intimate relationship? What are the dangers in this?
4. To what degree should we listen to the opinions of close relatives in considering the choice of a husband or wife?

3. Erotic arousal

The five senses are brought into play in the Song:

Taste

His fruit is sweet to my taste (2:3)

. . . and taste its choice fruits (4:16)

I have eaten my honeycomb and my honey (5:1)

. . . your mouth like the best wine (7:9)

Smell

Pleasing is the fragrance of your perfumes (1:3)

. . . my perfume spread its fragrance (1:12)

. . . perfumed with myrrh and incense (3:6)

. . . the fragrance of your perfume (4:10)

. . . the fragrance of your garments (4:11)

Touch

. . . your love [caresses] is more delightful than wine (1:2)

His left arm is under my head, and his right arm embraces me (2:6; also at 8:3)

I held him and would not let him go (3:4)

Hearing

. . . let me hear your voice (2:14)

Listen! My beloved is knocking (5:2)

You who dwell in the gardens . . . let me hear your voice! (8:13)

Sight

Do not stare at me because I am dark (1:6)

. . . show me your face (2:14)

You have stolen my heart with one glance of your eyes (4:9)

Turn your eyes from me; they overwhelm me (6:5)

. . . come back, that we may gaze on you! (6:13)

A *general state of arousal* underlies the following verses:

. . . your love is more delightful than wine (1:2)

. . . resting between my breasts (1:13)

. . . his fruit is sweet to my taste (2:3)

I am faint with love (2:5)

. . . he browses among the lilies (2:16; also at 6:3)

Until the day breaks and the shadows flee, turn, my beloved, and be like a gazelle, or like a young stag on the rugged hills (2:17)

I will go to the mountain of myrrh and to the hill of incense (4:6)

You have stolen my heart (4:9)

. . . my heart began to pound for him (5:4)

. . . my hands dripped with myrrh, my fingers with flowing myrrh, on the handles of the bolt (5:5)

Why would you gaze on the Shulammite as on the dance of Mahanaim? (6:13)

I will climb the palm tree; I will take hold of its fruit (7:8)

The mandrakes send out their fragrance, and at our door is every delicacy, both new and old, that I have stored up for you (7:13)

I would give you spiced wine to drink, the nectar of my pomegranates (8:2)

Under the apple tree I roused you (8:5)

Kissing is alluded to in several places:

Let him kiss me with the kisses of his mouth (1:2)

Let him lead me to the banquet hall (2:4)

Your lips drop sweetness as the honeycomb (4:11)

His mouth is sweetness itself (5:16)

. . . your mouth like the best wine. May the wine go straight to my
    beloved, flowing gently over lips and teeth (7:9)
I would kiss you, and no one would despise me (8:1)

**A *state of undress*. The following verses indicate, if not a state
of undress, then at least a very strong imagination:**
Your graceful legs (= rounded thighs) (7:1)
Your navel (7:2)
Your waist (lit. belly) (7:2)
Your breasts (7:3)

The woman's initiatives

Let him kiss me (1:2)
Take me away with you (1:4)
Tell me, you whom I love (1:7)
. . . turn, my beloved, and be like a gazelle (2:17)
I looked for the one my heart loves (3:1)
I will get up now and go about the city (3:2)
I will search for the one my heart loves (3:2)
Let my beloved come into his garden (4:16)
I arose to open for my beloved (5:5)
Come, my beloved, let us go to the countryside, let us spend the night
    in the villages (7:11)
. . . there I will give you my love (7:12)
Under the apple tree I roused you (8:5)
I would kiss you (8:1)
Come away, my beloved (8:14)

The man's initiatives

He has taken me to the banquet hall (2:4, lit.)
Arise, my darling, my beautiful one, come with me (2:10)
. . . show me your face (2:14)
Come with me from Lebanon (4:8)
My beloved is knocking (5:2)
I will climb the palm tree; I will take hold of its fruit (7:8)

The times of intimacy

. . . resting (= spending the night) (1:13)

Until the day breaks and the shadows flee (2:17)
Let us spend the night in the villages (7:11)
Let us go early to the vineyards (7:12)

The places of intimacy

Let the king bring me into his chambers (1:4)
. . . where you rest your sheep at midday (1:7)
The beams of our house are cedars, our rafters are firs (1:17)
Let him lead me to the banquet hall (2:4)
. . . over the hills (2:8)
. . . in the clefts of the rock, in the hiding-places on the mountainside (2:14)
I . . . brought him to my mother's house (3:4)
. . . let us go to the countryside (7:11)
I would lead you and bring you to my mother's house (8:2)
Under the apple tree (8:5)
You who dwell in the gardens (8:13)

The need for restraint

Do not arouse or awaken love until it so desires (2:7; 3:5; 8:4)

Discussion questions

1. Do you think that the Song undermines the gender stereotypes of our modern society?
2. What practical steps can be taken to ensure that we 'do not arouse or awaken love until it so desires'?
3. What degrees of intimacy are appropriate for particular stages in a developing relationship?
4. Are sexual fantasies always an indication of lust?
5. How far may we articulate to our spouses the particular intimacies which we find most pleasurable?
6. When does our desire for intimacy degenerate into a selfish desire for sexual gratification?

4. Betrothal and marriage

Look! It is Solomon's carriage . . . the day of his wedding, the day his
   heart rejoiced (3:7–11)

. . . my bride (4:8, 11)
My sister, my bride (4:9, 10, 12; 5:1)

Discussion questions

1. Is it helpful for single people to fantasize about their own possible future marriage?
2. What can we do to keep our own marriages from falling into a rut?
3. Is 'falling in love' a necessary prerequisite for a successful marriage?
4. What are the advantages of an arranged marriage?
5. What is the purpose of a wedding as a public ceremony?
6. In our secularized Western culture, cohabitation is becoming increasingly prevalent. In the light of Scripture, what would you say to such an unmarried couple?

5. Consummation

Let my beloved come into his garden and taste its choice fruits (4:16)
I have come into my garden, my sister, my bride (5:1)
. . . there I will give you my love (7:12)

Discussion questions

1. Make a list of the biblical passages which endorse marriage as the only legitimate context for sexual intercourse.
2. If the Bible regards the sexual act as a God-given part of creation, should we be embarrassed by it?
3. The Song says virtually nothing about the procreation of children. Do you find anything significant in this?
4. What are the benefits and drawbacks of books about techniques?
5. Why did Adam and Eve cover themselves with fig leaves? What is the connection between sexual self-consciousness and sin?
6. What importance should be attached to sexual satisfaction in a married relationship?
7. Discuss the capricious, whimsical nature of the sexual instinct.

6. The permanency of love

Place me like a seal over your heart, like a seal on your arm;
> for love is as strong as death (8:6)
Many waters cannot quench love (8:7)

Discussion questions

1. Do you think that love is primarily an emotion, or is it an act of the will?
2. How is it possible to maintain love if physical attraction wanes?
3. In what ways ought human love to mirror the love of God?
4. Read 1 Corinthians 13:8–13. In what sense does love 'remain' when other things pass away?
5. 'Love comes from God' (1 John 4:7). What is *this type* of love whose origin is divine? Does all love have its origin in God?
6. What is the difference between love, passion, desire, lust, infatuation, affection and friendship?

Listen to God's Word speaking to the world today

The complete NIV text, with over 2,300 notes from the Bible Speaks Today series, in beautiful fine leather- and clothbound editions. Ideal for devotional reading, studying and teaching the Bible.

Leatherbound edition with slipcase
£50.00 • 978 1 78974 139 1

Clothbound edition
£34.99 • 978 1 78359 613 3

The Bible Speaks Today:
Old Testament series

The Message of Genesis 1 – 11
The dawn of creation
David Atkinson

The Message of Genesis 12 – 50
From Abraham to Joseph
Joyce G. Baldwin

The Message of Exodus
The days of our pilgrimage
Alec Motyer

The Message of Leviticus
Free to be holy
Derek Tidball

The Message of Numbers
Journey to the Promised Land
Raymond Brown

The Message of Deuteronomy
Not by bread alone
Raymond Brown

The Message of Joshua
Promise and people
David G. Firth

The Message of Judges
Grace abounding
Michael Wilcock

The Message of Ruth
The wings of refuge
David Atkinson

The Message of 1 and 2 Samuel
Personalities, potential, politics and power
Mary J. Evans

The Message of 1 and 2 Kings
God is present
John W. Olley

The Message of 1 and 2 Chronicles
One church, one faith, one Lord
Michael Wilcock

The Message of Ezra and Haggai
Building for God
Robert Fyall

The Message of Nehemiah
God's servant in a time of change
Raymond Brown

The Message of Esther
God present but unseen
David G. Firth

The Message of Job
Suffering and grace
David Atkinson

The Bible Speaks Today:
New Testament series

The Message of Matthew
The kingdom of heaven
Michael Green

The Message of Mark
The mystery of faith
Donald English

The Message of Luke
The Saviour of the world
Michael Wilcock

The Message of John
Here is your King!
Bruce Milne

The Message of the Sermon on the Mount (Matthew 5 – 7)
Christian counter-culture
John Stott

The Message of Acts
To the ends of the earth
John Stott

The Message of Romans
God's good news for the world
John Stott

The Message of 1 Corinthians
Life in the local church
David Prior

The Message of 2 Corinthians
Power in weakness
Paul Barnett

The Message of Galatians
Only one way
John Stott

The Message of Ephesians
God's new society
John Stott

The Message of Philippians
Jesus our joy
Alec Motyer

The Message of Colossians and Philemon
Fullness and freedom
Dick Lucas

The Message of 1 and 2 Thessalonians
Preparing for the coming King
John Stott

The Message of 1 Timothy and Titus
The life of the local church
John Stott

The Message of 2 Timothy
Guard the gospel
John Stott

The Message of Hebrews
Christ above all
Raymond Brown

The Message of James
The tests of faith
Alec Motyer

The Message of 1 Peter
The way of the cross
Edmund Clowney

The Message of 2 Peter and Jude
The promise of his coming
Dick Lucas and Chris Green

The Message of John's Letters
Living in the love of God
David Jackman

The Message of Revelation
I saw heaven opened
Michael Wilcock

The Bible Speaks Today:
Bible Themes series

The Message of the Living God
His glory, his people, his world
Peter Lewis

The Message of Prayer
Approaching the throne of grace
Tim Chester

The Message of the Resurrection
Christ is risen!
Paul Beasley-Murray

The Message of the Trinity
Life in God
Brian Edgar

The Message of the Cross
Wisdom unsearchable, love indestructible
Derek Tidball

The Message of Evil and Suffering
Light into darkness
Peter Hicks

The Message of Salvation
By God's grace, for God's glory
Philip Graham Ryken

The Message of the Holy Spirit
The Spirit of encounter
Keith Warrington

The Message of Creation
Encountering the Lord of the universe
David Wilkinson

The Message of Holiness
Restoring God's masterpiece
Derek Tidball

The Message of Heaven and Hell
Grace and destiny
Bruce Milne

The Message of Sonship
At home in God's household
Trevor Burke

The Message of Mission
The glory of Christ in all time and space
Howard Peskett and Vinoth Ramachandra

The Message of the Word of God
The glory of God made known
Tim Meadowcroft

"*The Spirituality of Paul* is needed in the ongoing conversation about spiritual formation and Christian spirituality. Les Hardin, a fellow pilgrim and friend, writes with clear prose, Spirit conviction, and a voracious appetite—like Paul—to imitate Christ. Les resembles Paul in many ways: tough-minded, tenderhearted, Scripture-grounded, Jesus-tethered, and holy habits–anchored. With grace and freedom, Les offers a book worthy of reading and living. I, for one, am grateful."
—J. K. Jones, director of the MA in Spiritual Formation, Lincoln Christian University, Graduate Division, Lincoln, IL

"Written with Hardin's trademark wit, *The Spirituality of Paul* is at turns deeply personal and scholarly. Hardin offers a corrective to the caricatures of Paul we often see, presenting him as a real man, whose own spiritual struggles were like our own, and whose example can guide us as we pursue our own spiritual disciplines. Accessible to the general reader while copiously footnoted for the scholar, *The Spirituality of Paul* is an excellent read for Christians seeking to grow in spiritual maturity."
—Dr. Richard Scott Nokes, professor of medieval literature, Troy University

"Dr. Hardin takes us not only on a journey through the life and faith formation of perhaps the greatest leader in the first century church, but also on a personal journey into the life of the believer. Using Paul as a model for all of us who call ourselves Christ-followers, we gain insight and appreciation for the practices, struggles, and commitments of the Christian life; even engaging suffering as part of the road to Christlikeness. The book reflects both Dr. Hardin's capabilities as a scholar of the New Testament and his embrace of a distinctively Christian spiritual formation. *The Spirituality of Paul* challenge its readers to a deeper walk with Christ through a significant engagement with the life and faith of Paul."
—James Estep, professor of Christian education, Lincoln Christian Seminary

"Les Hardin provides a wealth of insight into the spiritual life of the apostle Paul. He is indeed well suited to do so, having previously published *The Spirituality of Jesus* (Kregel, 2009). Defining spirituality as an ongoing 'practical partnership with the Spirit,' he elaborates nine prominent features of what he calls Paul's 'Jesus-style spirituality.' Written in an engaging, energetic style, this book is grounded in academic study, ministerial experience, and the author's own spiritual journey."
—Jeff Miller, PhD, professor of Bible, Milligan College

"Thoroughly informed, clearly conceived, and warmly presented, Les Hardin's *The Spirituality of Paul* will bring insight to those who want Christian spirituality made accessible. Writing with a scholar's knowledge and a disciple's experience, Hardin vividly describes Paul's spiritual disciplines as they emerge from his life and letters. As much an introduction to Paul's thought as a guide to spiritual growth, *The Spirituality of Paul* is a model of exegetical fidelity, pastoral integrity, and personal honesty. It is a worthy follow-up to the author's *The Spirituality of Jesus* but readily appreciated by those who have never read its predecessor."
—Jon Weatherly, professor of New Testament and dean of the College of Bible and Theology, Johnson University

"*The Spirituality of Paul* provides unique insights into Christian spirituality, which is only accomplished by being both intensely biblical and intensely practical. As with his previous work, *The Spirituality of Jesus*, Dr. Hardin masterfully integrates the disciplines of New Testament studies with spiritual formation to provide much more than a simple how-to on spiritual disciplines; rather, it brings Christian spirituality to life by drawing from the amazing spiritual journey of Paul—a preeminent example of what it means to be Christlike. Deep, yet accessible, this work will be helpful to anyone seeking to pursue a thoroughly grounded spirituality."

—Brian D. Smith, PhD, president of Dallas Christian College

"In *The Spirituality of Paul* Les Hardin cuts through the mystery surrounding contemporary Christian spirituality. Instead of whatever feels spiritual, he provides a biblically based guide to the ways in which Paul partnered with the Spirit to be shaped into the image of Jesus. So just as Paul imitated Christ, the reader may learn Paul's practices to also become 'spiritual'—like Christ. Hardin's extensive reading, coupled with accessible prose in a practical arrangement, make *The Spirituality of Paul* useful for individual study or Bible classes and a rich resource for the recovery of biblical Christian spirituality.

—Dr. Glenn Pemberton, author of *Hurting with God: Learning to Lament with the Psalms*

"Dr. Hardin's work is a graceful balance of simple and scholarly insight into the not-so-Pharisaic spiritual disciplines of this much-beloved ex-Pharisee."

—Rebecca Owens, professor of English, Boise Bible College

"This book is a welcome companion to Hardin's *The Spirituality of Jesus*. Using our knowledge of Paul from his letters and from Acts, Hardin compiles a very practical and eminently readable study. Hardin's topical organization of Paul's teaching highlights both the theological backgrounds of Paul's thought, and the ethical implications for the modern reader. Hardin's conversational style expertly mixes within his presentation of both historical and autobiographical illustrations. The tone of the work is most inviting.

"This book will serve very well for teaching adults (Hardin's acknowledged gift) and as a welcome supplement for an undergraduate course on Paul. The topical layout would also work admirably for a series of weekly Bible studies.

"I heartily recommend this book. This is no elitist scholarly tome, but a very accessible look into this important topic. Hardin regularly points the reader to further literature, and provides a helpful bibliography, as well as explanatory footnotes."

—Thomas Scott Caulley, associate professor of Biblical Studies,
Kentucky Christian University

"Who better to imitate in spiritual formation than Paul? Both well-informed and written in popular style, this latest volume by Hardin fills a unique niche among books written about Paul or his writings. It could be a great first book on Paul or complement a substantial library on Paul."

—William R. Baker, professor of New Testament, Hope International University;
editor, *Stone-Campbell Journal*